Reading Obama

Reading Obama

Dreams, Hope, and the
American Political Tradition

With a new preface by the author

James T. Kloppenberg

Princeton University Press • Princeton and Oxford

Copyright © 2011 by Princeton University Press

Published by Princeton University Press, 41 William Street,
Princeton, New Jersey 08540
In the United Kingdom: Princeton University Press,
6 Oxford Street, Woodstock, Oxfordshire OX20 1TW
press.princeton.edu

Fourth printing, and first paperback printing, 2012
Paperback ISBN 978-0-691-15433-6

THE LIBRARY OF CONGRESS HAS CATALOGED THE CLOTH EDITION
OF THIS BOOK AS FOLLOWS
Kloppenberg, James T., 1951–
Reading Obama : dreams, hope, and the American political tradition
/ James T. Kloppenberg. — 1st ed.
p. cm.
Includes bibliographical references and index.
ISBN 978-0-691-14746-8 (cloth : acid-free paper) 1. Obama,
Barack—Philosophy. 2. Obama, Barack—Knowledge and
learning. 3. Obama, Barack—Knowledge—History. 4. United
States—Politics and government. 5. Political culture—United
States. I. Title.
E908.3.K55 2011
973.932092—dc22   2010020721

British Library Cataloging-in-Publication Data is available
This book has been composed in Times New Roman

Printed on acid-free paper. ∞

Printed in the United States of America

5 7 9 10 8 6 4

For Annie and Jay

Contents

Preface to the
Paperback Edition

H AVE THE FIRST THREE YEARS of the Obama
presidency made necessary a reconsideration of
the arguments presented in *Reading Obama*?
The short answer is no. To the contrary, Obama's successes and his failures have reflected the characteristics of
the worldview and the approach to democratic decision
making presented in this book. The criticism and the obstacles he has faced, both from the left wing of his own
Democratic Party and from the unprecedentedly intransigent right wing of the Republican Party, likewise bear out
the arguments I advance to explain why Obama's approach to leadership and problem solving seems so out of
touch with our times.

Reading Obama shows how and why Barack Obama
became the champion of moderation we have witnessed in
the White House so far. The book explains why he prefers
conciliation to provocation. His continuing effort to work
with his Republican opponents, a tendency that has exas-
perated many of his devoted followers in the Democratic
Party, springs from a deep-seated commitment to conciliation. He has refused the temptation to demonize conservatives not because he lacks backbone, as many critics
charge, but because he holds a particular conception of

the democratic process rooted in his understanding of American history. He has resisted the chorus advising him to portray contemporary politics as a war between good and evil, a morality play in which white-hatted heroes battle black-hatted villains, because that way of framing the issues, at least from his perspective, only intensifies the passions he wants to calm. *Reading Obama* lays out the evidence, drawn from his books and his speeches and the people who have known him at various stages of his career, that Obama has long been a moderate Democrat, a master of mediation drawn toward deliberation rather than drawing lines in the sand. Observers differ concerning the value and appropriateness of those qualities for the president of the United States in a time of hyperpartisan fervor, but those qualities should not come as a surprise. *Reading Obama* explains why Obama adopted the strategy of conciliation that has infuriated his critics. It is a strategy that has succeeded for him throughout his life; it springs from his understanding of American democracy. Nothing in Obama's performance as president so far calls into question the basic picture presented in this book: Obama's approach to politics is deeply grounded in an American tradition originating in the eighteenth century, with Thomas Jefferson and James Madison, and articulated in a particular form by many of those whose ideas most powerfully shaped Obama's own sensibility as he was coming of age.

To some of Obama's critics, *Reading Obama* might thus be interpreted as an explanation of the reasons Obama has turned out to be such a disappointing president. Without disputing all such criticism and without trying to defend all the decisions Obama has made, which I have no intention of doing, I intend in this preface to distinguish what *Reading Obama* does from what it does not do. The book seeks to establish the origins of Obama's view of American politics and to show the powerful effect of the tradition of American pragmatism and of the upheavals in late-twentieth-century American thought in shaping his worldview. I argue neither that such ideas explain everything about him nor that they provide an all-encompassing playbook from which every decision he has made must be derived.

The political sensibility and philosophical outlook shown in Obama's writings might well have expressed itself—and might yet express itself—in specific presidential decisions different from those we have seen. Indeed, as I make clear in *Reading Obama*, careful readers of *The Audacity of Hope* would have had good reason to expect a much more aggressive approach to some problems, the problem of economic inequality in particular, than he has shown so far. Obama's philosophical pragmatism leads him to prefer experimentation to dogma, but the particular form those experiments have taken—whether in the case of the stimulus, health care reform, consumer protection, or foreign policy—was not predetermined by his commitment to pragmatism. Indeed, the very idea of a lock-step relation between philosophical pragmatism and particular policy decisions is inimical to the philosophy of William James and John Dewey, both of whom advocated pragmatism as a method of testing hypotheses, not as a set of formulas. Obama's writings and speeches indicate the depth of his commitment to the values of freedom and equality. He has laid out a clear narrative of American history, one in which progressives demanding justice have challenged the prerogatives of power. Nothing in *Reading Obama* disputes the depth of his commitment to that project. Deciding on the most efficacious measures to advance toward those goals, however, is a matter of judgment, and that judgment depends on one's reading of the political climate and one's assessment of the possibilities. Not only are disagreements about those particular decisions inevitable, they are the lifeblood of democratic politics. *Reading Obama* examines the intellectual foundations of Obama's approach to making such judgments. Without offering an indictment or a defense of the particular decisions he has made so far, the book aims to illuminate the reasons he thinks about democratic decision making as he does, and why, as a matter of conviction rather than convenience, he seeks mutually satisfactory solutions and tries to resolve rather than intensify differences. Unfortunately, both for him and for the United States, plenty of people disagree with his approach to problem solving.

Partisan passions run deep in the history of the United States. Ever since the first party split developed during George Washington's presidency, intense criticism of the president has been the rule rather than the exception.

Americans should not have expected it would end with the election of Barack Obama.

The nation was born when men with deep convictions gathered in Philadelphia in the summer of 1787 and forged a compromise that required all of them to give a little. No one was entirely satisfied with the result, but they understood it was the best they could do given the chasms that divided them. On many questions, including how to choose a president and how much power the president should have, whether the number of senators from each state should be determined by population, and surely the question of slavery, profound disagreements separated delegates who argued about principles and wrangled about power. When they submitted their compromise to the state ratifying conventions, rancorous debates continued for a year. The Constitution was finally adopted, over the furious objections of a large minority, and Americans have been arguing about politics ever since. Some people never accepted the idea of a distant national government, which they feared would be run by elites. Others saw such objections as a smoke screen masking preferences for small-scale government that local notables could manipulate more effectively in their own interests. Even before George Washington concluded his two terms as president, old friends and fellow patriots were at each other's throats. Some fervent followers of Washington's successor, John Adams, considered his chief critic, Thomas Jefferson, and Jefferson's allies guilty of treason.

Conciliation, however, is an American tradition just as

old as partisanship. After his election as president in 1800, Jefferson declared in his inaugural address that "we are all Republicans, we are all Federalists." He meant that they had in common something deeper than their disagreements: their shared commitment to popular sovereignty. The people had spoken with their ballots, and in a democracy, one must be willing to accept defeat as well as victory. The alternative, as has been shown countless times from the ancient world to the present, is the death of democracy, civil war. Since Jefferson's election in the "revolution of 1800," as both sides called it, Americans have played the game of democracy by the rules, even when they did not like the outcome, and accepted the results of elections.

Except once. In 1860, the southern states interpreted the election of Abraham Lincoln as a threat to the institution of slavery. Despite Lincoln's declaration that the Constitution would not allow the federal government to touch slavery in the states where it was legal, the southern states seceded to form the Confederacy. After more than 600,000 deaths, and the unanticipated termination of slavery, the war ended and the southern states rejoined the union. The wounds, however, have not entirely healed. In the hearts of some Americans, the legacy of hatred persists, sanctified by bloody sacrifice and sustained by memories still fresh one hundred fifty years later.

In 2008, Barack Obama was elected president of the United States. His election was greeted by many Americans as the final triumph of the principles of racial equality for which they believed the Civil War was fought. For some other Americans, his election stung. It represented nothing less than a repudiation of the nation's defining principles. They refused to accept the legitimacy of their new president. He was not born in America, they insisted. He did not earn the degrees he was awarded by prestigious universities. He did not write the books he said he wrote. He was a Muslim. He was a socialist. He was black.

Some of those who celebrated Obama's election treated the abuse that rained down on the new president with the contempt they thought it deserved. They had endured eight years of George W. Bush, a president many rejected as illegitimate because of the contested results of the 2000 election. They savored the victory that had sparked such bitterness among Obama's foes. But their joy was short-lived. The president faced intractable problems stemming from the economic collapse, the two wars, the shrunken tax revenues, and the deep partisan divide that he had inherited from his predecessor. Shrill criticism of Obama's presidency began immediately and escalated quickly.

The measures President Obama proposed to address the economic crisis antagonized critics to his left as well as his right. The stimulus package that Congress passed, a compromise between those in the Democratic Party who thought it too big and those who wanted much more, squeaked into law. The Republican opposition conveniently forgot that every Republican president since Herbert Hoover had injected money into the economy when it faltered. Obama's compromise stimulus package, they shrieked, was socialist, un-American, and unaffordable. Obama put health care reform on the table, then waited while Congress hammered out a compromise that would leave the insurance industry in control of health care. As soon as that watered-down legislation, which was all the president could persuade his own party as well as Republicans to accept, passed by a slim margin in Congress, it was immediately denounced as socialist, un-American, and unaffordable. The deregulation of banking and real estate practices had led to excesses that plunged the nation into its worst recession since the 1930s. The financial reforms designed to rein in those out-of-control industries were again watered down to meet objections. As passed, the package would do little more than bring back the regulatory regime in place for sixty years, from the New Deal through the early 1990s, the years of the greatest sustained economic growth in American history. Yet critics screamed that the legislation was socialist, un-American, and unaffordable.

Many of those who protested against the stimulus, health care reform, and the new financial regulations came together in an apparently spontaneous movement that called itself the Tea Party. By the 2010 election season, the Tea Party had united many dissident Republicans around calls for lower taxes, lower government spending, and the repeal of measures passed during the first two years of Obama's presidency. To the dismay of those who supported the president, American voters sent a Republican majority to the House of Representatives, elected Republican governors in a substantial majority of states, and took control of a majority of state legislatures. Many of those new legislators, in the nation's Capitol and in state capitols, insisted against all evidence that America had once been a free-market paradise in which the economy had operated free of government oversight. Repeating that mantra with the fervor of true believers, they vowed to oppose any tax increases and shrink government spending dramatically.

The new Republican majority in Washington successfully blocked all the president's initiatives. In the immediate aftermath of the 2010 election, Congress struck at the heart of Obama's demand for fairness by preserving the Bush-era tax cuts for the wealthiest Americans. Some Republicans began challenging the constitutionality of health care reform. Most Republicans in Congress embraced a radical budget proposal that would further reduce government revenues and spending, a plan that included privatizing Medicare. Congressional Republicans nearly brought the federal government to a standstill in the spring of 2011 before finally approving the federal budget, then played an even more dangerous game in the summer.

The nation's debt ceiling had been raised routinely by Republican as well as Democratic presidents. A simple assumption—that the nation had no alternative to paying for expenditures Congress had already authorized—undergirded a bipartisan consensus. The debt ceiling was raised seven times during the presidency of George W. Bush, and Republicans did not make an issue of it. Since the last budget surplus of the late 1990s, the deficit had increased primarily because of rising health care costs and because the Bush administration had declined, for the first time in American history, to raise taxes to pay for the wars it initiated. When the debt ballooned throughout the Bush presidency, Republicans remained unruffled. Ronald Reagan, it was said, had shown that deficits do not matter.

Objecting to raising the debt ceiling, like objecting to deficit spending more broadly, was a deeply cynical move given the fragile condition of the United States economy. Recessions can be attacked only by deficit spending of the sort that earlier presidents and congressmen from both parties had judged necessary and unproblematic for decades. But now, as the economy remained stalled, Republicans labeled deficit spending a double evil: it would deepen the debt without contributing to economic growth. Because their stubbornness threatened the nation's credit rating and thus global economic stability, not only Democrats and some Republicans in the United States but business leaders and conservative politicians in Europe and Asia described the Republicans' intransigence as reckless and counterproductive. Republican lawmakers, such critics observed, were holding the American economy hostage to their own partisan agenda.

At that point, in the late summer of 2011, President Obama's already shaky support among independents and Democrats began to crumble. Even though the crises over the budget and the debt ceiling had been manufactured by

an increasingly radical Republican Party leadership, commentators blamed the president. Obama was too weak,
pundits wrote. He should have learned that you can't
compromise with thugs. He had to stop being so reasonable and start fighting. He needed a new storyline, a fable
with feisty, down-to-earth Americans slugging it out
against the nasty giants of Wall Street.

Exactly how the president was to lay down the law or
enforce his will against a Republican majority in the House
of Representatives was left unexplained. The advice to
get tough rested on Hollywood fantasies of presidential
power. Neither the Constitution nor historical experience
supports the claim that presidents who lack a majority
in Congress can simply tell Congress what it must do.
Presidents who have enjoyed great success have had substantial majorities in both houses of Congress. Obama
achieved modest results in his first two years because his
party held a slim majority in the House and a filibuster-
proof majority in the Senate. All except the most conservative members of his party went along with his initiatives, but only after they had been watered down to suit
their taste, as the stimulus package, health care, and financial reform all were. Yet consistent with the partisan criticism all presidents have had to face, Republican officials
and conservative commentators savaged the president
anyway. In the first two years of his presidency, when he
showed a willingness to compromise and enjoyed a majority in Congress, he was accused of ramming radical ideas
down America's throat. When he lost his majority and

still showed a willingness to compromise, he was said to lack backbone.

Liberal commentators, understandably impatient as the wars and the recession dragged on, wanted results. With the benefit of hindsight, they declared it obvious that Republicans were never going to compromise and mocked Obama's naivete. They ignored or forgot the speeches he had given repeatedly since his election, speeches in which he emphasized that his proposals to address the nation's problems were being rejected on the basis of extreme anti-government views held by no more than 20 percent of the American people. Many of Obama's critics on the left competed in a protracted disillusionment sweepstakes, vying to demonstrate who among them was the most deeply disappointed. As *Reading Obama* shows, Obama had made clear in his books and his speeches that he is a moderate Democrat committed to forging consensus. He had explained at length the reasons he favors deliberation over provocation. He had used examples from American history to show how a democracy solves problems. But some of his most avid supporters, who had projected onto him their expectations of far-reaching social and political change, felt betrayed. He had not turned out to be the fiery progressive they imagined him to be. Instead he was the calm, professorial mediator he had been his entire life. He had not slain the evil dragons of conservative activism. The tables had turned. Obama's supporters had lost; the other side had won. On both sides, there was plenty of anger to go around.

As I acknowledge repeatedly in *Reading Obama*, the president's strategy and his sensibility may prove ill-suited to our hyperpartisan moment. Although partisanship is as old as the United States, it has waxed and waned in intensity. Rarely has it been more heated than it is now. In the America of 2012, nuance is out, caricature is in. Inconvenient facts can be ignored and other "facts" invoked or, if necessary, invented. Attention often goes to the one who shouts the loudest. In that world, the thoughtful, empathetic, moderate Barack Obama can seem out of place.

Perhaps Obama's critics are right. Perhaps he must begin raising his voice and simplifying the issues. Perhaps he will, particularly when the presidential campaign heats up in the summer and fall of 2012. But if Obama is driven to adopt a more strident tone in the campaign of 2012, as so many Democrats are advising him to do, it will be a sharp departure from the steady calm that catapulted him to the presidency. There is nothing in Obama's past, or in his writings or speeches, that suggests he is likely to adopt that approach. *Reading Obama* seeks to explain how Obama thinks and who he is. Whether the American people want the man they elected in 2008—a man of unusually probing intelligence who sees the multiple dimensions of problems—to occupy the White House for another term depends on many contingent factors, most of which lie beyond his control. Even venturing a prediction about the 2012 election seems to me impossible. *Reading Obama* is the work of a historian, not a soothsayer.

Responses to *Reading Obama* have bolstered my confidence in its argument. Since the book appeared I have heard from many people who have known Barack Obama at different stages of his life, and in very different circumstances. All of them have told me they think I have him right. Here are just a few examples. One of his closest friends from Occidental College allowed me to read a set of long, remarkable letters that Obama wrote during his senior year at Columbia. Those letters reveal an already mature, penetrating mind—and reflect a serious engagement with difficult philosophical ideas—as well as the kindness for which he has been known throughout his life. One of Obama's good friends at Harvard Law School, one of his associates in Chicago politics, and a current U.S. Senator all told me that the careful, deliberative problem solver, the man known for seeing the nub of issues as well as cooling tempers and resolving disputes, was the man they knew. The author of the book I consider the best study of Obama and a member of Obama's U.S. Senate staff told me independently that *Reading Obama* clarifies the conciliatory and deliberative bent—the "on the one hand, and on the other hand" approach—that they had seen in action but did not understand. A former head of a European government assured me that my discussion of Obama's empathy captures the most distinctive feature of his sensibility as a statesman; and a former member of Obama's presidential administration has admitted that, although he values that quality somewhat less highly than

I do, he agrees it is the president's trademark. All of those responses, and many others, have confirmed my commitment to the value of the arguments in *Reading Obama*.

Little that has happened since the publication of *Reading Obama* has surprised me. The fierce partisanship of American politics, the depth of the problems Obama has faced, the moderation of his responses, and the resulting frustration of Right and Left were all predictable. But I have been surprised by the reluctance of some academic reviewers to consider the possibility that anyone elected to the presidency might take ideas seriously. Millions of Americans venerate education and work hard to achieve it. But distrusting educated people is also one of our nation's oldest traditions. As the Tea Party demonstrates, that tradition is as healthy as ever. Given the rancor common in the blogosphere, I have not been surprised by people who contend, without bothering to read his books, that the author of *Dreams from My Father* and *The Audacity of Hope* lacks intellectual firepower. I have been surprised, though, by the cynicism of scholars who discount the importance of Obama's education and his writings. I wonder why teachers who dismiss the value of what students learn continue to write and teach themselves. In contrast to the self-proclaimed realism of such observers, who minimize the importance of what Obama learned as a student and refuse to take seriously what he wrote in his books, I remain convinced from the evidence that ideas have mattered to Obama since he was in his teens, that they matter to him now, and that understanding those ideas should matter to anyone who wants to understand him.

If Americans are puzzled by Obama's refusal to take the bait offered by his opponents, if they want to know why he has persisted in his principled commitment to respectful disagreement and the search for compromise, they should pay attention to what he has said about those issues himself. Making clear the reasons he values deliberation is the purpose of *Reading Obama*. Of course, other factors matter, including Obama's upbringing and his family, American race relations, political life in Chicago, the dynamics of Washington politics, and Obama's own temperament and character. *Reading Obama* focuses on one dimension of the many that have shaped Obama's life—his ideas—a dimension that I think has received less attention than it deserves.

The constraints and opportunities Obama has faced as president differ from those he felt when he was fresh out of law school or new to the United States Senate, but the point of *Reading Obama* was neither to predict every decision he would make as president nor to provide a standard of judgment for evaluating his performance. Nor did I describe him as a "philosopher president," a phrase that took on a life of its own after it appeared in Patricia Cohen's October 27, 2010, *New York Times* article about *Reading Obama*. Taking philosophical ideas seriously does not make one a philosopher. My point instead was to illuminate, based on what Obama had written and said by the time my book went to press early in 2010, how he sees the world and why. Obama has called himself a "Christian and skeptic." Chapters 1 and 2 of *Reading Obama* explain how he can embrace both Christianity and skepticism by examining the cluster of ideas—perspectivalism, historicism, antifoundationalism, and philosophical pragmatism—that help clarify his outlook. Such ideas surely do not exhaust the person he is or limit the choices he can make.

Attempts to locate Obama's way of thinking in the conventional categories of Left and Right, liberal and conservative, can be misleading. He comes out of a long tradition of European and American thinkers who have been assailing the idea of absolute truth since the late nineteenth century. That assault opened the door to a wide range of philosophical and political possibilities. The revolution in thought accomplished by thinkers such as Friedrich Nietzsche and Max Weber in Germany and William James and John Dewey in the United States left many people unchanged. But others saw the world in a new way. They thought the philosophical foundations on which political ideologies stood had become unstable. Certainty had to give way to experimentation, and results had to be evaluated critically according to standards that were themselves open to scrutiny and debate. In the early twentieth century, progressives and social democrats in the United States and Europe renounced the dogmas of laissez-faire and Marxian socialism and launched reform movements that transformed industrial capitalist societies by introducing the graduated income tax, economic regulation, and social insurance. A century later, we inhabit the world that generation created.

After World War I, their intellectual revolution looked very different to a generation confronting the explosive arrival of foundational philosophies such as fascism, Nazism, and bolshevism. Many people on both sides of the Atlantic recoiled from experimentalism and returned to their own foundational philosophies, most often grounded in religious traditions. But the skeptical and experimental approach of those who embraced uncertainty did not disappear entirely. Non-doctrinaire reformers in Europe and America, including many who designed the most ambitious aspects of the New Deal and the programs of social provision undertaken by northern European social democratic governments after World War II, deliberately followed the lead of earlier thinkers such as William James and John Dewey in the United States, L. T. Hobhouse in England, and Jean Jaurès in France. Their legacy of incremental reform informed by an experimental, pragmatist method of trial and error went out of fashion during the early Cold War, but it returned and was appropriated by many thinkers in the years when Obama came of age.

Those ideas are hardly foolproof. Embracing antifoundationalism or philosophical pragmatism hardly assures political success. Asserting the beneficial consequences of doubting settled truths is a gamble under the best of circumstances. When people are clamoring for certainty, as members of the Tea Party do, and when people view skepticism as a threat to their cherished ideals, as many radicals as well as conservatives do, these ideas are particularly vulnerable. But neither does the drumbeat for dogmatism, no matter how pronounced, necessarily disprove the scientific method or the historical sensibility that sees change as constant and fruitful. As James and Dewey both acknowledged, there is a congruence between the experimentalism built into American democracy and the philosophy of pragmatism. Just as the Constitution was left open to amendment, and was ratified largely because the first ten amendments were added to it, so American democracy is open-ended by design. So is philosophical pragmatism. Whether that approach helps those who embrace it to solve problems or paralyzes them with uncertainty is a question students of pragmatism have debated since World War I. Different people give different answers. The jury is out.

Americans have elected plenty of presidents who never doubted their judgment, including Obama's predecessor. Not all Americans long for a president who shoots first and asks questions, if at all, only when it is too late, and who never admits a mistake. Whether readers find Barack Obama's approach to decision making a refreshing change from that of George W. Bush or consider Obama overly circumspect, *Reading Obama* explains some of the reasons for his commitment to conciliation and his aversion to dogma.

When Lincoln was elected president in 1860, he faced opponents whose intransigence was far greater than that of contemporary Republican legislators. They were ready to secede from the union and go to war on the battlefield, not on television talk shows. Their threat was not rhetorical but real. In his first inaugural address, Lincoln reaffirmed his promise not to act against slavery in the South, an action that he considered unconstitutional, and to enforce the fugitive slave law that Congress had passed, a law many northerners considered an abomination. These were his closing words to those ready to make war: "We are not enemies, but friends. We must not be enemies. Though passion may have strained, it must not break our bonds of affection. The mystic chords of memory, stretching from every battle-field, and patriot grave, to every living heart and hearthstone, all over this broad land, will yet swell the chorus of the Union, when again touched, as surely they will be, by the better angels of our nature."

The man examined in *Reading Obama*, like Lincoln, calls himself a Christian and a skeptic. He has firm beliefs, but he does not consider his own political judgments infallible. Like Lincoln, and like Jefferson before him, he does not consider those who disagree with him the enemy. As he said in his moving and memorable speech on January 12, 2011, after the shooting that killed six people in Tucson, he believes Americans need to see those unlike themselves with greater empathy, not with deeper hatred: "The forces that divide us," he said that day, "are not as strong as the forces that unite us." Those who recommend that

Obama begin vilifying his opponents, who insist that he abandon his commitment to deliberation and become as unyielding and unreasonable as those who oppose his every move, do not understand the dynamics of America's unfinished democracy as he does. In *The Audacity of Hope* and in many of his speeches, Obama has offered his own narrative of a diverse and divided people struggling to move forward, in fits and starts, toward the ideals of equality and freedom. Although he has stated and restated that story, he admitted after the 2010 elections that he needs to do a better job of communicating his message. With critics left and right assailing his willingness to compromise, he needs to explain why, to use the phrase of Ralph Ellison's *Invisible Man*, he continues calmly to "affirm the principle" of democracy and call for empathy, not antipathy, as the means toward the end of justice. At a time of intense partisanship, why does Barack Obama see American democracy as he does? Why he does continue to seek conciliation? *Reading Obama* answers those questions.

Introduction

AMERICA LOOKS DIFFERENT from the other side of the Atlantic. As I watched the twists and turns of the presidential campaign in the fall of 2008, I was following the drama from a distance. Living in England, lecturing to students at the University of Cambridge on the American political tradition, and trying in countless informal conversations to explain the unexpected emergence and election of Barack Obama, I began to see connections that had eluded me. Reading and rereading Obama's books, listening closely to his speeches, and thinking about the dynamics of American culture that made possible his rise to the presidency, I began piecing together the patterns traced in this book.

Barack Obama's intellectual and political persuasions emerged from a particular matrix, formed not only from his personal experience but also from the dynamics of American history. Obama's sensibility was shaped both by the period of his own intellectual formation—the years between his birth in Hawaii in 1961 and his ascent to national prominence with his election to the United States Senate in 2004—and by the longer history that stretches from the Puritans to the present. Perhaps because I was thinking about Obama simultaneously in relation to my

Cambridge lectures on the American past and my anxieties about the American future, I was alert to particular themes in his books *Dreams from My Father* and *The Audacity of Hope*. I became convinced that these books illuminate certain neglected aspects of American history and point toward a very different vision of the present than I had seen in any of the commentaries on the election.

Barack Obama is the product of three distinct developments. First, it was the history of American democracy, the long, unfinished project stretching from the seventeenth-century establishment of English colonies through the achievements of the civil rights and feminist movements, that produced the institutions and the cultural characteristics that made possible Obama's rise. Those same democratic institutions, and that same unfinished cultural project that we call American democracy, now constrain him as president. The immediate circumstances that led to Obama's election—public dissatisfaction with the greatest economic collapse in the United States since the Great Depression of the 1930s—have now become the single greatest obstacle impeding the realization of his most ambitious plans. The economic crisis resulted directly from policies of deregulation put in place during the preceding two decades by his predecessors Bill Clinton and George W. Bush. Yet many of the Americans who now hold Obama himself responsible for failing to restore prosperity also criticized the steps he took, the stimulus package and bank bailout, which most observers agree helped prevent an even deeper crisis. So incoherent is American pub-

lic debate that Obama's critics simultaneously blame him
for an economic situation he did nothing to cause and oppose larger infusions of money into the economy through
much greater government spending, the only option that
might directly address the problem. The impasse in which
the nation finds itself stems directly from the American
people's limited access to power—and their equally limited access to responsible sources of information about
how the American economy works. Because shrill, partisan simplifications dominate public debate, Obama's cautious, measured approach to economic reconstruction has
infuriated the Right without satisfying the Left. The penetrating analysis that Obama offers in *The Audacity of
Hope* explains the short-circuiting of American democracy in the twentieth century and illuminates the reasons
why he faces such intractable political as well as economic
problems as president. His conundrum, as he understands,
is the product of long-term, unresolved problems in American history.

Second, America's principal contribution to the Western philosophical tradition, the philosophy of pragmatism
that originated over a century ago in the writings of William James and John Dewey, has provided a sturdy base
for Obama's sensibility. It has become a cliché to characterize Obama as a pragmatist, by which most commentators mean only that he has a talent for compromise—
or an unprincipled politician's weakness for the path of
least resistance. But there is a decisive difference between
such vulgar pragmatism, which is merely an instinctive

hankering for what is possible in the short term, and philosophical pragmatism, which challenges the claims of absolutists—whether their dogmas are rooted in science or religion—and instead embraces uncertainty, provisionality, and the continuous testing of hypotheses through experimentation. The distinction between vulgar pragmatism and philosophical pragmatism is not always clear in practice because philosophical pragmatists can and sometimes do recommend what seems simply practical. But I will insist on the difference. The philosophical pragmatism of James and Dewey and their descendants has played an important part in shaping progressive politics since the early twentieth century. The close connection between the philosophy of pragmatism and the culture of democratic decision making illuminates crucial dimensions of Obama's thinking—and the fierce opposition he faces.

If philosophical pragmatism informs Obama's political outlook, the history of pragmatists' engagement in politics also suggests the reasons why pragmatism may be particularly ill-suited to our own cultural moment. At a time when partisans left and right vie to proclaim rival versions of certainty with greater self-righteousness, the pragmatists' critique of absolutism and embrace of open-ended experimentation seems off-key, unsatisfying, perhaps even cowardly. Pragmatists have debated the political consequences of the philosophy for over a century. There is general agreement concerning the tight connection between philosophical pragmatism and democracy. Both are committed to open-endedness and experimentation.

But there never has been—nor, I think, can there be—a clear, explicit, singular lesson to be drawn from the philosophy of pragmatism for a particular political dispute. Indeed, the idea of such a formula is inimical to pragmatism, which is a method for testing beliefs in experience rather than measuring them against a yardstick of unchanging absolutes. Precisely because consequences matter to pragmatists, one can never say dogmatically, in advance, that one policy or another follows necessarily from the commitment to experimentation. Pragmatism is a philosophy for skeptics, a philosophy for those committed to democratic debate and the critical assessment of the results of political decisions, not for true believers convinced they know the right course of action in advance of inquiry and experimentation. Pragmatism stands for open-mindedness and ongoing debate. The flexibility of pragmatist philosophy, which helps explain Obama's intellectual acuity and suppleness, may paradoxically undercut his ability to inspire and persuade the American electorate and the United States Congress at a time when strident rhetoric and unyielding partisanship have displaced reasoned deliberation and a commitment to problem solving.

Third, Obama's sensibility reflects the intellectual upheavals that occurred on American campuses during the two decades he spent studying at Occidental College, Columbia University, and the Harvard Law School, and teaching law at the University of Chicago Law School. Those struggles emerged for complex reasons and are difficult to summarize, but they played a crucial role in shaping Obama's ideas. Again and again he encountered struggles between universality and particularity, and between the ostensibly unchanging and the historical or contingent. Between college and law school, Obama spent three crucial years working as a community organizer in Chicago, and observers unsurprisingly take for granted that there must be a difference between what he learned on the streets of the far south side and what he learned in the seminar rooms of elite universities. To a striking degree, however, the lessons were congruent: Democracy in a pluralist culture means coaxing a common good to emerge from the clash of competing individual interests. Bringing ideals to life requires power. Balancing principles and effectiveness in the public sphere is hard work, an unending process of trial and error. No formulas ensure success.

Many commentators have already examined Obama's personality, his family background, and the role of race in his rise to the White House. Those issues are crucial, and I have learned a lot from such studies. But other factors in addition to psychology and family dynamics have shaped his way of thinking. Race, although it obviously has been and remains one of the crucial issues in American history, is only one of the contexts that matters. Obama will no doubt continue to fascinate biographers and political commentators, who will enrich our understanding of his life and times. My goal here is different. I want to focus on his ideas. Locating Obama's development in the frameworks of the history of American democracy, the ideas of philosophical pragmatism, and the intellectual turmoil of the 1980s and 1990s reveals how Obama thinks and why he sees American culture and politics as he does. Reading Obama requires not only examining the central arguments contained in his books and speeches, although that is clearly the first step. Understanding him as a writer, and as a politician, also requires placing his ideas in the deeper and broader contexts of the American political tradition, which neither the pundits nor prophets who dominate contemporary American public discourse have shown much interest in doing. Beginning that process, by placing Obama's ideas in the frameworks of American history and thought, is the modest aim of this little book.

Chapter 1 traces Obama's intellectual development by examining the distinct stages of his education, from his childhood through college, from his years as a community organizer and a law student through his emergence as a contender for national political office. Chapter 2 places Obama's ideas in the turbulent currents of intellectual debate during the closing decades of the twentieth century. Chapter 3 locates the arguments of his books in a much wider historical context, that of the long trajectory of American democratic theory and practice. Almost all historians appreciate the depth of the ideas that some presidents, notably John Adams, Thomas Jefferson, James Madison, John Quincy Adams, and Abraham Lincoln, carried with them to the White House. Many historians now also acknowledge that crucial dispositions and innovative policies of presidents Theodore Roosevelt, Woodrow Wilson, and Franklin Roosevelt likewise depended on ideas, in their case the revolutionary ideas of the pioneers of philosophical pragmatism, William James and John Dewey. Like his eighteenth-century and early twentieth-century predecessors, Barack Obama is a man of ideas. By linking his writings to the intellectual traditions on which he has drawn, quite clearly and deliberately, in *Dreams from My Father* and *The Audacity of Hope*, this book provides the first attempt to locate Obama in the contexts of American political and social thought.

In my field of intellectual history, it is customary for scholars who engage in the practice known as contextualism to trace the relation between texts and contexts, between ideas and the circumstances of their historical production and transmission. Those historians who study European ideas typically conceive of contexts primarily in the relation between selected canonical texts and other canonical texts in the history of philosophy or political theory. That is certainly a legitimate and valuable approach, particularly when examining the work of thinkers whose ideas often did not have much immediate impact on anyone except other thinkers.

In the historical study of American political thought, however, it is not enough to focus exclusively on the writings of philosophers, important as they may have been. Many of those who have actively shaped American politics, from the second, third, and fourth presidents to the forty-fourth, have not only drawn explicitly on the ideas of philosophers, they have worked quite consciously, deliberately, and sometimes successfully to translate those ideas into policies. Some have even engaged in serious political thinking and writing themselves, including of course those who played major roles in producing the most prominent and enduring products of the American Enlightenment, the Declaration of Independence and the United States Constitution, two documents that reflect the creative work of a generation of Americans. The same was true of Lincoln, whose carefully crafted speeches beginning in 1854 manifest his serious engagement with traditions of moral philosophy and political economy as well as with the writings of predecessors such as John Adams, Jefferson, Madison, and John Quincy Adams. Evidence of that tendency to link policies with theories has seemed less clear in recent decades. But scholars are now showing that serious ideas lay beneath the apparent anti-intellectualism of recent American conservative politicians, and a rising generation of historians is excavating the foundations of those ideas in the transatlantic discourse of the 1930s, 1940s, and 1950s.

Likewise, beneath Obama's politics lies a sustained engagement with America's democratic traditions, and this book illuminates those connections. Much has been written already, and much more is sure to come, concerning the crucial personal and social influences that also affected his personality and outlook. This book concentrates on his ideas. Chapter 1 narrates Obama's intellectual development. Chapter 2 focuses on formal political philosophy and social theory to explain the intellectual contexts that shaped Obama's own ideas. Chapter 3 shows how his understanding of American history informs his approach to politics. It would be false and foolish to claim that the issues discussed in this book exhaust the factors shaping Obama's sensibility. In addition to being a thoughtful and deft writer, Obama has proven that he is a shrewd and savvy politician who has learned a lot from the rough-and-tumble of community organizing in Chicago and from the notoriously down-and-dirty world of Illinois electoral politics. But intelligence and caginess are not mutually exclusive. Just as Lincoln emerged from courtroom wrangling and partisan scuffles full of high-minded principles as well as hard-won lessons, so has Obama, and not much has been written about the ideas he imbibed and the ideals to which he has declared allegiance.

Many of the disillusioned, self-consciously tough-minded, and sometimes cynical commentators who shape public attitudes toward contemporary politics seem disinclined to take ideas seriously, but Obama's books demonstrate that he sees things differently. Ideas matter to him. For that reason understanding what those ideas are, where they have come from, and what difference they have made in shaping the sensibility of the forty-fourth president of the United States should matter to us.

Chapter 1

The Education of Barack Obama

O N THE NIGHT HE WAS ELECTED president of the United States, Barack Obama proclaimed that "our nation's greatest strength" is "the enduring power of our ideals." That claim not only signaled Obama's clear repudiation of the self-conscious tough-guy realism of the preceding eight years, it also suggested a dimension of the new president's sensibility that has not received the attention it deserves. Most observers emphasized the novelty of Obama's campaign, with its reliance on grass-roots contributions and its unprecedented use of electronic communications, and not surprisingly stressed the break from the American past represented by his election and his emphasis on hope and change. Many writers linked Obama with the recurrent American impulse to begin again, the Adamic aspiration that has manifested itself in our culture's obsession with sloughing off the old and celebrating the new.

Irresistible as that reading may be given Obama's age and his race, it is a mistake. As he understands, he is a product of America's past. Obama has demonstrated an exceptionally sophisticated and sustained engagement with the history of American thought and political culture. His approach to politics seems new only to those who lack his acquaintance with the venerable traditions of American democracy: respect for one's opponents and a willingness to compromise with them. His commitment to conciliation derives from his understanding that in a democracy all victories are incomplete. In his words, "no law is ever final, no battle truly finished," because any defeat can be redeemed and any triumph lost in the next vote. Building lasting support for new policies and substantive changes is not the work of months or even years but decades.

Obama's writings show his debts to earlier American traditions and demonstrate that he has a deeper interest in, and a firmer grip on, America's past than has any president of the United States since Theodore Roosevelt and Woodrow Wilson. The strands on which Obama has drawn, however, differ from those that have appealed to many Democrats in recent decades. In part for that reason, and even more significantly because his sensibility reflects the profound changes in American intellectual life since the 1960s, Obama's ideas and his approach to American politics have thrown political observers off balance. His books, his speeches, and his political record make clear that he represents a hybrid of old and new, which explains why he puzzles so many contemporaries—supporters and critics alike—who see him through conventional and thus distorting lenses. Placing him in American intellectual history illuminates both the genuinely novel dimensions of his worldview, which have gone largely unnoticed, and the older traditions he seeks to resurrect. Obama's vision of American history and his understanding of its present condition both reflect the profound changes American culture has undergone in recent decades. If we want to understand him, we must understand how he sees the present in light of the past, and also how he envisions the future in light of his own—and his nation's—place within a global community that has undergone dramatic and unprecedented cultural transformations. As Obama put it when he accepted the Nobel Peace Prize in Oslo on December 9, 2009, the rise of transnational institutions such as the United Nations, movements such as the demand for human rights, and the process of globalization have caused people everywhere to "fear the loss of what they cherish in their particular identities—their race, their tribe, and perhaps most powerfully their religion." Balancing those apparently irresistible dynamics against the persistent appeal of local cultural traditions, finding a way to reconcile the apparently irreconcilable tugs of the universal against the particular, is the central dynamic of the twenty-first-century world. Obama has shown that he understands the sources of that struggle and the reasons why it is so much more difficult to resolve than most commentators on the left and right admit.

A powerful wave of enthusiasm washed over the world in the wake of Obama's election, so there were not many cynics among those listening when Obama spoke in Chicago on election night. In the light of day, however, skeptics might have been tempted to dismiss his observation about "the enduring power of our ideals" as just another piece of charming but empty rhetoric. Which parts of the American populace shared his understanding of "our ideals," including his understanding of the specific ideals he listed: "democracy, liberty, opportunity, and unyielding hope"? Surely the 48 percent of the electorate who voted for Republican Party candidate John McCain cherished a sense of America's intellectual inheritance quite different from that of Obama and his supporters. Moreover, Obama's choice of words suggested those of a discredited predecessor, the last Democrat elected to the presidency. Soon after Bill Clinton used similar terms in his first inaugural address in 1993, he began wandering down a path of personal and political miscalculation that led in the opposite direction. Instead of resuscitating the weakened tradition of progressive democracy that he invoked, Clinton spent eight years "triangulating," seeking a "third way," and squandering the chance to draw sustenance from—and breathe new life into—American democratic ideals. He left office with his party scrambling to extricate itself from his presidency and his nation even more polarized than it was when he was elected. In short, Clinton's presidency suggested that hearkening back to American ideals can prove to be no more than an empty gesture. Hadn't Americans heard such talk about "ideals" before?

Yes and no. Obama has written two serious books, *Dreams from My Father* and *The Audacity of Hope*, the first widely praised for its prose, the second more often dismissed, incorrectly, as a typical piece of campaign fluff. His third book, *Change We Can Believe In: Barack Obama's Plan to Renew America's Promise*, does fit comfortably within that old and undistinguished tradition of ephemera; it is useful only because it provides the texts of several of Obama's important speeches. But *Dreams from My Father* and *The Audacity of Hope* should be acknowledged as the most substantial books written by anyone elected president of the United States since Woodrow Wilson, who enjoyed a successful career as a political scientist before ascending to the presidency of Princeton University, then the governorship of New Jersey, and finally the White House. *Dreams* and *Hope*, taken together, provide not only a window into Obama's nuanced understanding of American history and culture but also his blueprint for American politics. Yet American journalists, stuck on the treadmill of an ever accelerating news cycle, necessarily attend obsessively to the news—and especially the scandals—of the day, and many political commentators themselves display limited interest in or familiarity with the history of American thought. As a result, Obama's books have received less careful scrutiny than they deserve.

Dreams from My Father is an eloquent and moving memoir that Obama wrote in 1994, after he was elected by his peers as the first African American president of the *Harvard Law Review* (*HLR*). The title president is somewhat misleading because it suggests executive authority for a position that more nearly resembles that of editor in chief. Coincidentally, I published a long review essay in that journal on the relation between law and intellectual history just a year after Obama's term as editor ended. That experience acquainted me with some of the talented and ambitious kids—and most of them are kids, after all, in their early to mid-twenties—who run the *HLR*. Like many of those who have written for law reviews or taught students from top-flight law schools, I found their intelligence and self-confidence more striking than the breadth of their experience. Being elected president—or, in other words, principal editor—of the *HLR* is a notable achievement. Yet serving in that position did not seem to me necessarily the best training for thinking carefully and critically about oneself and expansively about American history. For that reason, the self-conscious and convincing performance of personal modesty in *Dreams from My Father*, as well as the book's searching and unconventional analysis of the challenges of multiculturalism, took me by surprise. Not only as an account of Obama's own odyssey but also as a provocative meditation on personal identity, the book belongs in the distinguished tradition of American memoirs.

The Audacity of Hope appeared in 2006, after Obama had been involved in electoral politics for a decade. By then the junior United States Senator from Illinois was clearly beginning to entertain aspirations for the presidency. Such ambitions would have seemed far-fetched— or laughable—when he wrote *Dreams from My Father*. At that stage he had already begun to think about electoral politics, but his imagination seems to have carried him to the mayor's office in Chicago rather than the White House. *The Audacity of Hope*, much more than Obama's first book, provides his diagnosis of contemporary American problems and offers a roadmap of political possibilities. It also presents along the way a refreshingly serious and cogent account of American political and cultural history. It shows that Obama has wrestled with the central challenges posed by the multiple traditions of American political thought, and it establishes him as one of the few prominent figures in national politics who have made original and important contributions to those traditions in recent decades. These two books, together with his major speeches, demonstrate that when Obama makes references to American history and "our ideals," he knows what he's talking about. Skeptics have wondered whether Obama himself wrote these substantial books. He concedes that friends, associates, and staff members read drafts, suggested changes, and helped him refine his arguments. Every author depends on such help. But since I began investigating Obama's ideas, no one who knows him has expressed any doubt to me that both books are his work.

Locating Obama in American intellectual history presents a number of challenges. In the introduction to *Dreams from My Father*, Obama explains that he envisioned writing a book about American race relations before he found himself "pulled toward rockier shores." He had been invited to write the book because of his race, yet he found himself drawn toward anxieties, longings, memories, and stories that took him in surprising directions, toward the tangled roots of his own personal identity as well as America's persistent race problem. In the final chapter of his memoir, musing on the cacophonous voices of his African and American families, he likens the persistent questions he posed to members of his extended family to "rocks roiling the water." Obama's voyage into the past plunged him into currents he did not expect and did not know how to navigate. The man who emerged from those journeys earned wisdom that provided little consolation. Neither his mother's family, rooted in the heartland of America and transplanted first to Hawaii and then, when she remarried, to Indonesia, nor his father's, spread across the breadth of Kenya and beyond, offered him even a modest degree of stability, let alone tranquility.

Instead both America and Africa presented endless challenges and puzzles, the "rockier shores" on which his and his relatives' fantasies ran aground. His American and African families, like all families, had constructed dramatic tales of heroism and tragedy, most of which unraveled when Obama examined them carefully. His investigations repeatedly interrupted the flow of his families' narratives, creating eddies and pools where family members' memories mingled with Obama's own hopes. Beneath the surfaces of family sagas lay undertows that upset his equilibrium, complicated his own sense of self, and, even more treacherously, disrupted the personal and cultural narratives that had inspired him as a child.

Obama admits at the outset that *Dreams from My Father* should be read as a meditation on the central themes of his life rather than a strictly accurate account. He kept journals at some stages of his life, but the record is incomplete. Some characters are composites, some events out of chronological order. Reconstructed conversations only approximate what was said. But if *Dreams* is best read as a fable or an allegory, as a text hovering in the turbulence between fiction and nonfiction, it nevertheless reveals the depth of Obama's reflections on the problems of self-knowledge and cultural understanding. What he learned from his explorations into his American and African families left him perched between cultures, stranded, uneasy, puzzled.

Obama's explorations of American society and politics likewise proved painful and disorienting. As a student, a community organizer, a civil rights lawyer, a law professor, and finally a legislator, Obama saw his ambitions crash repeatedly against unyielding realities. In *The Audacity of Hope*, Obama explained why contemporary American culture proves so resistant to the changes that he and other progressives seek. In the process he revealed not only personal resiliency but a sure grip on the numerous and multilayered obstacles confronting anyone attempting to use the levers of law or politics to alter the peculiar amalgam of democratic and antidemocratic elements that constitute American public life. Again and again Obama has found his own ideals of democracy, equal rights, community, and justice—and his strategies of reconciliation, experimentation, and consensus building—bouncing off the hard surfaces of individual self-interest and political partisanship. That experience too left him stranded, uneasy, puzzled.

This book places Barack Obama in two separate contexts in order to illuminate the cultural frameworks within which he came of age, the historical patterns that have shaped his sensibility. Obama's life journey has been not only an American tale, as many commentators have noted, but also a journey lived at a time of deep cultural self-examination and contestation, when thinkers were seeking, finding, and then rejecting foundations of many different kinds. That sense of dislocation comes not just from Obama's own multiple homes and the different traditions he inherited from his parents. It comes also from the nature of his formal and informal education, his cultural formation, the world he has inhabited for the last twenty-five years.

Obama's writings reflect the impact of that multidimensional education. The child of an American mother and an African father who met while studying at the University of Hawaii and married in a small civil ceremony, the details of which he admits are "murky," Obama spent his early childhood in that most exotic island outpost of the United States. Several years after his parents separated, he moved with his mother and her new husband Lolo Soetoro to Soetoro's native Indonesia, where Obama attended school from age six to age ten. "Your mother has a soft heart," he remembers Soetoro telling him. As a boy he needed to learn the toughness that enabled Indonesians to survive life's hard edges, the toughness he would need as a man. "Sometimes you can't worry about hurt," his stepfather advised Obama. "Sometimes you worry only about getting where you have to go."

Obama's mother, softhearted or not, soon realized that her husband's career exacted a price she was unwilling to pay. Even more than their long separations, the unsavory deals Soetoro brokered between the Indonesian government and American businessmen soured her on their life and convinced her that her son—and his new half-sister Maya—should return to the United States for their education. To that end she began tutoring Obama in the early mornings, shaking him out of bed long before dawn to study English and instill in him the values of her midwestern girlhood: honesty, fairness, straight talk, and independent judgment. Puzzled by the contrast between her rock-solid virtues and his stepfather's unvarnished cynicism, Obama reports that he was beginning to take refuge in a wide-ranging skepticism. His mother had enlisted as a "soldier for New Deal, Peace Corps, position-paper liberalism," in Obama's words. Although she had missed the civil rights movement, she remained a disciple of Martin Luther King, Jr., Thurgood Marshall, and Fannie Lou Hamer, and she tried hard to convince her son that he inherited a special destiny from his African father.

But Obama lacked her faith. As a curious boy chafing at her rules and beginning to wonder about the mysteries of racial difference revealed by American magazines and television programs, Obama felt himself shifting his allegiance to Soetoro's unblinking fatalism. Maybe individuals did not shape their destiny. Maybe his stepfather's eclectic cosmology, comprising elements of Islam, Hinduism, and animism, better equipped him to cope with an unfair and unpredictable universe. His mother's fascination with Asia never wavered; eventually she wrote her doctoral dissertation in anthropology on the subject of metal working in Indonesia. But she wanted her son to grow up an American, so she sent him from Jakarta back to Honolulu, where he lived with his maternal grandparents for four of the seven years he spent studying at a private college preparatory school, Punahou Academy.

As a teenager Obama wrestled with competing impulses. Because of America's one-drop rule, he was classified as black. Yet he lived with his white grandparents or—for the three years his mother spent, after she and Soetoro divorced, back in Honolulu working on her master's degree—with his white mother and Maya. His own father visited once, for a month, which added just one more voice to all those hectoring the boy. He must work harder.

Study longer. Make his family proud. Live up to their dreams for him. Obama admits that the exoticism of Africa fascinated him. He was tickled that his father's visit to the school impressed his Punahou classmates. But the month-long stay was only an awkward interlude. His father had no place in his family's life, and Obama was relieved when he returned to Kenya.

At Punahou Obama experienced the usual anxieties of adolescence, but the puzzles of race heightened the uneasiness he shared with every teenager who wonders where he belongs. He befriended another mixed-race boy, Keith Kakugawa, called Ray in *Dreams*, and together they navigated the hard-to-read straits of race in Hawaii. As teens they wondered if they were black—or black enough. What should they make of their white friends on the basketball team, or, to use Ray's phrase, "white folks" more generally? For Obama such questions had no clear answers. Not only did he live with "white folks," they were his family. He could understand, but he could not quite share, Ray's resentment. He remained an indifferent student, playing sports, doing drugs, getting by. Basketball gave him "armor against uncertainty" and a chance to be part of "a community of sorts," a feeling unavailable to him elsewhere. On his own he was reading books that piqued his curiosity about race and identity, books by W. E. B. DuBois, Langston Hughes, James Baldwin, Richard Wright, Ralph Ellison, Malcolm X.

Obama already knew firsthand what DuBois meant by the color line, "two-ness," and double consciousness. In the complex, shifting, multiracial world of Hawaii, such concepts were a fact of life. Consciousness was not just doubled, it was squared, perhaps cubed. He knew about the rage felt by Ray and others who did not have the cushion of a loving white family to ease their experience of racism. He plunged into the anger of Baldwin and Wright. He already sensed that blacks were always playing on an away court, a court where only whites felt at home. But the voices that spoke most profoundly to Obama seem to have been those of Hughes and Ellison, writers who laced their anger with doses of hope.

Although doubtless indebted to many models, *Dreams from My Father* echoes the tone of Ellison's *Invisible Man*. Ellison's protagonist, despite repeated rebuffs and deepening disillusionment, refuses despair. At the end of the novel—even after descending into hibernation, in a burrow deep beneath the streets of Harlem—he still chooses to "affirm the principle" animating the tragically flawed project of American democracy. The protagonist's grandfather had urged him, with his dying words, to say "yes" to the principle because it was "greater than the men, greater than the numbers and the vicious power and all the methods used to corrupt its name." Although the principle had been "violated and compromised to the point of absurdity," and African Americans "brutalized and sacrificed" for centuries by that betrayal, Ellison's protagonist nevertheless embraces the ideals of freedom and equality that the nation's failures had not tarnished. Yet affirming the principle did not explain how to live, day to day, according to the rules whites made. In Obama's words, "there was a trick there somewhere, although what the trick was, and who was doing the tricking, and who was being tricked, eluded my conscious grasp." Like Ellison's character Rinehart, a master of disguises who thrived by keeping everyone guessing among his multiple identities, Obama toyed with escaping the script his mother and her parents had laid out for him. Yet that option, he realized, meant "withdrawal into a smaller and smaller coil of rage, until being black meant only the knowledge of your own powerlessness." To Obama that path held no appeal.

Instead, like Ellison, DuBois, and Hughes, Obama was beginning to realize that the principle would be redeemed only if African Americans, systematically excluded from its promise, could transcend hatred. If Obama found in Ellison reasons to resist Ray's rage and sustain hope, he found in *The Autobiography of Malcolm X* an even more compelling tale of self-creation and, ultimately, an even more profound promise of reconciliation between blacks and whites through the affirmation of a wider human brotherhood. Although his family, his teachers, and his friends might have thought Obama capable of deeper commitment and higher achievement than he showed at Punahou, his early reading and thinking about race laid the groundwork for his exceptional self-awareness. Conversations with one of his grandfather's black friends, the poet Frank Marshall Davis, drove home the central insight of DuBois's and Ellison's writings: because of the veil that obscured him from whites, because of his invisibility,

Obama would never be known by whites as he could know them. As he became aware of that condition, and his double consciousness, he began to understand his predicament. Even though he was surrounded by a loving family, Obama "realized for the first time that I was utterly alone."

Obama showed enough promise in the final two years he spent in the classrooms and on the basketball courts of Honolulu to earn a scholarship to Occidental College in Los Angeles. His two years there were another pivotal period in his life. He studied history and political theory, first of America and then of Europe, in two year-long courses with the political scientist Roger Boesche. Boesche was immersed in writing a fine book about Alexis de Tocqueville, author of the widely quoted and too seldom read *Democracy in America*, and he was beginning to think about the subject of his later scholarship, tyranny from the ancient world to the present. Almost three decades later, Obama's experience in those courses remains significant enough that he invited Boesche to the White House, where they joked about the "B" Obama remembered (correctly) having received from Boesche. In those courses Obama encountered a wide range of thinkers. Among Americans he was exposed to the ideas of John Adams, Thomas Jefferson, James Madison, and some of the Anti-Federalists who opposed the U.S. Constitution; Transcendentalists Ralph Waldo Emerson and Henry David Thoreau; antebellum reformers including Frederick Douglass and Abraham Lincoln; assorted populists, progressives, and New Dealers; Protestant theologians such as Reinhold Niebuhr; and leading figures in the civil rights movement and radicals of the 1960s. On the European side, Obama encountered Greek and Roman political philosophy and the writings of Niccolo Machiavelli, Alexis de Tocqueville, Karl Marx, Max Weber, Friedrich Nietzsche, and Jürgen Habermas, complex thinkers who probed the possibilities and the limits of politics. In an interview during the 2008 campaign, Obama counted many of those writers among the most influential in his life, writers whose work he has continued to consult. Traces of their ideas pop up regularly in his books and speeches.

Obama reports in *The Audacity of Hope* that he decided to study political philosophy at Occidental because he was "looking for both a language and systems of action that could help build community and make justice real." Given that aspiration, he struggled with the contrast between Weber's and Nietzsche's iconoclasm and the idealism of American reformers. That contrast, between a valueless, post-Christian nihilism and the continuing struggle to "make justice real," was among the insights that led William James and John Dewey to construct the philosophy of pragmatism. Teaching at Harvard from the 1870s until his death in 1910, James helped shape the thinking of his students George Herbert Mead, Herbert Croly, Walter Lippmann, W. E. B. DuBois, Gertrude Stein, Horace Kallen, Alain Locke, and Robert Park, individuals who figured prominently in twentieth-century American thought and American politics. They also figured prominently among the progressive reformers whose work Obama first encountered in his studies with Boesche. From his first serious explorations of American political thought, then, Obama was made aware of the shaping influence of the philosophy of pragmatism on progressive political reformers.

When Obama was studying at Occidental, race and gender were not yet the central themes they have become for twenty-first-century American scholars, but Obama notes in *Dreams* that he did begin to read the work of writers critical of Western imperialism and gender hierarchy while in Los Angeles. He learned enough to be able to quote Frantz Fanon, the Caribbean-born theorist of the Algerian Revolution, whose book *The Wretched of the Earth* made him the spokesman for third-world revolutions and the darling of many American radicals. Obama also knew enough about anti- and postcolonial literature to consider himself, like his fellow black and Asian students at Occidental, alienated from white America. When he eventually had a chance to travel to Europe, he reports having felt equally disconnected from European cultures. Unlike generations of Americans from Benjamin Franklin, John Adams, and Jefferson to DuBois, Baldwin, and Richard Wright, all of whom relished the chance to soak up the atmosphere of European capitals, Obama reported feeling only emptiness. In Europe he was living someone else's fantasy, not his own.

Obama arrived at Occidental a less than devoted student. More interested in basketball than in struggling with difficult ideas, he self-consciously projected a cool demeanor yet bristled when whites complimented him for it. But as he spent weeks wrestling with texts such as Nietzsche's *Beyond Good and Evil* and *On the Genealogy of Morals*, or probing the arguments in Lippmann's *Drift and Mastery* or DuBois's *Souls of Black Folk*, something clicked. During the two years Obama spent amid the eucalyptus and orange trees that dot Occidental's campus, he began hanging out with students more interested in ideas and politics than basketball and parties, and he began to think more critically himself. Under the influence of his friends and his literature professors Anne Howells and Eric Newhall, he began to cultivate a new self-image as a writer. Novels now vied with political tracts for his attention. He was drawn into the South African divestment campaign and the Committee in Solidarity with the People of El Salvador, the student–faculty organization opposing American intervention in Central America. He was unpersuaded when one of his friends resisted the black identity others ascribed to her and proclaimed herself "multiracial." She was running away from the hard fact of race in America. Whatever individuals might think of themselves, to whites they were black. So was Obama. When black friends, prompted by the woman he calls Regina in *Dreams*, began to call him Barack instead of Barry, he accepted it as a sign of his authenticity.

Obama quickly grew into his new identity. He contacted members of the African National Congress and invited them to speak at Occidental. He wrote letters and argued strategy with other students. He agreed to deliver a speech at a rally on South African divestment, or rather to begin to deliver a speech, which the rally's organizers agreed would be truncated by a bit of guerilla theater. After Obama had begun speaking, white students dressed in paramilitary gear would forcibly remove him from the stage, dramatizing the difference between the situation on American campuses and in South Africa.

Readers familiar with Ellison's *Invisible Man* will hear echoes of the novel in Obama's account of his first, transformative experience with political activism. Like Ellison's protagonist addressing the Brotherhood for the first time, Obama reports finding himself surprised by the power of his words and his bond with the crowd. When he was interrupted, as planned, he did not have to feign resistance. He genuinely did not want to be dragged from the stage. In Ellison's words, "I feel your eyes upon me," and "I feel suddenly that I have become *more human*. . . . I feel strong. I feel able to get things done. . . . With your eyes upon me I feel that I've found my true family!" Or, as Obama puts it in *Dreams*, "If I could just find the right words, . . . everything could change—South Africa, the lives of ghetto kids just a few miles away, my own tenuous place in the world." Like Ellison's protagonist, in a "trancelike state" he found spontaneous eloquence. The struggle in South Africa demanded a choice, as he put it, "between dignity and servitude. Between fairness and injustice. Between commitment and indifference. A choice between right and wrong." As in Ellison's *Invisible Man*, Obama reports having hesitated at that moment, waiting for the crowd to inspire him, only to see in their enthusiastic response that "I had them, that the connection had been made." When he was pulled away, "I had so much left to say." Not only had he discovered the seductive power of politics, he had discovered his voice. He did indeed have a lot to say. Like many bookish students flirting with politics before and since, Obama reports that he began to think harder about the world beyond parties and sports. Boesche had criticized Obama's lackluster academic performance and chided him for failing to realize his potential. Stung by those comments and increasingly engaged with ideas, Obama began exerting himself more in his studies.

But Boesche wasn't the only one pushing him. Black friends like Regina also thought he was selling himself short, shrinking back from a deeper engagement into the shell of indifference—the "armor of uncertainty"—that shielded him from his fear that he belonged to neither the black nor the white world. As he reflected on Regina's challenge, her words blurred into the similar challenges laid down by his teachers, his mother, his grandparents, and by unknown people in South Africa, Central America, Indonesia, and across America forced to endure poverty and injustice. All were demanding more from him. "They all asked the same thing of me, these grandmothers of mine." They asked just what the grandfather in *Invisible Man* demanded. They wanted him not just to survive or endure, they demanded that he shoulder a burden that he did not ask for, but that fell to him nevertheless, a responsibility to affirm the principle. But there was a problem. Obama was attracted more to the questioners—to Emerson, Nietzsche, James, and Niebuhr—than to those with the dogmatic certainty animating political activists. How could he reconcile his own doubts with his grandmothers' pleas?

When Obama learned that Occidental had an exchange program with Columbia University in New York City, he decided to look into it. He wanted to explore the heart of black urban life, and when the chance came to trade Occidental's mostly white community for a neighborhood next door to Harlem, he took it. Obama spent his junior and senior years at Columbia exploring books and beginning to envision a career as a writer of fiction. Although he read plenty of novels and took plenty of courses in literature, he was still seeking a way to connect ideas with action, so he majored in political science. He contributed to a student publication entitled *Sundial*, where he deployed ideas drawn from some of the thinkers he had read at Occidental. Obama wrote a sympathetic article about student protests against the Reagan administration's efforts to expand America's nuclear arsenal. But the moderation that has become his trademark was already apparent: he was clearly less enamored with the idea of a nuclear freeze than were many Columbia students. Instead he took up the idea of nuclear nonproliferation. In an essay he wrote senior year, as part of a year-long seminar with Michael Baron on international relations, he reasoned that negotiating with the leaders of the Soviet Union might prove more productive than trying to intimidate them.

During Obama's years in New York, the Reagan administration proposed requiring all draft-age Americans to register, a move widely seen as a step toward reinstituting the draft. When Columbia students organized to protest that proposal, and to protest against expanding the number of nuclear weapons America possessed, Obama wrote an article detailing their efforts. "The most pervasive malady of the collegiate system specifically," he wrote in *Sundial*, "and the American experience generally, is that elaborate patterns of knowledge and theory have been disembodied from individual choices and government policy." Student activists at Columbia were grappling with that problem. The protesters were not wasting their time making pointless gestures. Instead they were trying to "bring the words of that formidable roster on the face of Butler Library, names like Thoreau, Jefferson, and Whitman, to bear on the twisted logic of which we are today a part." By working to "deprive us of a spectacular experience—that of war," students at Columbia and across America were doing their best to "enhance the possibility of a decent world." Although his *Sundial* article was primarily a straightforward account of the organizers' ideas and activities—and a deliberate effort to beef up his thin résumé—Obama took the opportunity to reflect on the wider purposes of political protest.

From his days as an undergraduate, Obama showed the capacity and inclination to mobilize America's intellectual traditions to bolster democratic political action. He remained too focused on reading and writing—a journal, some fiction, and "some really bad poetry," as he puts it in *Dreams*—to be characterized as a political activist or a journalist during his time in New York. He still felt marginalized from student life at Columbia. Yet he was growing more attuned to the issues attracting student protests and to the problem of poverty that continued to plague American cities. Exposure to the remaining shards of black radicalism convinced him the civil rights movement, whatever it had offered an earlier generation, had "shattered into a thousand fragments." Marxists and black nationalists shouted epithets at bourgeois reformers, but Obama saw through their bluster: no one knew what to do.

Obama had come to New York in search of a black community. He found only ruins. After a stint working in the worlds of business consulting and public interest research, he decided to change course. His grandfather's friend Frank Davis had warned him, when he was leaving Honolulu for Occidental, to be careful of the world he was entering. "They'll train you," Davis said, then "eventually they'll yank the chain." With the lure of a comfortable office and a prosperous life still shimmering in his imagination, Obama chose not to be yanked away from the challenge his "many grandmothers" had posed. Filled with a vague uneasiness about black urban life in Reagan's America, he resolved to abandon the world of upward mobility and become a community organizer. Somehow. Somewhere. Unfortunately, he did not know exactly what community organizers did, nor how to begin, and his determination might have withered had he not received a call from a community organizer in Chicago who wanted to hire a trainee.

Equipped with little more than sentimental images of Chicago's black community and a job offer, Obama plunged into the far south side of Chicago. Looking back a decade later, he remembered that he saw Richard Wright in every mail carrier, Duke Ellington in every jazz musician, Ella Fitzgerald in every singer, and his Chicago-born friend Regina in every black girl he encountered. At twenty-five, he knew he lacked experience, but he was ready for the next stage in his development. He was going to work. Obama now calls the three years he spent as an organizer in Chicago "the best education" he ever got. It's not hard to see why. Obama was recruited by Gerald Kellman, called Marty in *Dreams*, to work in the Developing Communities Project, an offshoot of the Calumet Community Religious Conference. From Kellman, from Mike Kruglik, and from Gregory Galuzzo of the Gamaliel Foundation, Obama learned the techniques of community organizing by being thrown into the deep end of the pool.

Kruglik contends that most of Obama's core beliefs were already formed by the time he reached Chicago.

Obama knew from experience—and from reading St. Augustine and Niebuhr—that humans are prone to selfishness. He knew that the promise of American democracy had been squandered by plutocrats and that progressive reformers had tried but failed to redeem it. He knew that political ideas such as liberty, equality, and justice are always at risk because of the pervasiveness of evil and the tragic disconnect between noble intentions and unanticipated consequences. He knew from Madison and Tocqueville that American politics begins with individual interest, and he knew from the *Federalist* and *Democracy in America* that democracy can work only if people create institutions, associations, and political strategies to transform self-interest into the public good. He knew about affirming the principle, but he knew that a gulf separated individuals' existential choices from effective political mobilization. Obama arrived in Chicago with a mantra he said he had learned from Martin Luther King, Jr.: Love without power is mere sentimentality. Power without love is dangerous. Love plus power equals justice. Obama wanted to learn how to do the sum. Whether he knew it or not when he began working in Chicago, the mantra he attributed to King was also that embraced by the founding father of community organizing, Saul Alinsky.

Obama filled out his education in American history as well as politics while he was working in Chicago. Mike Kruglik had been a doctoral candidate in American history at Northwestern before he became an organizer, and when he and Obama talked, they discussed the reasons why a nation supposedly dedicated to freedom and equality provided so little of either. They talked about the differences between the populists and the progressives and the reasons why ordinary people never seemed to get anywhere in modern America. Kruglik recalls that Obama had a special interest in the work of the radical historian Howard Zinn. It was clear that Obama had read a lot of philosophy, political theory, and fiction. But he was equally interested in history from the bottom up, in the struggles fought by ordinary people, black and white, to improve their lot. Kruglik and Obama also discussed the short stories Obama liked to write on the weekends, stories peopled with characters patterned on the African Americans he was getting to know in the far south side, people unlike those who had raised him and taught him in school. Obama already knew a lot about politics in the abstract. In Chicago he learned the techniques of mobilizing people to act.

Kellman, Kruglik, and Galuzzo taught Obama a version of Alinsky's principles of community organizing. Alinsky created the Back of the Yards Organizing Council in 1939 to extend the confrontational strategies of John L. Lewis from the shop floor to the neighborhoods of Chicago. Alinsky was trained in sociology at the University of Chicago by Ernest Burgess and Robert Park, and he worked in the field of criminology before he decided that the approach Lewis used to build the Congress of Industrial Organizations could be applied outside labor relations to empower communities. With help from Lewis and his daughter Kathryn, from the reform-minded Catholic bishop of Chicago, Bernard Sheil, and from the Chicago philanthropist Marshall Field III, Alinsky established the Industrial Areas Foundation (IAF), which sponsored a network of community organizers eventually stretching from the factories of upstate New York to the farms of California. Besides learning Alinsky's strategies from his Chicago mentors, Obama attended an IAF training program in Los Angeles. Soon he was training organizers himself. How did Obama, lacking any experience as an organizer, learn the ropes so fast? In Galuzzo's words, "nobody teaches a jazz musician jazz. This man was gifted."

Kruglik explains Obama's genius by describing two approaches community organizers often use. Trying to mobilize a group of fifty people, a novice will elicit responses from a handful, then immediately transform their stray comments into his or her own statement of priorities and strategies. The group responds, not surprisingly, by rejecting the organizer's recommendations. By contrast, a master takes the time to listen to many comments, rephrases questions, and waits until the individuals in the group begin to see for themselves what they have in common. A skilled organizer then patiently allows the animating principles and the plan of action to emerge from the group itself. That strategy obviously takes more time. It also takes more intelligence, both analytical and emotional. Groups can tell when they are being manipulated, and they know when they are being heard. According to Kruglik, Obama showed an exceptional willingness to listen to what people were saying. He did not rush from their concerns to his. He did not shift the focus from one issue to another until they were ready. He did not close off discussions about strategy, which were left open for reconsideration pending results. Obama managed to coax from groups a sense of what they shared, an awareness that proved sturdy because it was their doing, not his. From those shared concerns he was able to inspire a commitment to action. In the time it takes most trainees to learn the basics, Obama showed a virtuoso's ability to improvise. As Galuzzo put it, he was gifted.

But Obama was also dissatisfied, particularly with the way Alinsky's principles translated into practice. He could not understand why organizers distrusted electoral politics, or why alliances across denominational lines or racial lines proved so difficult to sustain. In short, why were the differences between groups—the factions Madison had identified in the 1780s—always getting in the way of creating a shared sense of purpose, a common good? Why did Tocqueville's voluntary associations keep splintering into squabbling interest groups unable to cooperate with each other? From Obama's perspective, organizers like Kellman lacked the necessary connection with the communities they wanted to organize. Kellman dismissed his concern as a sign of immaturity or softheartedness, a longing for poetry instead of politics.

When Kellman wanted to transfer Obama to Gary, Indiana, Obama refused. He had become convinced that self-interest had to be tied to community, and making that connection required sinking down roots. Perhaps Obama had retained some of the lessons from Tocqueville he learned from Boesche. Obama knew that many American communities originated in religious congregations, yet the inheritors of Alinsky's method had lost the thread that originally tied them to the tradition of the social gospel. Obama himself saw empathy as an essential piece of organizing. He wanted to know what made people tick, whether he was meeting them in church basements, in school auditoriums, or as individuals panhandling on the streets. He wanted poetry as well as politics. He wanted to connect with the people he was trying to organize, and soon after he arrived in Chicago he began to show a knack for doing just that. The withdrawn adolescent, who had kept his distance from commitments, was giving way to a self-confident young man beginning to envision a career in public life. In his own way, he was preparing himself to affirm the principle in practice.

Much has been made, quite properly, of the years Obama spent working as a community organizer in Chicago. But different observers take different lessons from his experience there. To some critics, such activity seems naive or misguided. It proves that Obama doesn't understand how the American system works but instead seeks solutions to urban poverty in government handouts rather than personal initiative. To other, equally disenchanted observers at another point on the political spectrum, such work enabled the once starry-eyed idealist to learn firsthand that politics is a contact sport and that Chicago politics is a particularly rough form of hardball. He learned, in other words, how to cut a deal. From Kellman, Galuzzo, and Kruglik, and from Chicago African American politicians such as Emil Jones, Jr., the "ward heeler" whom he first challenged and later cultivated as a mentor, Obama is said to have found out that book learning won't get you very far when you have to negotiate with landlords, labor leaders, machine bosses, and gang members. Still other observers emphasize Obama's engagement with his coworkers, activists from the Catholic Church who employed him to work with parishes in Chicago's far south side and acquainted him with the powerful resources available to people immersed in religious institutions and community life. I do not think it is necessary or possible to choose among these three options. As Obama himself has made clear, all these lessons made a difference.

In 1988, after Obama had been working for several years as a community organizer, he wrote a revealing article entitled "Why Organize? Problems and Promise in the Inner City," published in the journal *Illinois Issues*. He conceded that most people do not understand what community organizers do or what motivates them to do it. He conceded that he had questions himself. He could not understand why, within the organizing community, issues were framed in terms of stark choices: "accommodation or militancy, sit-down strikes or boardroom negotiations." Such disagreements echoed earlier divisions within the civil rights movement between champions of integration and black nationalism. Like those divisions, rifts among organizers generated animosity and blunted their effectiveness. The goal, according to the twenty-seven-year-old Obama, should be instead "to bridge these seemingly divergent approaches."

In "Why Organize," Obama drew on a wide range of sources to advance an ambitious analysis of the problems facing African Americans. He cited the research of William Julius Wilson, a scholar then teaching at the University of Chicago, who had identified the absence of jobs, the departure of middle-class blacks, and the consequent hollowing out of inner-city communities as the central problems facing urban America. Obama insisted that only a combination of electoral politics, economic development, and community organizing could address this multidimensional crisis, yet different groups focused their attention myopically on one or another facet of the problem. Advancing an argument familiar to readers of Tocqueville, Obama identified the problem as cultural as well as political and economic. We must find a way to "knit together the diverse interests" of people's "local institutions. This means bringing together churches, block clubs, parent groups and other institutions in a given community." How can that be done? As Tocqueville had observed and Dewey had confirmed a century later, the secret is participation in public life. Engaging people in common projects, Obama wrote, paraphrasing one of the central arguments in *Democracy in America*, "enables people to break out of their crippling isolation from each other, to reshape their mutual values and expectations and rediscover the possibilities of acting collaboratively—the successful prerequisites of any successful self-help initiative." Professor Boesche would have been proud of his pupil.

The young man was not above pointing out the successes that his own organization, the Developing Communities Project, had enjoyed. Schools, he claimed, had become "more accountable." Moreover, "job training programs have been established; housing has been renovated and built; city services have been provided; parks have been refurbished; and crime and drug problems have been curtailed." Looming over those particular (and exaggerated) accomplishments, however, was another, of even greater significance: "plain folk have been able to access the levers of power, and a sophisticated pool of local civic leadership has been developed." These successes testified to the wisdom of scrapping the old Alinsky playbook, with its reliance on angry confrontations between "the people" and "the outside powers" who hold them down. Instead community organizers in the far south side had begun pooling their resources "to form cooperative think tanks like the Gamaliel Foundation," where organizers can "rework old models to fit new realities." The solution lay in flexibility and experimentation, not fealty to outdated formulas.

Obama concluded his essay by emphasizing the potential of "traditional black churches," which contain not only financial and potential political resources but also "values and biblical traditions that call for empowerment and liberation." By the time Obama wrote "Why Organize," he had already become acquainted with the Reverend Jeremiah Wright and had already joined Wright's church, Trinity United Church of Christ. He had seen how Wright could mobilize his congregation. Too many older pastors, unfortunately, had resisted joining forces with community organizers. They preferred the more familiar approaches of electoral politics or charity. More direct forms of social action made them nervous. But if the community organizers could soften their demands for confrontation, and if the ministers could expand their usual strategies, their union would produce "a powerful tool for living the social gospel."

This 1988 article testifies powerfully to the different sources of Obama's emerging political sensibility. It shows the roles played both by central themes in American political thought and by Obama's immersion in community organizing. The article deploys ideas from Madison and Tocqueville, the social gospel, the civil rights movement, the Alinsky organizing tradition, and contemporary social science to advance a subtle analysis concerning the principles and strategies that produce democratic social change. It is also beautifully written. Readers who wonder how Obama produced the lyrical prose of *Dreams from My Father* should consider the concluding paragraph of this essay, written seven years earlier:

> Organizing teaches as nothing else does the beauty and strength of everyday people. Through the songs of the church and the talk on the stoops,

through the hundreds of individual stories of coming up from the South and finding any job that would pay, of raising families on threadbare budgets, of losing some children to drugs and watching others earn degrees and land jobs their parents could never aspire to—it is through these stories and songs of dashed hopes and powers of endurance, of ugliness and strife, subtlety and laughter, that organizers can shape a sense of community not only for others, but for themselves.

Obama himself knew at least one organizer who had found that sense of community, and he was trying to figure out how to make the most of it. From his first week in Chicago, Obama had been impressed by the effect of the city's first black mayor, Harold Washington, on Chicago's black community. When Washington died, his galvanizing force died with him. But his example had convinced Obama that community organizers' aversion to electoral politics prevented them from tapping a rich vein of community energy. Whereas Kellman thought sensible organizers should pick up stakes and move when brighter prospects appeared, Obama's experiences and education taught him the opposite lesson. Strength came from forging links to a community. Equipped with that knowledge, he began thinking about how he might use the overlapping lessons learned at Occidental, Columbia, and in the far south side of Chicago—the lessons of theorists Madison, Tocqueville, and Dewey, and of activists Alinsky,

Jones, and Jeremiah Wright—to prepare himself to follow in the steps of Harold Washington. Multiple influences shaped Obama's political sensibility.

As Obama mapped his strategy for a political career, he decided that a law degree would provide the missing piece in his preparation. Buoyed by letters of recommendation coming from different parts of his background, he applied to several prestigious schools of law. He wanted to learn "about interest rates, corporate mergers, the legislative process"; about businesses and banks and real estate. He wanted to "learn power's currency in all its intricacy and detail," knowledge that he would bring back to Roseland, to Altgeld Gardens, to the people of St. Catherine's. Obama accepted admission to an institution that he thought could teach those lessons, Harvard Law School. One of his letter writers was John McKnight, professor of education and social policy at Northwestern, one of the scholars whose work Obama cited in "Why Organize." McKnight had written critically about the narrow, "consumer advocacy" approach of some community organizers, and he recommended instead the more eclectic, multipronged, and nondogmatic approach that Obama endorsed. When he left Chicago for Cambridge, Obama had already demonstrated a penchant for drawing on different traditions, a talent for blending apparently incompatible ideas, and a strong preference for flexibility over dogmatism. Those predispositions prepared him well for the very different challenges and conflicts he was about to face.

At the time when Obama decided that a law degree would make him a more effective advocate for residents of Chicago's poorest neighborhoods, the faculties in America's elite law schools were in turmoil. Immersion in that intellectual maelstrom not only shaped Obama's approach to law, it left a permanent imprint on his ideas about American history and politics. The Reagan revolution had already propelled the Supreme Court to the right. Legal scholars on the left, cherishing memories of the Warren Court, still believed that the law could serve as a lever for progressive social change. Professors wielding new philosophical and political ideas battled over the nature and sources of the law, how it should be taught and practiced, and what purpose it should serve.

On the one hand, legal conservatives were flexing their muscles. Some conservative scholars championed the idea of "original intent," a conception of the Constitution as the repository of timeless truths that could be marshaled to restrain radicals who, they insisted, had been operating for decades in the judicial as well as legislative branch of government. By retrieving the fundamental and unchanging principles of the American founding, principles such as individual rights—especially property rights—and resistance to government, conservatives could recapture the legal system. Only then, they thought, could American public life return from the long and disastrous detour that began with the New Deal and culminated in the judicial activism of the Warren Court. Other conservative law professors took a strikingly different approach, arguing that the principles of the free market provide the best guide for the judiciary. Although champions of market-oriented solutions sometimes allied with the first group, known as originalists, for strategic purposes, the two groups of conservatives disagreed with each other almost as passionately as both groups disagreed with disparate insurgents on their left flank.

Leftists on law faculties were even more contentious. Radicals began to accuse their erstwhile allies, liberals and moderate progressives, of unwitting complicity with reactionaries. They splintered into groups according to their judgment of the principal sources of injustice. Critics of patriarchy constructed a lively discourse called feminist jurisprudence, which fractured over debates on questions ranging from pornography to heteronormativity. Critics of racism clustered around ideas known as critical race theory. They disagreed about strategic choices and about the relation between the American battle against white supremacy and the struggles being waged by people of color around the world. Others who joined together—loosely—around the banner of critical legal studies, often influenced by radical European theorists such as Michel Foucault, were intent on demonstrating that the American law, despite the reverence it evokes, serves no purpose other than preserving the status quo. Finally, other progressive law professors invoked the American tradition of legal realism. Adherents to this way of thinking, descended from the seminal early twentieth-century writings of James's friends and fellow philosophical pragmatists

Oliver Wendell Holmes, Jr., and Louis Brandeis, saw the law as a way of addressing social problems. Legal pragmatists believed that the law is a product of history and culture, a set of rules designed to facilitate social interaction based on changing values and aspirations. They denied that the law rests on bedrock, a stable foundation of unchanging principles. But they disagreed with "crits," as the advocates of critical legal studies were called, about the futility of trying to use the law as a lever for social change. Like early twentieth-century progressive reformers and New Dealers, most legal pragmatists on the left saw themselves inheriting from Dewey, and from the legal realists of the 1930s whom he inspired, an agenda of social democratic reforms that depended on understanding law as a weapon that can be deployed for a variety of purposes.

Problems of nomenclature further muddled this already confusing array of positions. Those interested in "law and economics" often gravitated to the idea of "rational choice," the belief that individuals make choices consistent with their perception of their own self-interest. But adherents to law and economics divided between those who used such tools to advocate free-market solutions to social problems and those who sought instead to identify the optimal degree and form of state regulation. Most legal realists during the New Deal years considered themselves progressives as well as philosophical pragmatists. They sought to use the law as a method of challenging conservative dogmas and unsettling traditional alliances between economic privilege and political power. But now a few conservative champions of law and economics, including most notably Richard Posner at the University of Chicago Law School, also began calling themselves pragmatists. Posner was inspired more by the Nietzschean nihilism of Holmes than by the idealistic crusades for social justice that animated Brandeis. Posner reasoned that if pragmatism destabilizes inherited truths, the ostensibly neutral mechanism of the free market provides the best way to resolve the resulting confusion. To make these waters even murkier, some radical literary critics took to studying law as a species of literature. A few of them who were attracted to the ideas of the French poststructuralist Jacques Derrida, notably the prolific critic Stanley Fish, likewise designated themselves pragmatists. Not surprisingly, many legal pragmatists on the left, including some feminists and critical race theorists, considered both Posner's and Fish's hijacking of the term pragmatism a travesty, a repudiation of the egalitarian commitments and democratic activism of James, Dewey, and their followers in the progressive and New Deal coalitions.

When Obama entered Harvard Law School in the fall of 1988, he unwittingly found himself in the center of these storms. The volumes of the *Harvard Law Review* published during the three years when Obama was involved—first as a research assistant to Professor Laurence Tribe in 1988–1989, then when he served on the editorial board in 1989–1990, and finally during his term as president (or editor in chief) in 1990–1991—illustrate just how heated such disputes had become. The law school had experienced a protracted battle between traditionalists and radicals of various stripes. When the more conservative Robert C. Clark replaced the more progressive James Vorenberg as dean, it was widely interpreted as a sign that the prevailing winds had shifted. But many left-leaning Harvard faculty continued to fight the tide of conservatism, and the *HLR* reflects the continuation of those battles.

Among the favorite weapons wielded by progressives in the legal academy was a cluster of ideas drawn from the fields of American history and political theory. Known variously as civic republicanism, communitarianism, and deliberative democracy, this way of thinking transformed legal scholarship in the 1980s. Legal scholars attracted to these ideas counterposed the importance of the public interest—a conception of a shared, common good, emerging through the process of lively debate between champions of competing points of view—to the ideas of both conservatives and radical leftists of the Marxist and post-structuralist persuasions. Some conservatives invoked the notion of an unchanging Constitution, the "original meaning" of which they insisted had established once and for all the American commitment to individual freedom and a market economy. Some radicals, by contrast, dismissed the law as a tool of oppression used by rich white males to preserve their power. Positioning themselves between those poles, civic republicans and deliberative democrats countered that eighteenth-century Americans shared commitments to republicanism and democracy as the central animating principles of the new nation. Faculty members at Harvard Law School, the teachers with whom Obama studied, participated prominently in—indeed, helped to shape—all these controversies.

Debates over civic republicanism had already transformed the historical profession. In the most influential book on the founding published in the second half of the twentieth century, *The Creation of the American Republic, 1776–1787* (1969), Gordon Wood demonstrated convincingly, through an exhaustive examination of the evidence, that the architects of the United States were animated by a passion for civic virtue as well as liberty. They not only sought independence from Britain to establish freedom for individuals; in addition, they prized equality and justice as the ends of government, and they framed the United States Constitution for that purpose. Wood concluded his analysis by claiming that the promise of civic republicanism, which required individuals to balance self-interest against the interests of the community, was betrayed almost immediately by a rapacious individualism that quickly supplanted virtuous citizens' concern with the common good. Variations on the central arguments from Wood's masterful history—and countless other contributions to a burgeoning literature that appeared during the 1970s and early 1980s—slowly seeped into other disciplines such as political science, sociology, and law, and the discourse of civic republicanism transformed debates about the Constitution in law schools across America.

Now long-standing conservative claims concerning the primacy of individual rights had to reckon with new challenges. Besides the evidence of a vibrant tradition of civic republicanism, scholars also unearthed solid evidence that John Locke was a more fervent Calvinist than he was a prophet of rights consciousness. Other scholars probed the ethic of sympathy that the founders drew from Christianity and from Scottish commonsense philosophy. The belief that the founders had intended to insulate government from the people had to confront equally clear evidence that those whom Wood called "the people out of doors"—ordinary Americans including blacks, women, and white men disfranchised by their poverty, people brought to life in dozens of detailed studies by a generation of social historians such as Alfred Young and Gary Nash, Linda Kerber and Mary Beth Norton—themselves played a central role in winning independence and creating the new nation. The United States, according to this line of argument, was designed from the start to be a democracy in which the people would deliberate together to discover the meaning of justice and advance the common good. Obama had first encountered this way of thinking, under Boesche's tutelage, at Occidental.

That Boesche introduced Obama to the American founding through the arguments of Wood and other historians who advanced variations of the republican synthesis is among the most striking facts about Obama's intellectual formation. Whereas members of an earlier generation of Americans had been taught versions of the nation's history that stressed the importance of individual rights in the founding, Obama from the beginning learned the importance of community, the centrality of obligations, and the shaping influence of civic virtue in American democracy. From the courses he took, the books and articles he read, the papers he wrote, and the professors with whom he discussed his developing ideas, Obama's legal education reinforced and sharpened that understanding.

In the second issue of the *HLR* published with Obama on the editorial board, the issue published in December 1989, University of Chicago Law School professor Cass Sunstein published a long article entitled "Interpreting Statutes in the Regulatory State," a crucial text that illustrates what was happening within the legal academy. A year before, Sunstein and Harvard Law School professor Frank Michelman had published in the *Yale Law Journal* two of the most widely read articles on what was called the "republican revival." Both Sunstein and Michelman emphasized similar themes drawn from recent scholarship on eighteenth-century America: the centrality of deliberation, the importance of social as well as political equality, and the participation of citizens. Such republican values, they argued, did not necessarily contradict older liberal emphases on individual liberty. Instead late twentieth-century Americans should see, as did the founders themselves, the compatibility between civic republicans' emphasis on virtue and liberals' emphasis on freedom. Only virtuous citizens, as John Adams, Thomas Jefferson, and

James Madison agreed—and as Tocqueville later confirmed—were capable of exercising freedom responsibly. Without community norms constraining the use of individual freedom, liberty would degenerate into license, the undisciplined and destructive excesses that had doomed earlier experiments with popular government. If the shared civic values that united members of the American national community were to vanish, only a degrading scramble for wealth would remain, and the founders denigrated such selfishness as antithetical to the civic virtue they prized. Against conservatives' insistence that the U.S. Constitution sanctified individual rights over any other concerns, Sunstein and Michelman resurrected the founders' broader ethical preoccupations, their emphasis on social responsibility as the complement without which freedom lacked value.

Now, writing in the *HLR* a year later, in 1989, Sunstein added a second dimension, drawn from the tradition of philosophical pragmatism, to his earlier endorsement of "liberal republicanism." He argued that the meaning of legal statutes is never self-evident. Understanding the law requires interpretation, which in turn requires shared "background understandings" that rest on social norms. Meaning, in other words, depends on "culture and context." Lawyers and judges should abandon the illusion that they can proceed by focusing attention narrowly on precedents in the common law tradition. Instead they must face the inescapable conclusion forced on them by philosophers operating in the pragmatist tradition ever since James and Dewey: when competing principles collide, interpretation is necessary to resolve conflicts. The goal of this approach to the law, Sunstein concluded, was to "generate a series of interpretive principles" that could "promote the goals of deliberative government." Neither originalists who presumed to declare a fixed meaning in the Constitution nor leftists who insisted on the radical indeterminacy of law offered adequate solutions. Instead, Sunstein concluded, the law must proceed by means of interpretation, which requires a sophisticated understanding of cultural history, and experimentation, a willingness to engage in what the pragmatists called critical inquiry concerning the consequences of legal decisions. To that end, and within those constraints, the insights both of the law and economics movement and of deconstruction might prove fruitful. Sunstein cited both Posner and Fish repeatedly, but he used their work to bolster his progressive and egalitarian arguments, not to endorse their own quite different conclusions. Instead Sunstein treated as his guides Michelman, Madison, and Dewey. Michelman, having already written seminal articles on welfare rights, stood as the champion of sympathy and the interests of the underdog; Madison, as a deliberative democrat, a statesman who saw the inevitable clash of competing views and called it, if not good, at least potentially productive of the public interest; and Dewey, as the apostle of philosophical pragmatism.

The other seven issues of the *HLR* published in that volume—the one with Obama on the board of editors, the one preceding the volume published during the year in which Obama served as president of the *HLR*—show the range of controversies roiling the legal academy. Several articles engaged feminist jurisprudence, others addressed critical race theory, and the questions about power raised by critical legal studies provided a steady drumbeat running through the footnotes of such texts. But controversies between newly energized conservatives, who were relishing their dominance on the Rehnquist Supreme Court, and still shrill radical critics had to share space with other, somewhat more moderate sensibilities. For example, Joan C. Williams, who later became one of the preeminent legal theorists of pragmatist feminism, struck a chord that resonated with the tone of articles such as Sunstein's and Michelman's. Reviewing a book on urban government law by Gerald Frug, one of the stalwarts of critical legal studies, Williams complained that Frug drew too stark a contrast between oligarchy and participatory democracy. Instead she urged legal scholars to follow Tocqueville. The author of *Democracy in America* saw that individualism untempered by responsibility can "deteriorate into mere selfishness," but deliberative democracy, by engaging citizens in public life, provides an alternative that can keep alive a sense of shared purpose. That line of analysis, in its historical sensitivity and its accurate characterization of Tocqueville's unclassifiable political position, echoed the arguments of Boesche's scholarship on Tocqueville and those Obama offered in "Why Organize."

The clearest indication of Obama's own understanding

of such issues, however, surely comes from the volume of the *HLR* published during the year of his presidency. The election of the first African American to that position—usually seen as a springboard to prominence and power—sparked noisy celebrations and generated considerable public attention. Then came the grueling work of actually producing the journal and seeing it into print. The person elected president would have to inspire, then herd, his or her fellow editors through that process. Although his title would be president, Obama's job would be that of editor in chief: he would lead the discussions about what articles to publish, and he would bear ultimate responsibility for putting out the eight issues of the *HLR* published that year.

But first a fire had to be extinguished. For the first round of the competition among students vying to be chosen for the editorial board of the *HLR*, a designation that traditionally opened doors to prestigious clerkships and law firms, the journal had inaugurated a policy of affirmative action. Some minority students, notably Jim Chen, had protested that they felt stigmatized by that policy, since outsiders might assume they were less well qualified than other students. Some female law students, on the other hand, insisted that because they too were historically disadvantaged, they should be accorded a status akin to that of minority students. As the newly elected president of the *HLR*, Obama responded to those quite distinct complaints in a way that shows his already considerable political skill and his already firm commitment to democratic deliberation. In a letter to the student-run *Harvard Law Record*, Obama first explained the rationale for not including women in the affirmative action program: many women had made law review in recent years. But he expressed his willingness to put the matter to a vote if the students chose to do so. He then defended affirmative action for minority students. He conceded freely that he had "undoubtedly benefited" from such programs during his academic career. But he assured Chen and others that he had "not personally felt stigmatized within the broader law school community or as a staff member" of the *HLR* as a result of those policies.

Obama's letter calmed the storm, but dealing with such unrest was only one of the president's worries. Decisions had to be made about articles, reviews, and case notes. Authors and topics had to be selected. Submissions had to be vetted, then shepherded through the sometimes painful process of editing multiple drafts from distracted or stubborn contributors (such as the odd historian unfamiliar with the time-honored traditions of law journals, which require citations for sources ranging from the Bible to the Beatles). Finally, the president was responsible for the final edit of everything to be published in the *HLR*. Thus it is reasonable to assume, as Obama's fellow editors did—and as I am assured that student members of the journal still do—that the president read with care everything that appeared on his watch. What does volume 104 tell us about the ideas that engaged Obama during this crucial year?

The first issue, dated November 1990, opens with a string of tributes to the recently retired stalwart of progressivism on the Supreme Court, William Brennan. Michelman's eloquent portrait of Brennan attributes to the justice precisely the values Michelman identified in his own article on civic republicanism and deliberative democracy published the previous year. Brennan understood that freedom is "a social and political, not just a personal, condition." Brennan saw the value of "judicial sympathy," which Michelman characterized as an ethical predisposition to take seriously the perspectives of other people, especially those affected by a judge's exercise of his or her power. Assessing Brennan's long career, Michelman cited much of the recent scholarship published by progressive insurgents in the legal academy, including his colleague Martha Minow, who had written in the *HLR* three years earlier urging lawyers and judges "to become and remain open to perspectives and claims that challenge our own." Michelman concluded that Brennan's commitment to that principle of deliberation, along with his "ethical responsiveness," helped account for his landmark achievements as a justice, which placed him alongside John Marshall as one of the greatest Constitutionalists in American history.

Michelman was hardly alone in cherishing such qualities—or in trying to perpetuate them. By all accounts it was Obama's own ability to empathize with others, and his persistent efforts inside and outside the classroom to find ways to resolve conflicts, that resulted in his election as president of the *HLR*. His own political views were well known. He was a man of the Left. He had worked as a community organizer before coming to law school, and he made no secret of his intention to become a civil rights lawyer afterwards. But his adversaries as well as his allies respected his efforts to find common ground, whether they were discussing issues of law, issues of politics, or issues having to do with the journal they produced. That year no fewer than nineteen candidates had thrown their hats in the ring for the presidency of the *HLR*. In recent years the journal had been wracked by divisive debates between women, blacks, and members of other minority groups, who felt excluded, and white men, who felt unfairly accused of sexism and racism because they just happened to continue to hold the most prestigious and powerful positions.

A highly charged atmosphere surrounded the election itself. According to Obama's friend Kenneth Mack, among those whom Obama "trounced" in the election, to use Mack's term, the decisive moment came when Obama received the endorsement of one particularly vocal conservative white male. Inside and outside the classroom, Obama had frequently gone out of his way to seek out conservative students and try to understand their perspectives, just as he had gone out of his way to try to understand the perspectives of conservative faculty members such as Charles Fried, who had served as Reagan's solicitor general. If Michelman was right, and if Justice Brennan's greatness derived from his commitments to the virtues of sympathy, open-mindedness, and deliberation, it seemed just as clear to most of Obama's fellow students that the one among them who best embodied those qualities was the man they elected their president.

So it was no surprise that the first issue of volume 104, Obama's volume of the *HLR*, opened with a reassuring chorus of praise for the liberal lion Brennan, but readers were then thrown into the jarring facts of life in contemporary America. The annual review of the Supreme Court's preceding term, a high-profile standard feature of the *HLR*, included two articles, the first by Robin West, who excoriated the court for its accelerating retreat from progressive principles, and the second by Charles Fried, who in the 1980s had helped to start and now celebrated just that retreat. The justices' "disavowal of liberalism," according to West, showed just how vulnerable progressive ideas had become. Assailed from the Right as well as the radical Left, the traditions of the New Deal and Warren courts had given way to an increasingly assertive conservatism. Although they occupied diametrically opposed positions, both West and Fried peppered their footnotes with references to the issues raised by feminists, critical race theorists, and champions of critical legal studies, counterposing that scholarship to the opinions, leaning overwhelmingly to the right, handed down by the Supreme Court in the previous year. West was apoplectic, Fried more or less content.

Further evidence confirming the conservative surge in

the broader culture showed up in the next issue of the *HLR*. The fact that Obama had been elected president of the review did not mean progressive sensibilities were on the rise outside Cambridge. To the contrary. During these years the so-called culture wars were at their peak, with writers and activists on the left and the right battling each other over issues ranging from abortion, affirmative action, education, and school prayer to immigration, gay rights, and gun control. The shock troops of the Reagan revolution were hard at work rolling back the cultural changes of the 1960s. With an eye to that larger conflict, the editors of the *HLR* decided that a volume entitled *Confronting the Constitution*, a collection of essays edited by the cultural conservative Allan Bloom—author of the controversial, best-selling polemic *The Closing of the American Mind*—should receive a critical review. Bloom's collection featured essays by many prominent followers of the philosopher Leo Strauss, including Joseph Epstein, Thomas Pangle, and Harvey Mansfield. The Constitution, according to these scholars, was under attack by critics who included, among others, pragmatists, historicists, Marxists, Freudians, and existentialists, a surly crew of radicals intent on prying the document away from its foundation in natural rights and natural law. The anonymous review disputed the Straussians' understanding of the Constitution, counterposing to their claims arguments drawn from Wood's *Creation* and other contributions to the republican revival. As that review indicates, even when the editors of the *HLR* acknowledged the prominence of conservatives in America's culture wars, they frequently registered their opposition.

Although many of the articles published during the year of Obama's presidency could serve to illustrate my argument about republicanism, deliberative democracy, community, and pragmatism, I will mention just two more. The first is a review of *Making All the Difference: Inclusion, Exclusion, and American Law*, by Harvard Law professor (and now dean) Martha Minow. The review stressed Minow's emphasis on dialogue as the only way that different groups can resolve their differences. Minow disavowed any attempt to stipulate a single method for reconciling such disagreements, which the anonymous reviewer admitted some readers might find unsatisfying or evasive. But Minow rejected that option on principle. She pointed out that early twentieth-century progressives had often failed to reach their goals precisely because they presumed to dictate to others how they should solve their problems. Better to leave the procedures open-ended, to emphasize the indeterminacy of a "relational approach," than to foreclose options and experiments that might nurture community better than anything scholars might prescribe.

Finally, in his article "Why the Liberal State Can Promote Moral Ideas After All," Stephen A. Gardbaum extended Michelman's and Sunstein's arguments on republicanism to lay out the substantive principles undergirding American democracy. Against the claims of an earlier generation of liberals that the nation should strive for a neutral, procedural regime in which rights are defended but no ideals enshrined, Gardbaum contended that yoking rights to responsibilities, individuals to communities, and liberty to equality is the American way. Difficult as it is to identify an overarching theme in a journal as multifaceted as the *HLR*, the persistent emphasis on the potential of philosophical pragmatism, civic republicanism, and deliberative democracy as the best methods for resolving differences during the year of Obama's presidency is hard to miss.

Of course the *HLR* was not exclusively concerned with questions of philosophy or social theory. Like the curriculum required of first-year law students, each issue of the *HLR* includes articles devoted to nuts-and-bolts issues concerning tort, contracts, property, procedures, and criminal law. Some of those articles are signed, others are shorter notes contributed by the student editors. One of those, a report on a recent Illinois case concerning fetal rights against mothers published in January 1990, was written by Obama himself, and it shows the scrupulous neutrality that his students at the University of Chicago Law School later reported as a characteristic feature of his teaching. Given the passions aroused by all questions concerning the unborn, there is something uncanny—or, depending on one's viewpoint, either disturbingly evasive or thoroughly professional—about the restrained tone of Obama's case note concerning *Stallman v. Youngquist*. He laid out the issues clearly, discussed the relevant cases succinctly, and provided just the sort of mind-numbing footnotes that have long made reading law reviews a superb cure for insomnia. He ended by striking a balance of the sort that has become his trademark. In this case, the court "rightly concluded that, at least in cases arising out of maternal negligence, women's interests in autonomy and privacy outweigh the dubious policy benefits of fetal-maternal tort suits." But he noted that more difficult cases, such as those involving pregnant women whose reckless behavior damages a fetus, had yet to be decided, and he advised, prudently, against the temptation to adopt "constitutionally dubious laws in pursuit of ill-conceived strategies to promote fetal health." Obama closed his skillfully crafted note with a ringing call for better "prenatal education and health care facilities," as clear and uncontroversial an endorsement of motherhood and apple pie as I have found in the pages of the *HLR*.

Significant as all these articles are, perhaps the most telling single measure of Obama's engagement with the upheaval in American social thought during these years is an article written by the Harvard Law School professor who taught Obama constitutional law, Laurence Tribe. Serving as Tribe's research assistant was the first job Obama had at the law school. The article that resulted from their labors, "The Curvature of Constitutional Space: What Lawyers Can Learn from Modern Physics," appeared in November 1989 in the first issue of *HLR* published after Obama's cohort had joined the editorial board. Because Tribe's article encapsulates so many of the most important ideas being debated in the legal academy during the years when Obama was in law school, it merits close scrutiny.

It might seem surprising that Tribe invited Obama, then a first-year student, to work with him on this article. From the beginning of his time in law school, Obama impressed the faculty—and his fellow students—for two reasons. First, his exceptional intelligence enabled him to master difficult concepts that left many of his classmates floundering. Tribe reports having been impressed by Obama's acuity and intellectual curiosity the first time he met with him to discuss issues in constitutional law. Second, Obama's striking ability to resolve conflicts earned him the respect of his professors and his fellow students. Whether in a seminar room, in the heated debates among the editors of the *HLR*, or on a basketball court, Obama showed the same skill. When tensions rose and positions seemed irreconcilable, he was able to cut through the froth of passion and posturing to find the heart of the dispute and, if possible, defuse it.

Observers had various ways of explaining Obama's knack for conflict resolution. It was a magic trick. It was a gift, like perfect pitch or the ability to roll one's tongue. It was a strategy, a deliberate attempt to avoid creating enemies by cooling tempers and making peace. It reflected his awareness that, as a black man, he could not show anger without evoking anxiety or alarm. It was the style, usually learned in elite prep schools and honed in tony colleges, of those who would become the power elite, and Obama's apparently effortless mastery of its nuances showed how he could balance the savvy of an insider with the persona of an outsider. But more than Obama's unusual self-restraint and self-awareness was at work. His vaunted poise, which later endeared him to America's youth and often flummoxed his adversaries, then earned him the respect of his fellow lawmakers in the Illinois state legislature and the United States Senate, has given him an edge in many political debates. But it derives from something besides his temperament. In order to understand how and why Obama has almost always tried, and has so often succeeded, in resolving disputes, it is necessary to dig deeper into the way he thinks and why. The explanation of his commitment to conciliation lies in his idea of democracy as deliberation, his sure grasp of philosophical pragmatism, his Christian realism, and his sophisticated understanding that history, with all its ambiguities and ironies, provides the best rudder for political navigation.

In "The Curvature of Constitutional Space," which brings together all those traditions and ways of thinking, Tribe acknowledged the help he received from multiple research assistants, including, among others, Barack Obama. The article pointedly challenges claims made by champions of the Reagan revolution who wanted to make sure its achievements were not reversed by wrong-headed liberal judges said to be legislating from the bench. Judges should understand, Tribe contended, that the law necessarily affects social relations. Whether judges practice "activism" or "restraint," the force of state authority shapes the culture, either directly or indirectly, much as a star "curves" gravity in the space that surrounds it. Like the myth of a purely free market economy utterly unaffected by state power, so the myth of judicial restraint obscures the role inevitably played by law in legitimating existing social, economic, and political arrangements. Because that understanding of the role played by government and law informs so many of the arguments advanced in *The Audacity of Hope*, because Tribe's article incorporates so many central issues in American intellectual life during the years leading up to its publication, and because it locates Obama in this constellation of ideas, I will highlight several of its themes.

First, Tribe argued that "the fundamental fairness of a society is best judged by an examination of its treatment of the least advantaged." This concept of fairness is a variation on a theme as old as the Hebrew Bible and the Christian scriptures, but Tribe and his team of research assistants bolstered it with a footnote invoking the writings of the most prominent political philosopher in late twentieth-century America, John Rawls. Instead of proceeding, as Rawls did in *A Theory of Justice* (1971), from a thought experiment involving isolated individuals reasoning in the abstract about what principles of justice they would choose, the article instead pointed toward historicism, specifically to the rich American tradition of pragmatist jurisprudence. That tradition, as I have noted, stretches from the work of William James and his friends Oliver Wendell Holmes, Jr., and Louis Brandeis to legal realists such as Jerome Frank and Benjamin Cardozo.

"The life of the law has not been logic," Holmes proclaimed. "It has been experience." The law is an instrument for getting things done, not a repository of eternal truths.

Tribe dismissed the idea that the law inhabits an unchanging space above social and political conflict, an "Archimedean point" from which jurists can dispassionately survey the scene. That denial has been a standard move of pragmatists from the start. From the pioneers James, Holmes, Brandeis, and Dewey to more recent contributors to the resurgence of pragmatism such as Richard Rorty, Hilary Putnam, Richard J. Bernstein, and law professors Minow, Sunstein, Michelman, and Tribe himself, generations of writers influenced by pragmatism have emphasized the need to consider the particular circumstances within which the law—like all ideas and all forms of authority—functions.

Tribe rejected conservatives' claims for constitutional originalism in favor of historicism. As its title suggests, "The Curvature of Constitutional Space" made use of arguments from Stephen Hawking and other physicists to establish the pragmatists' point: looking "to the natural sciences for authority—that is, for certainty—is to look for what is not there." That claim was sustained by citing the work of Thomas Kuhn, the historian of science who most clearly demonstrated how ideas change in the natural sciences. Challenging those members of the Reagan-era Rehnquist Supreme Court who believed in an unchanging Constitution and a judiciary disengaged from social conflict, the article also quoted the anthropologist Clifford Geertz. Lawyers, Geertz wrote, must explore the "*social meaning* of what the state has done," because "the state enacts an image of order" that is coercive. In other words, it inevitably curves the space around it.

Tribe's multiple references to contemporary philosophers and social theorists as well as earlier pragmatists, progressives, legal realists, and historicists—along with legal precedents—indicate the pervasiveness of such ideas in the legal academy at the time when Obama was studying law. These references came from work done by a team that included not only Tribe and Obama but also other students at the Harvard Law School, including Robert Fisher and Michael Dorf, the latter already an accomplished student of physics and later a distinguished scholar of constitutional law. The article makes clear that Obama, like Tribe, Dorf, Minow, Michelman, and many other students and faculty members at the time, was deeply immersed in the controversies addressed in it. Like the other articles published in the *HLR* in the following two years, when Obama was even more directly involved in producing the journal, "The Curvature of Constitutional Space" provides unmistakable evidence of the way in which he and many other members of his generation were learning to think about the law. Of course there were plenty of rival approaches, both to the right and to the left, but the testimony of those who knew him at Harvard, both students and faculty, and Obama's own mature writings have made abundantly clear his grounding in these pragmatist and historicist conceptions of knowledge, law, and politics.

In 1991 Tribe and Dorf published *On Reading the Constitution*. In that study they likened constitutional interpretation to "conversation," and they credited that metaphor to Robert Fisher and Barack Obama, who "influenced our thinking on virtually every subject discussed in these pages." From James and Dewey through the work of their many students, including many progressives and New Dealers as well as DuBois and Park, the ideas of philosophical pragmatism have spread so broadly through American culture that it has become almost impossible to identify the direct lines of their influence. But *On Reading the Constitution* clearly reflects that influence. Lacking a "mathematical algorithm of interpretation," according to Tribe and Dorf, the best we can do is to rule out the extremes of unbounded judicial activism and the fiction of pure judicial restraint by pointing out that the Constitution has changed over time. "A great many people have lost faith in the idea of the timeless, the universal, and unquestionable," Tribe and Dorf wrote. Yet we still manage, through conversation, to distinguish sound reason-giving from sophistry. In their account of "what it means to give reasons in a world unbolstered by ultimate truth," Tribe and Dorf cited the work of the pragmatist philosopher Hilary Putnam, among the most incisive late twentieth-century writers on William James.

In 1990 Harvard Law School hosted a conference on

the significance of philosophical pragmatism for the law, which attracted many of the leading contributors to debates over the legacy of James and Dewey. Many members of the faculty appeared on the program, and a number of them contributed articles to an issue of the *Southern California Law Review* devoted to the subject in 1991. A volume published that same year, *Pragmatism in Law and Society*, included articles by, among others, Posner, Fish, Rorty, Putnam, Minow, and other prominent contributors to pragmatist discourse, including Cornel West, Margaret Jane Radin, Joan C. Williams, Catharine Wells, and Elizabeth Spellman. Of course not all these writers agreed with each other. Indeed, the liveliness of their disagreements testifies to the vitality of the debates over philosophical pragmatism that raged in America—from the Harvard Law School to the University of Southern California Law School—during the years when Obama was studying law.

Obama's familiarity with philosophical pragmatism should come as no surprise. He encountered it in many forms, and in many separate circumstances, throughout his education. Through the pragmatist literary critic Kenneth Burke and through James's students DuBois and Alain Locke, pragmatism powerfully affected Ralph Ellison, and that impact is visible throughout *Invisible Man*. In Obama's first courses on American history at Occidental, he read the work of James's students Croly, Lippmann, and DuBois. His training in Chicago derived from Alinsky, who was himself a student of Robert Park at the University of Chicago in the 1920s. Before Park enrolled at Harvard to study with James in 1898, he had worked with John Dewey as a muckraking journalist in Chicago, and Park and Dewey had collaborated on the short-lived radical periodical *Thought News*. In his own teaching, Park repeatedly emphasized the importance of learning how to empathize with others unlike oneself. Achieving such mutual recognition, Park had written, is "prerequisite to achieving communication in a society composed of individuals as egocentric as most of us naturally are," and he characterized James's essay "On a Certain Blindness in Human Beings"—an essay Park said he first encountered in one of James's classes at Harvard—as the "most radical statement of the difficulty and the necessity" of seeing the world from others' point of view. James predicted that his philosophy of pragmatism would eventually "filter down into practical life," even if that process involved its spread "through the remotest channels." From literature through community organizing to law schools, the traces of James's ideas are unmistakable in various dimensions of American culture and clearly discernible in Obama's writings.

At Harvard Law School Obama encountered a culture infused with a mixture of intoxicating ideas and hardheaded lessons. No-nonsense professors taught inexperienced students the nuts and bolts of the law, making sure that those who arrived thinking they could use the law to change the world, as Obama did, came to see that justice is blind. Students learned that in the Anglo-American tradition of common law, precedents matter more than abstract principles. First-year students had to master the dry details of procedures, tort, property, administrative law, and so on, before they could explore other dimensions of the curriculum.

Yet technical as legal education in the 1980s and 1990s surely remained, Harvard Law School was already beginning to move in the direction that has recently led to a complete overhaul of the curriculum. Research from a variety of academic disciplines was leaking into legal education. From science studies, powerfully influenced by the debates over Kuhn, came awareness of the impermanence of all ideas. From philosophy, particularly from the evolving work of Rawls but also from his various critics, and increasingly from the neopragmatists and other historicists, came attention to the contingent quality of all principles. From history came a new and more complicated understanding of the American founding, a Tocquevillean ambivalence about the strengths and limitations of American democracy deepened by Lincoln's tragic sensibility, and an interest in the possibilities of using the law for progressive reform. From cultural anthropology came awareness of the variability and mutability of cultures and the inescapability of hermeneutics. Theorists of race and gender showed the essentially contested quality of the clusters of concepts purporting to explain black and white, male and female. Other political scientists and sociologists contributed a heightened awareness of civil society, the sphere of voluntary associations stressed in *Democracy in America*, and they examined both its problems and the prospects for its renewal. From the classrooms of Occidental and Columbia to the offices of the *HLR*, Obama spent years immersed in these debates.

He was also immersed in debates about race. Harvard Law School faculty members Charles Ogletree and Randall Kennedy provided role models of African Americans who had made it to the top of their profession, but no one at the law school—neither faculty nor students—could take such recent progress for granted. The first black faculty member awarded tenure there, Derrick Bell, ended his stormy stay in Cambridge in 1990, when he left to protest the institution's failure to appoint a woman of color, Regina Austin, to a tenured position. Bell had made a career of using Alinsky-style confrontational tactics to dislodge practices of racial segregation. He had worked in the U.S. Department of Justice and the NAACP before moving into the legal academy. In his writings Bell addressed the continuing evidence of racism throughout American culture decades after the 1954 decision in *Brown v. Board of Education*. Responses to Bell's challenges to hiring practices at Harvard Law School—including a hunger strike—exposed deep divisions within the faculty and within the student body. To his critics Bell was ignoring the strides the school had made and threatening the sacred principle of merit. To his defenders, including Obama, Bell was keeping alive the spirit of Rosa Parks and other heroes of the civil rights movement.

Another angry visionary made a lasting mark on Obama's thinking while he was studying law. Roberto Mangabeira Unger, a brilliant and prolific social theorist on the law school faculty, taught Obama in two courses—a core course, Jurisprudence, in his first year and an elective, Reinventing Democracy, in his third and final year. The unclassifiable Unger, who recently returned from a stint as minister of strategic affairs in his native Brazil, still considers himself Brazilian even though he has lived and taught in Cambridge during most of the last four decades. Initially Unger helped propel critical legal studies, then he turned against the crits when he thought their all-encompassing nihilism had blinded them to the prospect of progressive political action. A radical critic of capitalism, Unger has been equally critical of Marxism and of the centralized government apparatus on which European social democratic welfare states rest. Rather than embracing socialism, he has endorsed the market—if freed from the alliance between government and monopoly power that controls it—as a potentially creative force. Although the Catholic-born Unger no longer identifies himself as a Christian, he remains an avid advocate of Christian altruism. In *Democracy Realized: The Progressive Alternative*, the book on which Unger's course Reinventing Democracy was based, he advanced ambitious arguments well beyond the range of American law and politics. To realize democracy, Unger called for reconstructing government, the economy, civil society, and educational institutions through a process of "democratic experimentalism," and he aligned himself with Jefferson's ideal of decentralization and Dewey's pragmatism. Unger reports that Obama participated actively in the discussions in both classes, and his fellow students remember some sharp exchanges between the strong-willed professor and the self-confident student. Although students in his courses were not required to read the works of James and Dewey, Unger's own exchanges with Obama convinced him that Obama understands the pragmatists' critique of dogmatism and the democratic potential of pragmatist philosophy. Even more crucially, from Unger's perspective, Obama understands and sympathizes with the pragmatists' commitment to empowering individuals to engage actively in experimentation in the political, economic, and social spheres, the sensibility that Unger passionately champions in the most explicitly pragmatist of his books, *The Self Awakened, Pragmatism Unbound*. From Fried and others on the right to Unger and others on the left, at Harvard Obama wrestled with a wide range of ideas, from faith in the free market to confidence that individuals, if freed to exercise their imaginations, could enact a radically pragmatist democracy.

Obama had completed his law degree *magna cum laude*, and Minow was not alone in considering him one of the best students she had ever taught. The notoriety he earned as the first African American elected president of the *HLR* won him a contract for the book that became *Dreams from My Father*. On the strength of Obama's record and his promise, Abner Mikva offered him a prestigious clerkship with the United States Court of Appeals. Obama had made such a positive impression on one of the scholars whose work he edited for the *HLR*, Michael McConnell, that the right-leaning McConnell recommended the left-leaning Obama for a teaching position at the University of Chicago Law School, where McConnell himself taught. The Chicago law firm best known for civil rights work also offered Obama a position as an associate. Too many doors seemed to be opening at once. Obama turned down the clerkship because he wanted to return to public life in Chicago. But he found it difficult to manage the demands of writing, teaching, and practicing law, and his juggling act got tougher when he accepted an offer to head a registration drive for Project Vote.

One of the courses Obama taught at the University of Chicago Law School, a seminar entitled Current Issues in Racism and the Law, reflects with particular clarity the impact of his education and his commitments to deliberation and community. Instead of requiring each student to write a brief, a standard practice designed to help aspiring attorneys hone their skills marshaling evidence and making a persuasive argument, Obama stipulated that each student must offer "a thorough examination of the diverity of opinion that exists" on his or her chosen topic. The other principal course requirement was an hour-long group presentation, a project requiring hypercompetitive law students to cooperate with each other. Each group could choose its own issue involving the intersection of law and race. The list of suggested topics included many of the hot-button controversies that Obama's critics on the left have accused him of dodging—issues such as immigration policy, interethnic tensions, welfare and reproductive freedom, reparations, hate speech, affirmative action, and public school funding—and his brief descriptions identified the nub of each issue. The explicit aim of the group projects was to stimulate lively discussion, which meant that each group had to address "the full spectrum of views on the issue you're dealing with." The students were required to examine plenty of court decisions, but in addition they read works of historical interpretation, classics of political and legal theory, commentaries from contemporaries ranging from Robert Bork on the right to Randall Kennedy on the left, and central texts by African American writers including Frederick Douglass, Booker T. Washington, W. E. B. DuBois, Marcus Garvey, Martin Luther King, Jr., Malcom X, William Julius Wilson, and Derrick Bell.

At the University of Chicago Law School, Obama's colleagues included a number of luminaries with whom he would eventually forge close ties, among them his second Supreme Court nominee, Elena Kagan, Abner Mikva, Martha Nussbaum, Geoffrey Stone, and Diane Wood. Although the faculty might have been less noisily contentious than that of Harvard Law School, they ranged from free-market economists and prominent figures in the law and economics movement, including Richard Posner, to politically active progressives who were trying self-consciously to keep alive Dewey's philosophy of pragmatism and his ideal of participatory democracy. Although by the end of the twentieth century the University of Chicago was well known for its conservative economists and political theorists, the community also included scholars who cherished a different tradition. These were the heirs to the Chicago-based social activism associated with Jane Addams, founder of the first American social settlement, Hull House, and Robert Park and other crusading social scientists who sought during the Progressive Era and the New Deal to yoke Dewey's ideas to political reform. As a lecturer Obama rubbed shoulders with prominent members of this progressive community, notably one of his colleagues at the law school, a fellow graduate of Harvard Law School with whose work he was already familiar from the *HLR*, Cass Sunstein, who became and remained a good friend and confidant.

During the summer of 1989, after completing his first year at Harvard, Obama had worked for the Chicago law firm Sidley Austin. There he was supervised by a recent graduate of Harvard Law School, Michelle Robinson, who treated him with the time-honored disrespect that law-student interns are thought to deserve. He found himself attracted to her, even though, as his boss, she refused to see him socially. Eventually the awkwardness of their situation at work was resolved—Obama secured a different job in Chicago the following summer—and the two began dating. In the fall of 1992 they married. The Robinson family provided Obama the stability and community his own family lacked, and the couple put down roots in the University of Chicago's Hyde Park neighborhood, where they lived until they moved to the White House.

They enrolled their children Malia and Sasha in the university's Lab School, a remarkable institution founded by Dewey and his wife Alice. Still infused with its original spirit of democratic engagement, pragmatism, egalitarianism, and active learning, the Lab School counts a large number of scholars and political activists among its alumni, including the man who became Obama's chief campaign strategist, David Axelrod.

Through Michelle's friends Obama developed contacts with downtown Chicago foundations, and soon the rising young attorney was serving on the boards of several civic organizations. He completed *Dreams from My Father*, which was published in 1995, and the next year he was elected to the Illinois state legislature. He was on his way, self-consciously following the path that Harold Washington took from state to national office, still with his eyes fixed on the prize of serving as mayor of Chicago. But as Obama began his ascent to national stature, he built intellectual networks, including those among colleagues at the University of Chicago Law School, as well as political networks. The breadth of those contacts assured that what he had learned at Occidental, Columbia, and the Harvard Law School—as well as the lessons he had learned on the far south side of Chicago—stayed with him. The columns he wrote for the *Hyde Park Herald* during the late 1990s testify to his continuing commitment to building community. The separate pieces of his education were beginning to fit together as Obama established himself in Chicago's civic, academic, and political spheres.

During the years from 1997 to 2000, Obama participated in a series of two- or three-day gatherings called the
Saguaro seminar. Convened by the political scientist Robert Putnam, a professor at Harvard's Kennedy School of
Government who had written the influential article "Bowling Alone" (1995) about the decline of civic engagement in
America, these annual meetings brought together civic,
religious, and academic leaders, including Obama's law
school professor Martha Minow. Participants ranged from
prominent liberals such as *Washington Post* journalist
E. J. Dionne to influential conservatives such as Ralph
Reed of the Christian Coalition. The Saguaro seminar included bankers and union organizers, insurance executives
and civic activists, pastors and professors, and difficult-
to-classify figures such as Jim Wallis of Sojourners, former Republican congressman Vin Weber of Minnesota,
and the maverick modern choreographer Liz Lerman.

Putnam organized the seminars to address the problem
that he and several other American social scientists had
identified, the same problem, coincidentally, that Obama
had identified so clearly in his 1988 article "Why Organize." Americans were losing contact with each other and
with the public sphere. Not only were they dropping out
of community organizations such as parent–teacher associations, all major indices of civic engagement showed
shrinking participation. Rather than joining leagues,
Americans were "bowling alone." As Tocqueville and
later progressive reformers understood, the success of
American democracy had depended on citizens' involve-

ment in activities that brought them into contact with people of different backgrounds, values, and political affiliations. With signs of such engagement fading, Americans showed greater hostility toward each other, greater willingness to assume the worst about people unlike themselves, and an increasing distrust of government at all levels. According to Putnam and others involved in such research, these problems did not result simply from the Reagan revolution, Americans' turn to the right, or the conservative crusade against the legacy of the New Deal. The new culture of individualism reflected instead a broader and deeper transformation with consequences extending beyond America's periodic cycles of reform and retrenchment. The health of American public life depended on resolving these problems.

The Saguaro seminar, by bringing together people from various political persuasions and occupations, was intended to generate new ideas to regenerate civil society. In these seminars, Obama followed his standard practice. He listened intently, asked for the clarification and elaboration of arguments, and tended not to say much in the early stages of each meeting. Gradually, however, once all the ideas and disagreements were on the table, he began to assert himself. Paraphrasing positions to make sure they were correctly understood, identifying weaknesses in argument and evidence, teasing out assumptions and implications, and pushing participants to rethink and refine their positions, Obama established himself in his familiar role. As goad, peacekeeper, and conciliator, he elicited and contributed new and creative ideas.

Of course Obama was by then no stranger to the issues under discussion at the Saguaro seminars. He had first encountered Tocqueville as a freshman at Occidental. As a community organizer in Chicago he had experienced personally the strangulation of civic participation, and addressing that problem had remained among his central objectives since his return. At Harvard Law School he had taken a course entitled Civil Society, jointly taught by Minow and two of her colleagues on the faculty, conservative Catholic Mary Ann Glendon (later named by George W. Bush as United States ambassador to the Vatican) and Todd Rakoff (a specialist on administrative law who has also written extensively on the reform of legal education). During his time in law school, Obama probably spent as much time in class with Glendon as with any other member of the faculty besides Unger.

In light of Glendon's later trajectory, as an increasingly strident political partisan and relentless opponent of abortion, and in light of her dramatic refusal to accept an honorary degree from Notre Dame in 2009 because of the institution's decision to invite Obama to campus, Obama's repeat appearances in her courses might seem surprising. Instead their relationship reflects both the catholicity of his interests and what has happened to American public life (and perhaps to American Catholicism) in the intervening two decades. In the year that Obama completed his legal training, Glendon published *Rights Talk: The Impoverishment of Political Discourse*, a fascinating critique of the absolutist, hyperindividualist discourse of rights in American law. Contrasting such American dogmatism to European traditions that yoked rights to responsibilities, Glendon sounded themes from German social democracy and Catholic social doctrine concerning the importance of community, and she cited authorities ranging from Edmund Burke to Karl Marx, and from Tocqueville to Tribe, on the inadequacy of the idea that atomistic individuals bear unqualified absolute rights. The progressive Catholic journal *Commonweal* noted that Glendon in those days deliberately resisted being "ideologically pigeonholed." In the late 1980s and early 1990s, it was possible for Catholics such as Glendon to invoke the idea of duty and community in a way that appealed to American progressives troubled by Reagan's gospel of individualism. Twenty years later such alliances have become less common.

In the seminar on civil society that Glendon taught with Minow and Rakoff, Obama had another opportunity to read European social theorists, including Marx, Weber, and Emile Durkheim. Just as important, visitors to that seminar included prominent scholars and activists who explored the relation between law, religion, community life, and economic, social, political, and cultural change, precisely the issues later on the agenda at Putnam's Saguaro seminars. Guests of the Harvard Law School civil society seminar included Monsignor George Higgins, who discussed the tradition of partnership between religious congregations and labor organizations; Emmy Werner, who focused on economic development; and Anthony Cook, who connected Martin Luther King, Jr., with "reconstructive theology," the topic of an article he published in the *HLR*. Stewart Macaulay spoke on the "social context of contract," a question linked to Sunstein's *HLR* article "Interpreting Statutes"; noted feminist Carol Gilligan, on women and education; sociologist Alan Wolfe, on social science and moral obligation; and philosopher William Sullivan, a coauthor of *Habits of the Heart* (among the most widely read books published in the 1980s), on the intersection between individual choice, religious faith, and the American tradition of republicanism.

The presence of all those speakers in a single seminar illustrates the pervasiveness in the legal academy, during the years Obama was studying law, of concern with civil society and with the republican synthesis. These ideas, which Obama encountered as theory at Occidental and at Columbia, in practice working as a community organizer in Chicago, and then again in the classrooms of Harvard Law School, constitute another of the underappreciated dimensions of Obama's intellectual formation. Their centrality is reflected clearly in Obama's books, in his speeches, and above all in his emphasis on the obligations individual citizens have to one another in American culture. Just as the American Revolution was not made by rugged individualists but by responsible (albeit unconventional) Christians who concerned themselves with the common good rather than simply their narrow self-interest, so contemporary American society could solve its problems only by a renewed commitment to the health of the public sphere.

Americans usually associate an emphasis on individual freedom with liberals (think of the American Civil Liberties Union) and an emphasis on tradition with conservatives (think of the religious Right). Both the civic republican interpretation of American history and the communitarian sensibility that Obama encountered as an undergraduate, as a law student, and in the Saguaro seminar complicate that simple equation by highlighting how often in American history the work of radical reformers has been informed by, and has been driven forward through the work of, communities—frequently religious communities—that sustained and amplified the significance of individuals' efforts. To understand Obama's attitude toward American politics and his long-term commitment to breaking the logjam of American party politics, it is not enough to trace his sensibility to his formative years in Indonesia and Hawaii; to Los Angeles, New York, and Cambridge; to Illinois and Kenya. It is equally crucial to locate him within the frameworks of civic republican and communitarian discourse, within the tradition of philosophical pragmatism, and in relation to a cluster of complex ideas that emerged in the 1960s and 1970s.

Usually designated by a bundle of multisyllabic terms that signal their complexity, these ideas—antifoundationalism, particularism, perspectivalism, and historicism—

also decisively shaped Obama's sensibility. He first encountered them haphazardly, simply by virtue of having
to cope with the contrast between the attitudes of his
mother and his stepfather while living in Indonesia. As a
student in college and law school, he breathed an atmosphere saturated with the ideas of contingency and change.
As a community organizer and then as a lawyer and political activist in Chicago, he found himself practicing
forms of pragmatist improvisation as he tried to bring together multiple traditions and strategies of social action.
Whereas many Americans are upset—disoriented—by the
idea that values vary over time and across cultures, Obama
found that way of thinking congenial because it made better sense of his own experience, conformed to his emerging understanding of American democracy, and gave him
valuable tools for dealing with the philosophical and political puzzles he was trying to solve.

By antifoundationalism and particularism I mean the
denial of universal principles. According to this way of
thinking, human cultures are human constructions; different people exhibit different forms of behavior because
they cherish different values. By perspectivalism I mean
the belief that everything we see is conditioned by where
we stand. There is no privileged, objective vantage point
free from the perspective of particular cultural values. By
historicism I mean the conviction that all human values
and practices are products of historical processes and must
be interpreted within historical frameworks. All principles
and social patterns change; none stands outside the flow

of history. These ideas come in different flavors, more and less radical and more and less nihilist. To the most radical antifoundationalists, particularists, perspectivalists, and historicists, such as Nietzsche, no ideals stretch across time, across cultures, or even between individuals in the same culture. Everything is relative. Every judgment is deeply flawed and subject to unmasking. All that remains is power. By contrast, to moderate antifoundationalists, particularists, perspectivalists, and historicists, such as the American pragmatist philosophers James and Dewey, such insights into the contingency and variability of values have a different significance. They help us interrogate our own inherited ideals and subject them to critical scrutiny. They warn us against the self-satisfied recourse to dogmatism that most humans have found comforting, even irresistible. But—and this is the decisive point—they are not cause for despair of the sort that ensnared Nietzsche. Through interaction with others, and with the world, we can test our beliefs. Even if the results of those tests must remain provisional, open to further scrutiny and further testing, they provide sufficient stability to enable us to move forward, as members of communities located in history, aware of our traditions and self-consciously attempting to realize the ideals we choose to keep alive as our guides.

Versions of these ideas, as I have noted, first emerged in America in the late nineteenth and early twentieth centuries, in the work of James and Dewey, in the writings and programs of the progressive reformers and social scientists they taught or influenced through their writings, and in the work of a number of contemporaneous European thinkers and political activists. In the 1960s new versions of antifoundationalism and historicism found expression in the work of scholars such as those cited by Tribe in "The Curvature of Constitutional Space" and *On Reading the Constitution*, influential writers such as Kuhn, Geertz, and the neopragmatists, who profoundly unsettled American social thought. They showed that conventions and inherited traditions play central roles in all human behavior and cultural expression, which means that all ideas and beliefs must be historicized—placed in the context of a particular time and place—if they are to be understood. Obama's sensibility, his ways of thinking about culture and politics, rests on the hidden strata of these ideas.

Obama's books appeal so widely because they are pitched at a level different from the level of abstraction at which scholars and theorists operate. But the ideas are there, just beneath the surface. As a political speaker, he learned from practice how to breathe life into these abstractions. As a novice organizer in Chicago, he showed the flair for understanding and connecting with different people—people with diverse backgrounds, values, and aspirations—that led Kruglik to admire him and Galuzzo to call him gifted. When he returned from law school and entered electoral politics, Obama at first came across as a cold-eyed analyst of law and policy, a wonkish technocrat more comfortable teaching law than wooing voters. But in electoral politics, as in other domains, he proved a quick study. During the years since his election to the Illinois state legislature in 1996, Obama has become an accomplished storyteller, capable of bringing complex ideas to life by embodying them in narratives concerning individuals, either himself or those around him.

That quality too, like his talent as a conciliator, can be described as a trick, or a gift, or a personality trait. It is not. Obama's own books and speeches, and the issues of the *HLR* for which he was responsible, show him wrestling creatively and productively with the most challenging and difficult ideas of antifoundationalism, particularism, and historicism. The evidence of the shaping force of these ideas is as clear and compelling as the evidence of the impact of his time working as a community organizer in Chicago or the role played by his family's stories in forming his sensibility. Obama's conception of democracy as deliberation, like his conception of American history as a dynamic process and project of widening opportunities and inclusion, derives from the balance between his firm commitment to the principles of freedom, equality, and social justice and his realization that the road toward realizing those ideals remains as bumpy and as twisted now as it has always been in the past. Obama knows that balancing adherence to principles against the understanding that all principles change over time requires maintaining a delicate equilibrium, an equilibrium difficult enough to establish in the seminar room, the law review article, or the courtroom and nearly impossible to achieve in the maelstrom of electoral or legislative politics. Unfortunately, facing that challenge in a democracy is as inescapable as it is difficult.

Obama's commitments to philosophical pragmatism and deliberative democracy— to building support slowly, gradually, through compromise and painstaking consensus building— represent a calculated risk as political strategy. It is a gamble he may lose. But it is not a sign of weakness, as his critics on the right and left allege. It shows instead that he understands not only the contingency of cultural values but also how the nation's political system was designed to work. Democracy means struggling with differences, then achieving provisional agreements that immediately spark new disagreements. Only autocrats enjoy the luxury of vanquishing their opponents. That luxury is unavailable, by design, in the United States. Obama's inclination—and ability—to reconcile differences has distinguished him from an early age. Observers usually attribute this quality to his character or his temperament, but there is more to it than that simple description suggests. His predilection to conciliate whenever possible is grounded in his understanding of the history of American thought, culture, and politics.

America in the early twenty-first century has enemies. Perhaps for that reason, some Americans are inclined to treat dissent as evidence of treason and respect for other ways of thinking as spinelessness. But the denial that democracy depends on disagreements to sustain its vitality may in time prove as serious a challenge to American civic life as any threat launched from beyond our borders.

Given so many Americans' impatience with opposition to their own beliefs, conciliators are out of fashion. Given our culture's almost automatic impulse to brand compromise as cowardice, Obama's steely commitment to comity is rarely identified for what it is, a sign of principle. We need to uncover its sources.

Chapter 2

From Universalism
to Particularism

A MERICAN INTELLECTUAL LIFE in the last half century defies neat synthesis. So many inconsistent and cross-cutting ideas have emerged that a tidy account is almost impossible. Near the beginning of *Dreams from My Father*, however, Barack Obama captures the central dynamic with exceptional insight and such subtlety that readers might miss it. He paints a portrait of his mother and her parents that captures the mid-twentieth-century mindset of millions—perhaps even the majority—of Americans. From their origins in Kansas, Obama's maternal grandparents migrated to Texas, then to Washington, then to Hawaii, arriving in the nation's newest state convinced of what Obama calls "the seeming triumph of universalism over parochialism and narrow mindedness." They saw themselves playing a part in creating "a bright new world where differences of race and culture would instruct and amuse and perhaps even ennoble." His mother's mother, whom he called Toot, the Hawaiian term for grandmother, was proud to announce that she was part Cherokee. His grandfather, because his dark skin had caused some people to label him a "wop," told himself that he had shared the discrimination faced by members of other dark-skinned races. Once he arrived in Hawaii, he cultivated the friendship of a few African Americans. Obama knew his grandparents were exaggerating their struggles and their broad-mindedness, but he acknowledged "how strongly Gramps believed in his fictions, how badly he wanted them to be true." Even though they inhabited a safe, white space in a white nation, Gramps and Toot imagined themselves free of prejudice, particularly when their own daughter married an African.

Looking back at their rosy optimism, and that of their generation, Obama comments that they embraced "a useful fiction, one that haunts me no less than it haunted my family." To those who shared the idealism of those years, who applauded when the United Nations proclaimed the Universal Declaration of Human Rights and who celebrated the rise and apparent success of the American civil rights movement, Obama's characterization of such universalist principles as "a useful fiction" might seem strange. After all, these ideals animated the generation that won the Good War, established an international organization designed to keep the peace, and struggled to extend the American principles of liberty and equality to African

Americans and to women. If their conception of a single human community challenged a history of ethnic, religious, and nationalist warfare and proclaimed the "family of man," shouldn't they have earned admiration rather than suspicion? Why should Obama describe the values they cherished as a "fiction" rather than a sturdy set of ideals? Why should such ideas "haunt" rather than, say, inspire him? To answer those questions, one must appreciate the struggle between different worldviews that developed in America—and not only in America but worldwide, as Obama later realized—during his formative years.

Bringing order to the chaos of recent American intellectual life is a risky business; it requires simplifying and schematizing a dizzying array of diverse materials ranging from the natural sciences to the social sciences. In the field of political theory, however, such schematizing is made easier by the towering figure of John Rawls, the philosopher whose work dominated the landscape. Rawls's book *A Theory of Justice* has generated more commentary, both positive and negative, than any other work of political theory published since World War II. For that reason— and because his ideas can be shown both to have influenced Obama and to illuminate Obama's political convictions—I will use themes from Rawls's life and work to trace an arc that characterizes much of American thought in recent decades. Unless we understand that arc, we cannot understand the amalgam of deeply held principles and frankly admitted uncertainties that characterizes Obama's approach to public life.

American social thought since the middle of the twentieth century has been marked by a struggle between champions of foundationalism and universalism—that "useful fiction" animating champions of international law and interracial harmony—and challengers who deny the existence of unchanging truths. Obama's sensibility is a product of that conflict. He understands the reasons why the ideas of foundationalism and universalism proved useful: such ideals inspired the generation of his maternal grandparents and that of his parents. He also understands the reasons why such ideals proved vulnerable to a series of challenges: those who embraced those ideals aspired to more than any theory could provide. Even though Obama shares the skepticism of those critics who eroded the foundations on which mid-twentieth-century universalism stood, he nevertheless understands—and is "haunted" by—the residual appeal that timeless ideals continue to exert. As he has been throughout his life, as president he remains caught in the force field between universalism and particularism.

The ideological polarization that marks our own time would have surprised many of those who were writing about America at the time of Obama's birth in the summer of 1961. The savvy technocrats who flocked to Washington that year were not coming to Camelot. Instead of seeking romantic adventure, they thought of themselves as replacing partisanship with problem solving, ideology with expertise. But their confidence proved misplaced. The ink was scarcely dry on Daniel Bell's widely read book *The End of Ideology* when ideology began breaking out all over the Western world. Anticolonial struggles, challenges to racism, and the emergence of distinctive national forms of a New Left and, only slightly later, a New Right combined to shatter the brittle veneer of American unity in the bipolar contest between the United States and the Soviet Union that had seemed to many Americans to define the world after World War II. In similar fashion, the articles that Rawls published in the 1950s and 1960s—the articles that formed the core of his *Theory of Justice*—showed that American political theory was being resurrected even at the time when its death was being proclaimed. Many social scientists agreed with Bell: big ideas were out. Tinkering—otherwise known as social engineering—was in. Rawls proved them wrong.

When Rawls's *Theory of Justice* was published in 1971, it resuscitated American political theory, stimulating debate about fundamental principles and helping to inspire a scholarly renaissance. In the assessment of the philosopher Alexander Nehamas, *A Theory of Justice* stands among the few books educated Americans might be embarrassed not to have read. Yet of course plenty of Americans have not read it, and only a few have read it recently, so briefly reviewing the two principal arguments of the book may be worthwhile, because Rawls's arguments played a decisive role in debates about justice when Obama was studying political science, then law, and when he was teaching at the University of Chicago Law School. The first argument concerns a hypothetical condition that

Rawls called the "original position," in which those designing a just society come together to decide on the principles of justice. The second argument concerns the two principles of justice that would be chosen in those circumstances. Rawls borrowed from the seventeenth- and eighteenth-century tradition of social contract theory the notion of individuals meeting together to decide on the rules for their society. Of course he never imagined that any such meeting actually occurred. It was instead, in his words, "a purely hypothetical situation," useful only because it helps us see how people reason about justice.

Rawls added another wrinkle to the tradition usually associated with Thomas Hobbes, John Locke, and Jean-Jacques Rousseau. No one in the original position, Rawls hypothesized, knows what his own position in the society will be. Deliberations occur behind the "veil of ignorance," to use Rawls's evocative term. Thus no individual knows his class or social status, or his intelligence, strength, appearance, or anything else that would affect his chances of success. In a move that proved to be particularly controversial, Rawls further stipulated that those in the original position are also ignorant of what he called "their conceptions of the good or their special psychological propensities." The veil of ignorance was intended to insure that "no one is advantaged or disadvantaged in the choice of principles by the outcome of natural chance or the contingency of social circumstances." Because all persons are similarly situated, no one can try to design principles that would benefit himself or any particular individual. The principles of justice chosen under such conditions are thus said to be "a fair agreement or bargain," and Rawls's theory was dubbed "justice as fairness." Rawls's notion of fairness, which descends roughly from James Harrington's example of cake cutting in *Oceana* (one cuts, the other chooses) through Kant's ideas about the political implications of his ethics, is central to *A Theory of Justice*. Even though none of us will ever experience anything resembling the original position, Rawls argued that knowing what principles people in such circumstances would choose enables us to identify the principles of a just society. Whether one agreed or disagreed with him, no one in the scholarly communities of philosophy, political theory, or constitutional law could proceed in the 1970s or 1980s without coming to terms with Rawls. Before, during, and after the years when Obama was studying law, references to Rawls's writings peppered the pages of the *HLR*.

Rawls argued that people in the original position, despite the veil of ignorance, know that they will want certain things, including rights and liberties, opportunities and powers, income and wealth, and finally, self-respect. He reasoned that people with such desires would choose two principles of justice. The first, the principle of equal rights, "requires equality in the assignments of basic rights and duties." This principle Rawls assigned priority over the second, which is often referred to as the difference principle, or the maximin principle. Rawls stated his second principle in these terms: "social and economic inequalities, for example inequalities of wealth and authority, are just only if they result in compensating benefits for everyone, and in particular for the least advantaged members of the society." Rawls aimed, with his two principles of justice, to balance rights against redistribution, freedom against equality.

To a remarkable degree, Rawls's two principles align with the principles that Obama learned in Chicago as a community organizer, the principles animating Alinsky's approach to social action. People have interests. They have a legitimate right to express those interests. People understand that their own interests are in tension with the interests of other people. But it is the people at the bottom of the heap, the people who lack the resources to realize their life plans, who should be the focus of social policy. Democratic government should concentrate its resources not on rewarding the powerful but on improving the situation of the least advantaged. The challenge facing community organizers, from Alinsky's first forays into the Back of the Yards Neighborhood Council to Obama's work with the Developing Communities Project, has been to persuade people in power that they should make something like Rawls's difference principle their own rule of thumb. Confrontations, Alinksy insisted, force the issue, and for that reason they have the best chance of convincing the powerful that they should listen not only to those who already enjoy privileges. Their policies should aim, in Rawls's words, toward "compensating benefits for everyone," particularly those excluded from wealth and power.

It might seem jarring to find Rawls's principles of justice being hashed out in the church basements of Chicago's far south side. But according to Kruglik, that is what he, Kellmann, Galuzzo, and Obama knew they were doing. Organizers begin by encouraging disempowered individuals to express their aims. They are not meeting behind a veil of ignorance—although the poor are usually invisible to the rest of society—but through their discussions community members reach agreement about the goal they would like to reach. Then they decide on the forms of social action they consider most likely to tug policy makers toward awareness of their needs. To reiterate, "inequalities of wealth and authority," according to Rawls's difference principle, "are just only if they result in compensating benefits for everyone, and in particular the least advantaged members of the society." Community organizers, at least from Kruglik's perspective, work to enact Rawls's theory of justice. When Obama wrote "Why Organize," he was aiming to explain what organizers do and why they do it. He was not explicitly writing a commentary consistent with Rawls's *Theory of Justice*; nor was Alinsky when he explained himself in *Reveille for Radicals* (1946) and *Rules for Radicals* (1971). Nevertheless, both were effectively doing just that.

Although Rawls had worked out his arguments about justice in articles published before Gordon Wood began studying the creation of the American republic and Robert Putnam began studying civil society, striking resonances also exist between Rawls's theory of justice, Wood's republican sensibility, and Putnam's emphasis on civic engagement. Rights are important. So is freedom. True enough. But a commitment to equality emerged alongside the concern with individual liberty in the eighteenth century, and Americans built a nation on the templates provided by their experience of participating in local civic institutions. Americans of Obama's generation, who learned much of their political theory from Rawls, much of their American history from the republican synthesis, and much of their political science and sociology from the Tocqueville-tinged debates over civil society, knew that balancing freedom and equality, rights and obligations, self and community, had been Americans' goal from the beginning. Obama found those lessons confirmed in the strategies he learned—and practiced—as an organizer in Chicago.

Rawls was a realist, as was Madison. The founders had shown themselves to be hardheaded as well as highminded. If the republic were to nourish civic virtue, it had to survive human cupidity, the original sin of self-centeredness. Even Deists saw the logic of the argument in Genesis. Whether or not any Satan had tempted man to turn away from God's goodness, the evidence of egoism was inescapable. Operating in the purely secular thought world to which he had recently converted, Rawls identified at the outset one of the central assumptions animating *A Theory of Justice*: those in the original position should be thought of as "rational and mutually disinterested." This does not mean the parties are pure egoists, by which

Rawls meant individuals interested in nothing but "wealth, prestige, or domination." But he did conceive them as "not taking an interest in one another's interests." In other words, Rawls interpreted the concept of rationality "as far as possible in the narrow sense, standard in economic theory, of taking the most effective means to given ends." This form of reasoning, thanks to the law and economics movement, pervaded debates about law at the end of the twentieth century. In Kruglik's words, Obama wanted to know "how power operates." Or as Obama himself put it, "I think that oftentimes ordinary citizens are taught that decisions are made based on the public interest or grand principles, when, in fact, what really moves things is money and votes and power." "What I am constantly trying to do," Obama explained, "is balance a hard head with a big heart." One can characterize that challenge in terms of Rawls's two principles of justice, Madison's constitutional architecture, or the difference between Obama's softhearted mother and his hardheaded stepfather Lolo Soetoro—variations on the same theme.

Consider another way of framing these issues. At the dawn of the twentieth century, the German sociologist Max Weber had identified three forms of reason. His framework clarifies much of what had happened in the intervening decades between the time Weber wrote and the time Obama entered public life. Champions of Weber's first form, traditional rationality, calculate according to the demands of inherited customs, which dictate forms of action that, despite disastrous or at least unpalatable consequences, are accepted because they conform to long-accepted norms. These were the values that Obama, in "Why Organize," urged community organizers to respect, not dismiss as irrational, old fashioned, or counterproductive. Weber's second form of reason, value rationality, dictates following religious or ethical precepts laying out the good life, again regardless of the results of acting according to shared principles. Obama saw such reasoning at work in the church groups he wanted to mobilize for social action. The third form of reason, instrumental rationality, which Weber considered new—and characteristic of the modern world that was emerging in his day—rules out both cultural traditions and religious or ethical values. Instrumental reason focuses attention on the means whereby ends can be achieved in the world of action. This form of reason provides the sole guiding norm for those who value results—whether profits or victories of any kind—and of self-consciously tough-minded organizers, like Kellman (in Obama's account at least), who always think about which strategies will succeed—without thinking about the relation between those strategies and the traditions and values of the people involved.

Using that Weberian framework, the individuals in Rawls's original position might be said to reason instrumentally, an ironic and little noticed feature of a philosophy frequently aligned with the antiutilitarian philosophy of Immanuel Kant. This point about Rawls's second principle, the maximin, or difference principle—that it was selected because it was seen as useful even by individuals not interested in each other's interests—has often been overlooked. When we encounter Obama's strikingly different reliance on the idea of empathy to establish the desirability of equality, which is the point Rawls sought to establish with the difference principle, it is useful to keep in mind the contrast between this form of instrumental rationality and the older practices of traditional and value rationality that Obama knows persist in American culture. Although not identical to the contrast between universalism and particularism, the contrast between reasoning on the basis of tradition or values, on the one hand, and on the basis of means–ends calculations, on the other, also helps explain the depth of the disagreements raging in contemporary American culture. At stake in disputes over particular issues, at least occasionally, are buried disagreements about issues as basic as the meaning of rationality.

A Theory of Justice was widely understood as having clear implications for politics, even though Rawls himself said little in the book about contemporary political and economic issues. In law journals as in the rest of the academy and the popular press, the Left applauded and the Right jeered. Many of those who reviewed the book—and some Democrats outside the scholarly community who began to invoke it in support of their own ideas—thought Rawls's principles could provide a robust rationale for the ambitious (and still largely unrealized) programs of Lyndon Johnson's Great Society. They saw in the difference principle a warrant for a more steeply graduated income tax and a social safety net that would provide all individuals with an opportunity to make use of the formal and supposedly equal liberties they enjoyed in the abstract. In Michelman's portrait, Justice Brennan was a champion of the difference principle, as were Michelman's and Sunstein's liberal republicans and progressive legal interpretivists. From his perspective as a graduate student in American history who had shifted his attention from the academy to community organizing, Kruglik judged Alinsky's ideas congruent with Rawls's philosophy.

Conservatives who addressed *A Theory of Justice* argued instead that the book showed the fallacy of the welfare state. They reasoned that the maximin principle undercut the principle of equal rights; they insisted that progressive taxation diminishes individuals' incentives to work and their chance to enjoy the rights guaranteed by Rawls's first principle. Moreover, schemes of social provision, by siphoning off the resources of the most productive individuals, limit economic productivity, thereby insuring that less wealth is created for all to enjoy. From this perspective, Rawls had it all wrong. The American Revolution was fought to secure rights; the New Deal had to be dismantled to restore those rights.

At the same time that many Democrats and Republicans were invoking Rawls to bolster their own political positions, critiques of the book appeared that have continued to frame disputes in American political and legal theory. Charles Taylor, who taught at Oxford during these years before returning to teach in his native Canada and in American universities, developed a line of argument that has remained influential, an argument that shows up in both of Obama's books and most of his important speeches. Taylor challenged Rawls's assumption that those in the original position would be uninterested in each other's interests and that rationality should be understood in the narrow sense of economic theory. Why, Taylor asked, should we presume that any persons would reason without the most important—the constitutive—beliefs that give their lives meaning and direction? Why, in other words, should we rule out the religious or ethical convictions, or the cultural or national traditions, fundamental to every person's sense of self?

One of Taylor's students at Oxford was the American Michael Sandel, whose book *Liberalism and the Limits of Justice* (1982) became the most widely read version of Taylor's critique. From this perspective, Rawls not only ignored, he ruled out of bounds, the most precious of all human commitments, the basic commitments that make us who we are. Those who advanced this line of analysis, because they challenged the inadequacy of Rawls's conception of the individual person and stressed the importance of the communities and traditions in which each self is embedded, came to be known as communitarians. If *Habits of the Heart*, the most cited proclamation of this view before the publication of Putnam's "Bowling Alone," circulated more broadly at Harvard Law School than any other single statement of communitarian principles, it vied for prominence with Sandel's *Liberalism and the Limits of Justice*. Sandel, a professor in Harvard's Government Department, taught a popular seminar at the law school taken by some of Obama's friends. Many Harvard Law School students served as graduate teaching fellows in Sandel's wildly popular undergraduate course, Justice, which enrolled more students than any other course at Harvard—as it still does.

In the 1990s versions of communitarianism were ubiquitous. Although scorned by critics left and right as fuzzy-minded wishful thinking, communitarians self-consciously sought to amalgamate arguments from across the political spectrum. Like many on the right, communitarians prized religious, ethnic, and patriotic traditions; like many on the left, they savaged the hierarchical, exclusionary, and militaristic side of those traditions. Such eclecticism struck their critics as a sign of their incoherence. Their critics' lack of sympathy struck communitarians as evidence of the inadequacy of the prevailing conservative and radical options. The prevailing false binary shunted everyone into one camp or the other, resulting in impoverished intellectual life and unproductive public debate. Sandel argued repeatedly—and accurately—that he intended to supplement Rawls's arguments about justice rather than supplant them. Rawls had indeed included an account of "the idea of social union," and he protested that he did not deny the importance to individuals of participating in communities. He wrote near the conclusion of *A Theory of Justice*, "we depend upon the cooperative endeavors of others not only for the means of well-being but to bring to fruition our latent powers." Such formulations notwithstanding, Sandel's critique of Rawls struck a chord among political theorists of various stripes, and Sandel was routinely cast as a communitarian antagonist to Rawls's liberal individualism.

Critics accused communitarians of romanticizing American society, in which power and greed so often trump trust and benevolence. Sandel's book *Democracy's Discontent* offered a much fuller reply to such critics. He argued that American history offers the best evidence of the constitutive value of individuals' commitments to the traditions in which they are embedded. Viewed in relation to the issues of the *HLR* produced while Obama was studying at Harvard Law School, *Democracy's Discontent* reflects the influence of the republican synthesis, which Sandel used to supplement Rawlsian liberalism and to extend arguments made in law review articles by Sunstein, Michelman, and many others. Rejecting the idea of a procedural republic neutral in relation to substantive values, Sandel allied with those legal scholars to champion an American tradition incorporating responsibilities as well as rights, attentive to communities as well as individuals.

When Obama makes the case for the importance of neighborhoods and church groups and the necessity of sacrificing oneself for the greater good, his critics to the left label him a conservative. When Obama calls for redistribution and excoriates the greed of plutocrats, his critics on the right label him a socialist. Both sets of critics are wrong. He is a civic republican, committed to a revised version of Rawls's principles of justice as applied to law and politics by many of those with whom he studied, and whose work he read, in college and in law school, scholars such as Boesche, Minow, Michelman, Putnam, Sandel, Sunstein, and Wood. Critics of communitarianism are fond of pointing out that the Ku Klux Klan and the Weather Underground were also communities. Not all individuals who cluster together contribute to the resolution of civic problems. The time Obama spent in Chicago, with gangs and crooks operating inside as well as outside the law, inoculated him against naive celebrations of civil society as a panacea.

A second line of critique directed at Rawls emerged from the writings of feminists, who not only rejected the gendered language that Rawls, like most male academics writing in the 1950s and 1960s, used more or less unselfconsciously. Some feminists argued that Rawls's entire approach to justice was gendered male. According to such critics, women never have reasoned, and never would reason, in a way that fails to take into account the particularities of individuals, their relationships to others, and their fundamentally different needs. Women were too attuned to networks of caring to abandon those dependent on them or reason as if they did not exist. Obama had encountered these tensions at an early age. He watched his mother struggling to carve out an autonomous life in the male-dominated world of Indonesia, and when he returned to Hawaii, he became aware of the challenges facing his grandmother. Although she awakened at five a.m. every day to get ready for her bus ride to work, as a working woman she could never do enough to meet the expectations of her husband or the bank that employed her. She watched as less devoted men rose to executive status, while she was never able to break through the glass ceiling that prevented women from rising above midlevel positions no matter what they did. She understood the dynamics, but she did not see how to alter them. Instead she projected her aspirations onto her grandchildren. "As long as you kids do well," she explained to Obama, "that's all that matters."

But not all American women were equally willing to accept their condition with such resignation. As women challenged prevailing gender norms using different arguments, Rawls's arguments about justice popped up on all sides. Some feminists counterposed the idea of justice typically practiced within families to Rawls's flattened vision of calculating individuals concerned only with maximizing their own life chances. Other feminists such as Susan Okin took a very different approach, arguing that Rawls's principles of justice should be introduced into the family to destabilize the illegitimate privileges of husbands and fathers vis-à-vis their wives and children. Okin believed, as did Sandel, that theorists could supplement Rawls's model of reasoning by pointing out the role of empathy and the cultural embeddedness of all people. Still other theorists of feminism, who emphasized humans' historicity and sympathy for other persons, particularly Seyla Benhabib in *Situating the Self* and Joan Tronto in *Moral Boundaries*, urged feminists to leave Rawls behind and look instead toward the ideas advanced by the widely read German philosopher Jürgen Habermas, whose work Obama first encountered at Occidental. Habermas held out an ideal of communicative rationality—an ideal that emerges in different forms over time, in particular communities—oriented toward the aim of all human communication, the telos of mutual understanding. Explicitly challenging the domination of modern life by Weber's idea of instrumental reason, Habermas advanced arguments for social, political, and economic reconstruction premised on the values of equality and empathy latent in practices of "everyday communication." Many theorists attracted to feminist critiques of Rawls, or to those of Taylor or Sandel, found themselves moving toward the discourse ethics of Habermas, whose work strongly influenced many American social and legal theorists on the left, including Michelman and Sunstein, who were looking for alternatives to Rawls's emphasis on individual rights.

Given the proliferation of theories concerning gender and race during the 1970s and 1980s, it would be misleading to exaggerate Rawls's role in these domains. Many women did not need a theory of feminism; like Obama's grandmother and his mother, Stanley Ann Dunham Soetoro, they simply got on with the business of making careers for themselves. Obama's mother spent years doing field work in Indonesia, struggling to carve out an academic career as an anthropologist while she worked to help Indonesian artisans survive economically and preserve their traditional culture. From the examples of his mother and his grandmother, Obama knew about gender stereotyping and resistance long before he ever encountered feminist theory. But the need many theorists of gender felt to address Rawls's arguments—even though he discussed neither gender nor race in *A Theory of Justice*—reflects the centrality of his ideas during these years. Even those who ended up rejecting Rawls could not avoid him.

Finally, a very different line of criticism emerged from Robert Nozick and others who articulated varieties of libertarianism that appealed to many American conservatives. According to Nozick, who in his widely read book *Anarchy, State, and Utopia* called for a "minimal" state (even though he rejected the more extreme demand of some libertarians for an "ultraminimal state") to maximize the freedom of individuals, the successful are fully entitled to enjoy the fruits of their labors. In stark contrast to the challenges coming from various communitarians and even more diverse feminists, libertarians followed Nozick in contending that the maximin principle offered only a fig leaf to cover the injustice of taking from individuals what was rightfully theirs and unjustly redistributing it to those who had not earned it and did not deserve it. Descended from the writings of post–World War II free-market economists such as Friedrich Hayek and others associated with the Mont Pèlerin Society, and later given prominence through the efforts of think tanks such as the Cato Institute, such ideas gradually entered the mainstream of Republican Party rhetoric.

If such a schematic summary of the myriad responses to Rawls hardly does justice to the intricacies of the debates sparked by *A Theory of Justice*, it does at least identify some of the central arguments and points of view, all of which found expression in law journals such as the *HLR* as scholars explored the implications of these ideas for legal theory and practice. To cite just one example, one of the most comprehensive compilations of the varieties of feminist theory, which contains contributions from representatives of all the points of view I have described here, was published in 1990, in the middle of Obama's time in law school, under the title *Feminism and Political Theory*. Although almost all the contributors were women, the book was edited, and opened with an introduction written by, Cass Sunstein, who acknowledged the assistance, among others, of Obama's law school professor Martha Minow.

As these controversies raged, Rawls replied in careful articles, refining and eventually redefining his position in a way that has not received the attention it merits. Rawls's quiet reformulation of the basis for his ideas illustrates a crucial development in American culture during the 1970s and 1980s, the years when Obama was coming of age and American social theory was being decisively transformed. Subtly Rawls shifted away from what Obama later termed the "useful fiction" of universal ideals, away from the perspective that Rawls termed "an Archimedean point for judging the basic structure of society," toward a more modest form of particularism and historicism. First in a series of essays, notably a preface to the French edition of *A Theory of Justice* (1987) in which he distinguished the ideal of a "property-owning democracy" from the welfare state, Rawls emphasized the importance of reforming the distribution of wealth in ways that would make *re*distribution less necessary. If incomes were less unequal in the first place, then life chances would be more equal and recourse to the difference principle less necessary. This shift placed Rawls closer to the radical reconstructionist program of earlier economic populists such as Dewey and their contemporary heirs such as Roberto Unger. Unfortunately, few partisans of "property-owning democracy" articulated a strategy for realizing their ideals. Second, in Rawls's ambitious book *Political Liberalism* (1993), he substantially revised his earlier claims for the status of his ideas about justice. He now admitted that all any theory can provide are principles appropriate "for us" rather than for all rational people. He conceded that such principles do not derive from reason in the abstract but from what he called "our public political culture itself, including its main institutions and the historical traditions of their interpretation."

In *A Theory of Justice,* Rawls had acknowledged that philosophers can offer only "provisional fixed points," but now Rawls went beyond that deliberate oxymoron to admit that his historicist and communitarian critics were right: principles of justice do not derive from the disembodied process of rational reflection or exist in a timeless realm of truth. Rawls now placed the principles of justice firmly in the context of America's own liberal democratic culture and admitted that he was writing, in his words, "to help us work out what we now think." Thus he emphasized that our understanding of our history and, in particular, our awareness of "the plurality of incommensurable conceptions of the good" characteristic of America's fundamentally contested culture necessarily shape contemporary American philosophers' ideas about of justice. At the time when Obama the community organizer was trying to find a way through the thickets of competing strategies in Chicago public life, recommending in "Why Organize" a more capacious set of strategies attuned to the distinctive values of the different communities with which he had worked, Rawls too was becoming a pluralist. At the time when Obama was weighing the incommensurable arguments of Charles Fried and Martha Minow at Harvard Law School, across campus Rawls was completing the revisions of *Political Liberalism*. Timelessness and universality were out. Contingency and particularity were in.

In short, during the late 1970s and 1980s Rawls historicized his project. He brought *A Theory of Justice* down from the "Archimedean point" of universality, from the imagined exchanges among disembodied rational actors operating behind the veil of ignorance, and placed them in the particular context of modern American culture. Justice could no longer be conceived in terms of unchanging principles. It had become, in Rawls's terminology, the product of "an overlapping consensus" that acknowledged the persistence, indeed the necessity, of distinct and incompatible "comprehensive religious, philosophical, and moral doctrines." Rawls was at pains to insist that his new formulation did not require skepticism or indifference to such comprehensive doctrines, but he denied that partisans of such doctrines could legitimately impose them on others in a pluralist democracy. When disagreements inevitably arise, "political groups must enter the public forum of political discussion and appeal to other groups who do not share their comprehensive doctrine." They must be able to "explain and justify their preferred policies to a wider public so as to put together a majority." Their ability to persuade others with reasons, not the conformity of their position to the "Archimedean point" of justice, had become the litmus test. That conception of reason-giving informs the arguments of Tribe and Dorf in *On Reading the Constitution*, the arguments for understanding the Constitution as a conversation that they attributed to Fisher and Obama. Justice was no longer to be understood as universal but merely as a "useful fiction," to use Obama's terminology in *Dreams*. Even so, the idea of "an overlapping consensus," forged in the arena of public debate rather than deriving from disembodied rational actors in the original position, nevertheless continued to haunt even those who understood its contingency, its particularity, its historicity.

What had happened? How had the assumptions about reason that undergirded the articles Rawls published in the 1950s and 1960s, the arguments that came together so compellingly in *A Theory of Justice*, come unraveled by the time *Political Liberalism* appeared in 1993? If we want to understand Obama's sensibility, answering these questions is important, because he grew to maturity during these crucial and transformative years from the 1960s through the 1990s. The answer is complex; it requires a brief excursion into the professionalization of American philosophy and social science.

So let's back up. During the early twentieth century, when James and Dewey were among the dominant figures in American philosophy, critics and allies alike judged their pragmatism America's principal contribution to the history of philosophy. James and Dewey emphasized the close connection between uncertainty—our inability to answer with confidence the central questions in philosophy, theology, ethics, and politics—and democratic politics. They reasoned that within the domain of the human sciences, the painstaking, imprecise, but inescapable process of interpreting meanings known as hermeneutics could never yield answers with the precision of mathematical formulas. Despite the attractiveness of scientific method, no exact measurements are possible where the object of analysis is human choice. Even though individual choices are always conditioned by culture, they remain sufficiently open to be unpredictable. For those reasons the pragmatists argued that a culture of inquiry should supplant a culture of fixed truths. Processes of experimentation should replace proclamations of dogma. James and Dewey, and the generations of early twentieth-century social scientists and activists they influenced, saw in the extension of democracy from the political to the social realm the means to extend those insights from the seminar room to the culture as a whole. Their ideas—and similar ideas that emerged around the turn of the century in Europe— helped fuel a variety of reform movements that took shape under the banners of progressivism, social democracy, or the new liberalism. On the eve of World War I, such ideas seemed triumphant, well positioned to transform nations on both sides of the Atlantic by replacing reliance on inherited doctrines in philosophy, politics, law, and social thought with cultures of thoroughgoing experimentation.

At the same time, however, countermovements began to develop in philosophy, especially in England and Austria. These movements assumed many shapes and go by many names, but they took as their inspiration none of the strands of moral philosophy that had shaped eighteenth- and nineteenth-century American culture. These older traditions included Christian ethics; Scottish commonsense philosophy as formulated by thinkers such as Thomas Reid and Adam Ferguson; the revised, qualitative utilitarianism of English philosophers John Stuart Mill and Henry Sidgwick that stressed the importance of benevolence; and versions of the German idealist traditions of Kantianism and Hegelianism. Rejecting such traditions, some early twentieth-century English and Austrian philosophical renegades patterned their ideas on mathematics and the natural sciences. The English discourses of analytic philosophy and philosophy of language and the Vienna school of logical positivism rose to dominance not only in Britain and in many European schools of philosophy but, especially after World War II, also in the United States.

Anglo-American analytic philosophers and logical positivists aimed to use scientific procedures to establish certainty, which required heightened attention to issues of language and logic. Such thinkers scorned many older varieties of philosophy that they considered hopelessly imprecise, unscientific, and—to be blunt—unphilosophical. They rejected not only the traditions of idealism and pragmatism, but all varieties of ethics and political theory, as philosophically meaningless. If choices of values were merely matters of emotional response or aesthetic judgments about the good life, matters best understood, in other words, simply as irrational personal preferences and thus not amenable to proper philosophical investigation, then the domains of moral and political philosophy should be relegated to the margins of the discipline. If philosophy were to become a science at last, such questions, which had been at the heart of philosophers' quest for wisdom since the ancient world, had to be banished to the provinces of intellectual history or literary studies. There fuzzy-headed thinkers who still cared about such things could blather on about how these questions had been addressed in the past without doing much damage to the serious work of philosophical analysis. In the disciplines of history and literature, and in the discursive social sciences such as political theory, sociology, and cultural anthropology, less rigorous scholars and their students could luxuriate in disputes about the meaning of life posed by novelists, poets, and existentialists without interfering with the mature work of problem solving that engaged professional philosophers and serious—that is, quantitative or deductive—social scientists.

This shift toward science in the discipline of philosophy, and in much of political science, psychology, and economics as well, paralleled a broader shift in mid-twentieth-century American culture. As scientists and policy makers scrambled to meet military challenges from Germany and Japan during the 1940s, new ideas from the decision sciences, cybernetics, and game theory established themselves as valuable tools of analysis for a variety of purposes. Pragmatists such as James and Dewey would have been quick to acknowledge the usefulness of these new ways of thinking as long as they were deployed within consciously circumscribed frameworks, and as long as the purposes they were designed to serve were subject to open discussion. But instead the genie escaped the bottle, and the idea of rational choice was let loose on the academic world. This way of thinking, rooted in some of the ideas advanced by unsentimental eighteenth-century thinkers such as Bernard de Mandeville, elevated self-interest from a vice to a universal maxim of human behavior.

Some partisans of rational choice tried to trace their ideas to Adam Smith, but they tended to neglect the book Smith himself prized, his *Theory of Moral Sentiments*, and to emphasize arguments advanced in Smith's *Wealth of Nations*, which they found more congenial. From the perspective of historians, this selective reading got Smith exactly wrong. Smith believed that the point of free markets was to enable autonomous individuals—freed from the constraints of earlier, more rigid social and economic orders descended from feudalism—to act morally, not according to naked self-interest. But the qualms voiced by historians hardly registered. Attracting much more attention was the gathering enthusiasm for supposedly rational choice, which swept through the American academy in the postwar years. The urgency of the Cold War gave these ideas even greater momentum. In many spheres the idea of rational choice largely displaced the earlier historicist awareness of cultural particularity and the related wariness about the possibility of achieving certainty in the human sciences, the sensibility that James and Dewey bequeathed to the many progressives and New Dealers whom they influenced.

Instead the new disenchanted philosophy and the new hard-boiled decision sciences fueled enthusiasm for discovering rival versions of what constituted the "human," the "rational," the "universal." Multiple nominees for these designations emerged within each discipline, and it would be a mistake to equate them all. One emblematic version of this sensibility surfaced in the efforts by the Allied powers, which had called themselves the United Nations during World War II, to create a permanent international organization, perhaps not surprisingly to be known as the United Nations. This way of thinking sprang to life in the organization's signature achievement, the Universal

Declaration of Human Rights, proclaimed six decades ago at the peak of this universalist mania. This concept of universal reason might have been born in "the West," to use a term that also came into currency during these years. But it was considered applicable to all the particular civilizations in the world, including those cultures mired in tradition, superstition, and poverty, which were judged especially vulnerable to the irrational appeal of communism in its Soviet or Maoist forms. As the Cold War heated up, imperatives to expand the reign of reason became increasingly urgent, and the result was what Obama dubs "the seeming triumph of universalism over parochialism and narrow mindedness."

Philosophers, social scientists, and politicians joined in multiple campaigns of this midcentury crusade to uncover the ostensibly universal structure of human motivation, organization, and production. In America the fields of philosophy, psychology, sociology, political science, and economics have never been the same. Convictions about the justice of the Allied cause in World War II had a magical effect on Americans who had criticized their nation from the left during the 1930s. Scholars were hardly immune to that transformation. Awkward questions concerning economic inequality in America, questions that had persisted throughout the first half of the twentieth century and dominated debate during the years of the Great Depression, now slid from the center to the margins.

Race was the glaring exception to this celebration of American democracy. Gunnar Myrdal's prize-winning study *An American Dilemma* (1944) called attention to the anomaly of systematic racism prevailing in a culture that prided itself on commitments to freedom and equality. As dissatisfaction with segregation spread, ever-increasing numbers of African Americans mobilized against the racism legitimated by American law. Slowly, painfully, the civil rights movement uprooted the legal basis for Jim Crow. The triumphs of the familiar heroes and heroines of the civil rights movement—and of the countless anonymous participants whose efforts made the difference—testify to the power of midcentury universalist ideas. Throughout the long struggle for equal rights, invocations of an unchanging ideal of justice propelled moderates and militants alike.

But the legislative and judicial landmarks that transformed American race relations failed to change the distribution of wealth and power in America. The white males who continued to enjoy a disproportionate share of the privileges in post–World War II America conceived of themselves as a meritocracy, and America's most prominent cultural arbiters shared that spirit of self-congratulation. Critics of the prevailing distribution of power found their voices drowned out by celebrations of the "vital center," "modernization," and the "end of ideology." Social scientists' quest to establish universal, ostensibly value-free principles on the basis of empirical studies of reason, social structure, and behavior provided a scholarly echo of the political rush to moderation. Questions about what ought to be done were unceremoniously pushed aside in the rush to discover what is. Of course the scholars who embarked on these quests disagreed with each other, not only about the proper paths to truth within their disciplines but just as passionately about the political implications—if there could be said to be any at all, which many champions of value-free scholarship denied—of the laws or rules said to govern human behavior.

Although the arguments advanced in the preceding paragraphs shave many of the edges off a complex and multifaceted process of cultural change, they are not mine alone. In 1997 prominent practitioners from the fields of economics, literature, philosophy, and political science gathered to share their perspectives on what had happened in their disciplines since 1945. The resulting volume, published by the journal *Daedalus* under the title *American Academic Culture in Transformation: Fifty Years, Four Disciplines*, encapsulates the changes I have just described. Although some scholars would characterize the positive contributions of scientism more generously than I have done, there is general agreement concerning the larger contours of the shift in the disciplines of philosophy, economics, and political science. Much of the ferment in American universities in the 1980s and 1990s, which Obama encountered at Occidental, Columbia, and Harvard Law School, centered on insurgent scholars' dissatisfaction with scientism. The results of their challenges varied, but their efforts transformed legal discourse almost as dramatically as the civil rights movement transformed the Jim Crow South. Just as clearly as Obama's political success reflects the magnitude of the latter change, so his books testify to the depth of the former.

The wide variety of scholarly projects aiming toward Truth notwithstanding, one indication of the transformative power of that dynamic comes from looking at Rawls himself. If *A Theory of Justice* might reasonably be taken as the culmination of this urge toward the universal, and *Political Liberalism* as a sign of its rejection or at least of its reconsideration, then the senior thesis that Rawls wrote at Princeton in 1941–1942 illustrates just how far he had to travel before he could reach his postwar conviction that human reason could yield universal principles of justice. American culture during the 1940s was saturated with religion, and Rawls's senior thesis, entitled "A Brief Inquiry into the Meaning of Sin and Faith: An Interpretation Based on the Concept of Community," which has recently been rediscovered and published, testifies to its pervasiveness.

Surprisingly, the central argument advanced in 1942 by the young John Rawls bears an uncanny resemblance to the critiques of the mature Rawls offered by some of his communitarian and feminist critics such as Sandel and Sunstein, Minow and Benhabib. At Princeton, Rawls explicitly rejected social contract liberalism because it depended on the idea of isolated individuals. Drawing on Christian theology, Rawls argued that persons become persons only in communities of interdependence. In his words, social contract theorists "fail to see that a person is not a person apart from community and also that true

community does not absorb the individual but rather
makes his personality possible." Ideas of self-interest,
Rawls insisted, even "enlightened self-interest," were inadequate for capturing life as it was understood by contemporary theologians and inadequate for understanding
life in the contemporary United States. Writing with a
self-confidence typical of midcentury American Protestants sure of their culture's superiority to its rivals, Rawls
declared that "any society which explains itself in terms of
mutual egoism is heading for certain destruction." Where
did Rawls's communitarianism come from?

The young Rawls traced his intellectual debts primarily to the Christian scriptures and to the most important
of their contemporary neo-orthodox interpreters, the
Swiss theologian Emil Brunner, who taught at Princeton
while Rawls was an undergraduate there, and the American Reinhold Niebuhr. In recent years Niebuhr's neo-
orthodoxy, with its emphasis on human sinfulness, has
returned to the center of American debates about religion,
in part thanks to the pervasiveness since the 1980s of
phrases such as "the evil empire" and "the axis of evil"
and the association of terrorism with evil. But most references to Niebuhr betray little familiarity with what he actually wrote. Rawls, by contrast, had read Niebuhr carefully. In light of Rawls's later work, it is striking that in
1942 Rawls defined sin as the "destruction and repudiation of community." Rawls dismissed the naturalism that
has since become fashionable among philosophers and
stressed instead the role of God's grace in helping indi-

viduals turn away from their inclination toward sin, integrate themselves with their communities, and embrace the Kantian (and Christian) imperative to treat other people not as means to their own ends as individuals but as ends in themselves. In recent years Niebuhr has been trotted out as an American exponent of the idea that human sinfulness is fundamental and ineradicable. Niebuhr's writings about grace have attracted less attention. The columnist David Brooks in particular has written extensively about Obama's sustained engagement with the writings of Niebuhr, and Obama himself has often cited Niebuhr as an important influence on his thought.

Obama's tough-minded assessments of the dangers confronting America and the existence of evil, so-called Niebuhrian chords struck in several of his most notable speeches, have gratified some on the right and alarmed some on the left. But Niebuhr's Christian realism had two components. In addition to prudence concerning the threat represented by the Soviet Union and America's need to be resolute in confronting it, Niebuhr stressed the Christian message of love and forgiveness. He began as a radical champion of the social gospel, like his role model Walter Rauschenbusch and his ally John Ryan, practitioners of social Christianity who served as community organizers before Alinsky scripted the part. After Niebuhr moved from Detroit to New York City, he ran for Congress in 1932 as a candidate of the Socialist Party. He remained a consistent critic of Roosevelt's New Deal—from the left, roughly the same position occupied by Dewey in

the 1930s. Niebuhr never renounced the Christian imperative of the Beatitudes, even when the rise of Hitler and
Stalin prompted him to begin reminding Americans about
the need to be realistic about all humans' limited capacity
to live according to the law of love. When Niebuhr criticized Dewey for overlooking the propensity of humans to
self-interest, he was not repudiating the egalitarian principles that both of them shared and that both of them derived (at least originally, in Dewey's case) from the Christian law of love. Niebuhr wanted only to remind Dewey
that power must be met with power, in the domestic sphere
as in the international sphere.

Some recent invocations of Niebuhr simplify his complex ideas. Niebuhr was too aware of the danger posed
by human pride to pretend that he, as a fallen and sinful
man, could ever be certain he knew God's will. Likewise
Niebuhr's career as a vaunted champion of "realism" in
foreign policy was bounded by the emergence of totalitari-
anism in the 1930s and his criticism of America's intervention in Vietnam in the 1960s. It was Niebuhr's message
concerning God's grace, not simply Niebuhr's reminders
about man's sinfulness, that attracted the young Rawls to
neo-orthodoxy, and it is that complex amalgam that
Obama has endorsed. If we must remember, as Obama
put it in his Nobel acceptance speech, that pacifism would
not have stopped Hitler, we must also remember—as
Gandhi and King pointed out—that unchecked reliance
on war erodes the cultural resources on which international law and cooperation depend.

Given Rawls's religious convictions as a Princeton undergraduate, what happened to this vigorous Christian neo-orthodoxy between 1942 and Rawls's emergence as the philosopher of justice? The evidence points toward two explanations, which I will mention briefly both because they illustrate the ways in which intellectual changes are woven into the fabric of broader historical development and because they show the shift in midcentury American academic culture. First, during World War II Rawls served in the Pacific, where he was shaken by the horrors of the war itself and by the use of nuclear weapons to end it. The Holocaust, when he became aware of it, provided the coup de grace for Rawls's religious faith. World War II proved to him that the problem of theodicy—the problem of justifying the existence of evil given a benevolent and omnipotent God—simply could not be solved, even though neo-orthodox theologians had devoted considerable attention to that question. One further dimension of Rawls's life story helps illuminate the change in his worldview: Rawls later admitted that his religious faith had helped him cope with the fact that during his childhood his two younger brothers died of diseases (the first of diphtheria, the second of pneumonia) that they contracted from Rawls himself when he was seven and eight years old. When Rawls abandoned his religious faith in the aftermath of World War II, he found himself—unsurprisingly—preoccupied with the injustice of fate, or what he called "the arbitrariness of fortune," an issue that was obviously central to *A Theory of Justice*. Intellectual history can turn on such accidents of fate.

The second hypothesis, also biographical, turns on broader cultural developments within the academic world. Rawls returned to Princeton to study for a Ph.D. degree in philosophy at precisely the moment when the combination of analytic philosophy, logical positivism, and game theory was beginning to transform American philosophy and social science. Rawls, now adrift from his religious convictions, saw in the quest for certainty—certainty grounded on reason and science—an irresistible alternative to the Christianity he had abandoned. In short, a theory of justice that would rest solidly on reason rather than revelation beckoned to Rawls. One can acknowledge the importance of institutional contexts—whether for Rawls at Princeton or Obama in Chicago or Cambridge—without reducing individuals' ideas to those institutions.

But cultural change is messy. No sooner were varieties of universalistic and scientistic ideas established in the middle decades of the twentieth century than another, radically different set of ideas began to emerge. Or rather, to reemerge. These are the ideas that shaped Obama's sensibility as profoundly as did those of Madison, Tocqueville, Dewey, King, Ellison, or Alinsky. Updated versions of late nineteenth-century historicism and hermeneutics, articulated most prominently by Thomas Kuhn in the history of science and Clifford Geertz in cultural anthropology, challenged the new faith in science as the path to certainty. In *The Structure of Scientific Revolutions* (1962), Kuhn identified the decisive role of "paradigms" in providing frameworks within which "normal science" can proceed. Kuhn's work had the effect of breeding skepticism about the validity of science and the more general claims of so-called objective or value-free scientific inquiry. Kuhn contended that "paradigm shifts" occur when unexplained anomalies pile up. Standard explanations of the data cannot account for them, and a dramatic reorientation provides a new way of making sense of the available evidence. Commentators enthusiastic about the idea of paradigm shifts pointed to the changes of allegiance from Ptolemy to Copernicus in cosmology, from Linnaeus to Darwin in biology, and from Newton to Einstein in physics as examples validating Kuhn's radical account. If the natural sciences did not track on the world as it "really is" but instead reflected and depended on conventions destined to be superseded when demonstrated to be false, then perhaps the findings of the natural sciences—and the other disciplines modeled on them—were less stable than their champions claimed. It was no surprise that Tribe and other legal scholars often cited Kuhn in books and articles challenging the pretensions of originalists. Kuhn had exposed the vulnerability of the ideas of "timeless, universal, and unquestionable truth" that Tribe had in his sights. Historicism trumped universalism.

Clifford Geertz provided a framework that helps explain the power of Kuhn's challenge. Geertz had earned the respect of cultural anthropologists for his work on the

Middle East and Southeast Asia. Obama's mother, for example, was familiar with his writings on Indonesia as a result of her graduate studies in anthropology at the University of Hawaii. But it was the publication of Geertz's essay collection *The Interpretation of Cultures* in 1971 that made him a household name across the humanities and social sciences. Geertz denied that social science can provide general rules of human behavior. He urged his fellow scholars to surrender that aspiration and concede that they were engaged in hermeneutics: they were interpreting social meanings rather than discovering universal laws. Geertz opened his book with an account of a Western anthropologist visiting India. There he was told by a Hindu that the world rests on the back of a turtle, which also rests on the back of another turtle. When the anthropologist asked what that turtle rested on, he was told, according to Geertz, "Ah, Sahib, it's turtles all the way down." For at least twenty-five years, that phrase popped up repeatedly as a kind of shorthand in American academic life. Whenever claims were advanced about the supposedly universal status of Western ideas, particularly ideas drawn from the natural sciences or the social sciences patterned on them, someone could be counted on to remark, sagely, "No, it's turtles all the way down." Knowing nods would follow. Many readers now associate this story with Stephen Hawking's *Brief History of Time*, and older versions can be found in the writings of Bertrand Russell, William James, and even John Locke, all of whom used it at different times for somewhat different purposes. But in the late twentieth-century American academic world, the locus classicus was Geertz's *Interpretation of Cultures*.

Geertz had shown that scholars seeking certainty were doomed to find only stories—and beneath them only more stories. There was no foundation. Geertz defined culture as a "historically transmitted pattern of meaning embodied in symbols, a system of inherited conceptions expressed in symbolic forms by means of which men communicate, perpetuate, and develop their knowledge about and attitudes toward life." To understand such systems of symbols, we must attend to particularity and renounce the idea that at some level of abstraction the diverse phenomena of the world's cultures can be said to be the same. Whether one is writing about anthropology, as Geertz was, or about law, as Tribe, Minow, and Michelman were, the irreducible plurality and particularity of cultural meanings inevitably defeat attempts at universalism. It's turtles all the way down.

Kuhn and Geertz were but two home-grown intellectual revolutionaries writing at a time when the ideas of thinkers such as Frantz Fanon, Jacques Derrida, Michel Foucault, Pierre Bourdieu, and various theorists of race, class, gender, and postcolonialism on both sides of the Atlantic were throwing more monkey wrenches in the works of natural science, social science, and the humanities. By the late 1960s, the skepticism bred by such ideas was intensified in the United States by many other developments outside the academy. The challenges posed by the civil rights movement, second-wave feminism, and the antiwar and student movements caused many American intellectuals to conclude that the idea of a universal human nature had been routed. Histories of stable ideas gave way to studies of the multivalent texts in which they appeared. Stories of the rise of the West, staple fare from the end of World War I through the early years of the Cold War, began to seem embarrassingly parochial and narrow-minded. Radical critics exposed the concept of Enlightenment rationality itself as just one more regime of discipline imposed by the alliance between power and knowledge. Communities of discourse lost their sacred aura and appeared as scrums in which academic entrepreneurs scrambled to attain status rather than discover truth. The concepts of the West and the Male—along with the concept of Science—were revealed as forms of self-delusion with oppressive and sometimes murderous consequences. Some champions of critical race theory advanced versions of white hegemony so extreme that they left little space in which even dissent, let alone effective resistance, could emerge. According to Obama's friend and classmate Ken Mack, it was that pessimism, rather than the cogency of these critiques, that disturbed more activist-oriented African Americans such as Obama, who wanted to know what they could do to change things. So all-encompassing did such challenges sometimes become that even Kuhn and Geertz drew back. Kuhn distanced himself from the most sweeping denunciations of science. Geertz observed that although a germ-free environment is impossible, surgeons do not operate in sewers. The critiques of science and objectivity could go too far.

At that moment came the return of the repressed. The American tradition of philosophical pragmatism had fallen from favor when analytic philosophy, logical positivism, and rational choice theory rose to dominate American universities. The 1980s and 1990s, for a variety of reasons, witnessed a resurgence of pragmatism. When Habermas began to identify his widely influential theory of communicative action with the writings of American pragmatists Charles Sanders Peirce, Dewey, and James's student George Herbert Mead, young American radicals were caught off-guard. They were surprised to learn that ideas they found compelling had roots in the unlikeliest of places, the supposedly anemic American intellectual tradition, which they had been taught by the political theorist Louis Hartz was all about property holding and thus bereft of radical ideas they could use. Now that Habermas and Bourdieu, among others, were declaring themselves good pragmatists and social democrats in the Deweyan tradition, more Americans decided it was time to begin investigating their forgotten heritage.

Then came the Trojan horse of American philosophy, Richard Rorty. The most widely influential—if least characteristic—of the late twentieth-century American pragmatists, Rorty attacked the citadel of Anglo-American analytic philosophy from within, as a prominent member of the Princeton Philosophy Department. Rorty established his credentials with a series of well-respected papers on language and logic. In 1967 he edited *The Linguistic Turn*, which contained rigorous essays in the prevailing styles of linguistic and logical analysis. In his introduction to that volume, however, Rorty gently hinted that there might be a problem. The conflicts between the logical positivism of Austrian Rudolph Carnap, on the one hand, and the ordinary language philosophy of the Englishman J. L. Austin, on the other, were so fundamental that they would never be resolved. Rorty thereby issued a challenge to the idea of progress in problem solving that most American philosophers took for granted.

When Rorty's formidable book *Philosophy and the Mirror of Nature* appeared in 1979, many scholars hailed him as the most incisive critic of contemporary Anglo-American philosophy. As he continued to sharpen his critiques of the analytic tradition, he was excommunicated by the community of professional philosophers, most of whom ceased to consider him a member of their guild. Rorty left Princeton to become a professor of humanities at the University of Virginia, then a professor of comparative literature at Stanford. He urged philosophers to follow his lead. Like Geertz, he recommended that philosophers abandon the most ambitious claims of science for the more moderate aspirations of hermeneutics. They should shift their focus from "systematic" philosophers such as Locke and Kant, Austin and Carnap, to "edifying" philosophers such as James and Dewey. Philosophers should stop chasing the phantom of problem solving and concede they could do no more than contribute to what Rorty provocatively called "the conversation of the West." There could be, Rorty wrote in *The Consequences of Pragmatism*, no "extra-historical Archimedean point" from which to do philosophy. In his heretical words, "there is nothing deep down inside us except what we have put there ourselves, no criterion that we have not created in the course of creating a practice, no standard of rationality that is not an appeal to such a criterion." If philosophers had been shown to frame arguments not according to logic or reason but in line with conventions, then Kuhn's paradigms and Geertz's turtles had come to philosophy.

Rorty knew his arguments echoed those of James and Dewey, whose pragmatism he called "the chief glory of our country's intellectual tradition." In stark contrast to the pessimism of Nietzsche and Martin Heidegger, James and Dewey wrote in a "spirit of social hope" and asked us to surrender "the neurotic Cartesian quest for certainty." But Rorty sometimes struck readers as more similar to Nietzsche than to James. When critics charged him with relativism, Rorty replied that the charge is incoherent. From his radically historicist perspective, there is nothing for truth to be relative *to* except our traditions and our purposes. It's conventions, Rorty insisted, all the way down.

In Rorty's later writings, until his death in 2007, he increasingly emphasized history as the alternative to foundationalism in all its forms, scientific and political as well as philosophical. He reasoned that accepting the contingency of all beliefs, a cardinal principle of pragmatism that earlier critics had judged culturally dangerous, can actually strengthen our feelings of solidarity. "Our identification with our community—our society, our political tradition, our intellectual heritage—is heightened when we see this community as *ours* rather than *nature's*, *shaped* rather than *found*, one among many which men have made." Rorty also moved back in the direction of more conventional progressive politics. Reaching the goals laid out in *Achieving Our Country*, the title of Rorty's final book, would require a deliberate move away from what he dismissed as the "politics of the English Department," the narrow, obsessive, and futile insistence on ideological purity within the academic world, usually accompanied by cynical disengagement from the hopelessly corrupt world beyond the academy. Instead Rorty urged a return to the old-fashioned progressive politics of the Deweyan Left, the struggle for mundane improvements in the minimum wage, better health care, and attention to the environment. Since Rorty's radical philosophical critique of objectivity had been embraced by avant-garde literary critics such as Stanley Fish as a warrant for their own brands of postmodern radicalism—the politics of the English Department on steroids—Rorty's explicit repudiation of newfangled cultural critiques in favor of old-style social democracy disappointed many on the cultural left.

Rorty's shift came as a welcome change, though, to some of his fellow pragmatists, notably Richard J. Bernstein and Hilary Putnam, who interpreted Rorty's final turn back to social democracy as a tacit acceptance of arguments they had been making for decades. A few intellectual historians had also been uneasy about some of Rorty's claims, notably his denial that there was any particular relation between the philosophy of pragmatism and the politics of democracy. Such historians never tired of pointing out that both James and Dewey had insisted repeatedly on precisely that connection. Without absolutes, the early pragmatists had argued, the most attractive political ideas are those that have survived the rigorous historical tests of trial and error, and no politics offers as many tools for self-correction as does democracy. Bernstein and Putnam, having made precisely that point in their friendly critiques of Rorty's iconoclasm, were now vindicated.

Rorty and Bernstein had become friends when they were undergraduates together at the University of Chicago, and they remained friendly even as they sparred over the meaning and political potential of pragmatism. Bernstein established himself as a critic of what he called the "analytic ideology," his term for the most scientistic strands of analytic philosophy, and of the reductionist and uncritical empiricism of mainstream academic social science. When Yale denied him tenure, critics joined outraged undergraduates who lamented the narrowmindedness of professional philosophers. Bernstein proposed a more capacious range of alternatives to the kinds of philosophy preferred by many of his colleagues. He drew together ideas from the traditions of hermeneutics and existential phenomenology, the later writings of Ludwig Wittgenstein, and the critical theory of Habermas, whose Deweyan dimensions Bernstein was among the first Americans to emphasize.

Because Bernstein has advanced the version of pragmatism that seems to me closest to the ideas advanced in Obama's books—although Obama is hardly as systematic in the presentation of the philosophy—I want to outline the five dimensions of Bernstein's pragmatism. The first characteristic is fallibilism, or "the experimental habit of mind," which considers all knowledge to be as provisional as the latest results in a laboratory. Bernstein's formulation of pragmatism as "interpretive, tentative, always subject to correction" echoes throughout Obama's books, in his article "Why Organize," and in many of his speeches. Second, Bernstein emphasized the inescapably sociocultural character of individual experience, which means that so-called rational choice dissolves into the multiple cultural forms reason has taken in our own culture and continues to take around the world. There can be no concept of "rational choice" independent of particular, value-laden cultural contexts. As Tribe credits Obama for helping him to see, even the interpretation of a document as supposedly fundamental as the United States Constitution should be seen as a conversation, an interpretive process that never ends.

Third, Bernstein emphasized the participation of individual interpreters in a community of inquiry or discourse, the Deweyan conception of democracy that Obama had already internalized even before he began working as a community organizer in Chicago. From Bernstein's perspective, this conception of democracy, which extends far beyond elections, should serve as a model in the academy and the workplace as well as the polity. Fourth, Bernstein called for sensitivity to radical contingency and change, which James captured in his phrase "the open universe" and Dewey with his idea of "the precariousness of existence" in a world he dubbed "uncannily unstable."

Finally, in place of the midcentury longing of many academic philosophers and social scientists for unity, Bernstein embraced a pluralistic philosophy for a pluralistic universe—or "multiverse," to use James's preferred term. No single way of thinking, and no single conception of philosophy or any other discipline, could capture all the dimensions of the world's cultures or even its physical form or processes. During the years when legal scholars such as Michelman and Sunstein were wrestling with the implications of civic republicanism for American law, Bernstein's work provided the bridge that connected themes from eighteenth-century American history with Wittgenstein's notion of language games, Habermas's discourse ethics, and Dewey's deliberative democracy. References to many of Bernstein's books, like Rorty's, appeared regularly in the footnotes of law review articles and books, such as Minow's, at just the time when Obama was studying at Harvard Law School.

The other most significant contributor to the resurgence

of pragmatism among philosophers has been Hilary Putnam, who, like Rorty, established himself as a master of
the analytic mainstream through his pioneering work in
the philosophy of mathematics. Late in his distinguished
career, Putnam shifted his focus from mathematics
and returned to the early pragmatists, especially William
James, although with an emphasis quite distinct from
Rorty's. Putnam challenged one of the central dogmas of
many practitioners of Anglo-American analytic philosophy. He began urging philosophers to develop what he
called "a less scientistic account of rationality, an account
that enables us to see how reasoning, far from being impossible in normative areas, is in fact indispensable to
them" in fields ranging from ethics to economics. Re-
nouncing the principles of his teachers Carnap and Hans
Reichenbach, Putnam worked to demonstrate that the
logical positivists' division between analytic and synthetic
statements, and their banishing of all value judgments beyond the philosophical pale, were mistaken from the start.
Rather than promulgating dogmas inconsistent with the
way we think, talk, and live our lives, Putnam called instead for philosophers to embrace the earlier pragmatists'
tentativeness. In Putnam's words, "the solution is neither
to give up on the very possibility of rational discussion,"
as Rorty at his most insouciant sometimes seemed to do,
nor with the logical positivists "to seek an Archimedean
point, an 'absolute conception' outside of all contexts and
problematic situations." Instead we should, "as Dewey
taught his whole life long," continue "to investigate and

discuss and try things out cooperatively, democratically, and above all *fallibilistically*."

Putnam extended his critique from philosophy to the social sciences, drawing on the work of the economist Amartya Sen to challenge the prevailing assumption that rational behavior is self-interested. According to Sen, this widely accepted notion became dogma only after economists followed Lionel Robbins in converting to noncognitivism, the idea that there are no rational grounds for making value judgments. From the moment when Robbins embraced the idea that we cannot attain reliable knowledge in the domain of values, economists felt justified in denying any link between ethics and economics. They were then free to endorse the idea of a fact/value dichotomy, and from there they felt able to isolate the so-called rational choices of self-interested individuals as the engine driving human behavior. Bernstein, Putnam, Sen, Rorty, and others have challenged that argument head-on. Although Putnam resists the efforts of commentators to place him in the pragmatist tradition because he dislikes labels and intellectual categories, the resonances between his recent work and that of Rorty and Bernstein, James and Dewey, seem clear enough.

Perhaps not surprisingly, given Putnam's position as a member of the Harvard Department of Philosophy, he has been more frequently cited by Harvard Law School faculty members than have the other contemporary philosophical pragmatists. In "A Reconsideration of Deweyan Pragmatism," Putnam's stirring contribution to *Pragma-*

tism in Law and Society, the volume derived from the 1990 Harvard Law School conference on pragmatism, he invoked both Dewey and James—and tied their insights to those of Habermas—to make the case for a "radical" democracy that is pragmatist rather than foundationalist, participatory rather than elitist, and "more hardheaded and realistic" than the romantic ideas often espoused by some of Dewey's self-proclaimed heirs among educational reformers. The goal of Dewey's educational theory, Putnam concluded, "is to produce men and women who are capable of learning on their own and thinking critically." If one takes seriously the central ideas of philosophical pragmatism, Putnam insisted, it is a way of thinking inextricably linked to radical democratic participation, precisely the model laid out in Obama's "Why Organize" to justify the continuing effort to empower the disempowered.

Of course the influence of thinkers such as Kuhn, Geertz, Rorty, Bernstein, and Putnam, considerable as it has been in some spheres, has hardly ended the dominance of scientism in analytic philosophy and mainstream social science. Indeed, such thinkers themselves were always careful (indeed, more careful than I have been in this brief presentation of their ideas) to acknowledge the value of much of the work done in such fields, and the many champions of what continues to be called "rational choice" in many academic disciplines would understandably scoff at the suggestion that their predominance has been shaken. Yet the proliferation of rival claimants to the status of universality within and across academic disciplines helped fuel the rise of historicism and particularism. Although each of the candidates for universal status—arguments drawn from the rich and lively discourses of game theory, evolutionary biology, law and economics—seemed to explain some observed phenomena, their incompatibility remained a nagging problem. So did their apparent inability to generate the reliable predictions to which many social scientists aspired. To cite just one prominent example, no one predicted the cataclysmic changes kicked off by an East German official's offhand comment concerning new travel policies in the fall of 1989. The dramatic transformation of eastern Europe and the collapse of the Soviet Union mocked those who doubted the force of contingent human choices.

Despite the impossibility of arranging these multiple developments along a single axis, the influence of this unruly and heterogeneous band of critics, whether we call them antifoundationalists, historicists, or particularists, is nevertheless discernible in various dimensions of the culture. Decades will pass before we have access to the personal papers that might eventually make clear the lines of influence that ran between Putnam and his longtime Harvard colleague Rawls, for example, or the nature of Rawls's response to the work of Kuhn or Geertz, or his assessment of the writings of pragmatists and feminists who engaged his ideas. Given the deep debts these thinkers expressed to the traditions from which they emerged, how multifaceted each individual discipline became, and how dizzying the arrays of cross-disciplinary interaction are now, the schematic conflict I have sketched briefly here will have to be made much more complex and nuanced. Clarifying changes within those networks of relationships will be among the tasks facing the next generation of American intellectual historians.

Rawls himself denied that he could explain his own shift from the 1960s through the 1980s, and the words he did choose are revealing. He contended in *Political Liberalism* that "any story I would tell" to explain the change "is likely to be a fiction, merely what I want to believe." Beyond that arresting claim, he acknowledged only that the arguments of fellow philosophers Samuel Scheffler and Derek Parfit alerted him to the possibility that his *Theory of Justice* depended on a culturally contingent concept of personal identity. That astringent account, fictional or not, reflects even though it does not explicitly credit the waves of antifoundationalist critiques that crashed against the bulwarks of analytic philosophy during the decades while Rawls was revising his ideas. Between his graduation from Princeton and the publication of *A Theory of Justice*, Rawls had repudiated Niebuhr's theology and internalized the ideas of midcentury American philosophy and social science. If one likewise contrasts *A Theory of Justice* to *Political Liberalism*, one can see not only the impact of Scheffler's and Parfit's papers on identity but also the ways in which ideas similar to those of Kuhn, Geertz, Rorty, Bernstein, and Putnam filtered into Rawls's realization that we must envision justice not from the perspective of reason or for the ages but as it appears for us now.

Obama learned similar lessons. He shares with the young Rawls, Rawls the Princeton undergraduate, an appreciation of the indispensable role played by communities, often (although of course not always) religious. Obama shares with the Rawls of *A Theory of Justice* a commitment to the dual importance of individual rights and equality, the view that securing effective rather than merely abstract or formal rights requires minimizing as much as possible the gulf between rich and poor. Finally, he shares with the Rawls of *Political Liberalism* an awareness that these convictions do not descend directly from Reason or Natural Law but emerge from careful reflections on our own culture's particular historical experience. Obama embraces community, liberty, equality, and historicism, values often assumed to be in tension but, at least in Obama's writings, not only consistent but mutually constitutive.

One of the persistent dynamics in American intellectual life in recent decades has been the contest, sometimes vocal and visible, sometimes muted and submerged, between universalists (recently led by evolutionary biologists as much as by social scientists or analytic philosophers) and historicists. On one side of this blurred line are those who claim that an unchanging principle, often although not always that of rational self-interest, whether derived from our genetic makeup, from the way our brains are hardwired to act according to our sense of what choice will extend our gene pool, or from some combination of various features of human biology, underlies and therefore makes possible predictions about human behavior. On the other side are thinkers such as Kuhn, Geertz, Rorty, Bernstein, and Putnam, and others they have influenced, including legal scholars such as Minow, Michelman, Tribe, and Sunstein, who deny universalist claims and emphasize the particularity and mutability of human cultures and the voluntary nature of human choice.

Framing these debates schematically, in terms of that contrast between universalism and particularism, between timelessness and historicism, brings us back to Obama. In the summer of 2006 he accepted an invitation from one of his fellow Saguaro seminarians, Jim Wallis, to address a conference entitled "Building a Covenant for a New America." The theme of Obama's speech was the relation between politics and religion, and his arguments amalgamated many of the ideas I have been discussing in this chapter. Obama began by noting how wary most Democrats are about addressing religion; he warned that their wariness merely intensified the "mutual suspicion that sometimes exists between religious America and secular America." He recounted his misgivings about his own response, two years earlier, when his opponent in the race for the United States Senate characterized his position on abortion as "an abomination" utterly inconsistent with Christianity. Obama took refuge in the standard secular retort: because we live in a pluralistic society, he could not impose his views on anyone else. Most Democrats, he ob-

served, reflexively opt for such responses, equally fearful
of offending religious and secular voters. But Obama later
realized that his reply is exactly what evangelical conservatives want and expect. That response removes religion
from public debate and allows evangelicals to claim—
plausibly—that they speak for all religious Americans and
that their opponents represent only the tiny fraction of
Americans who say they do not believe in God. Surely
Democrats can do better than that, Obama went on, acknowledging "the power of faith" for the vast majority of
his fellow citizens. But what should he have said instead?

Obama began with Putnam's argument in "Bowling
Alone" and Robert Bellah's in *Habits of the Heart*. Americans going about their daily lives report that "something
is missing." They lack a "sense of purpose," a "narrative
arc." As he had seen for himself in Chicago and noted in
"Why Organize," Americans feel less closely attached to
their neighbors and family members. Obama reported
that, having grown up lacking religious faith himself, he
knew how they felt once he fell under the influence of the
Christians with whom he worked in the far south side of
Chicago. Compared to them, and lacking "a commitment
to a particular community of faith, at some level I would
always remain apart and alone." He reflected on the resources of the tradition of black Christianity, not only its
capacity to comfort the oppressed but its power to inspire
hope. That hope would not wash away doubts because
doubt is an ineradicable part of being human. Echoing
Niebuhr, he observed that certainty is not available to us

fallible creatures. With that "second insight," and feeling "God's spirit beckoning," Obama was able to "shed some of my skepticism," as he put it in *Audacity*, "and embrace the Christian faith." He joined Jeremiah Wright's congregation at Trinity United Church of Christ, thereby following in the footsteps of millions of Americans of all denominations who have converted to religious faith as adults.

Obama argued forcefully against the claim, standard among many Democrats, that the separation of church and state means religious arguments must be kept out of the public realm. He pointed out, accurately, that many of the most effective reformers in American history—Douglass, Lincoln, William Jennings Bryan, Dorothy Day, King—"were not only motivated by faith, but repeatedly used religious language to argue for their cause." Invoking religious ideas is a venerable American tradition, which Democrats have only recently abandoned. Obama urged a different course.

Having diagnosed the problem of purposelessness by using arguments from the scholarship on civil society, and having recommended a solution—tapping into the religious values most Americans espouse—straight out of the communitarian playbook, Obama next rejected the temptation of universalism that had lured many Americans toward versions of intolerant dogmatism. With so many rival convictions embraced by Americans, none of them can be made the official—and coercive—doctrine to which everyone must adhere. Obama understands, better than many members of the Democratic Party, that the decision to separate church and state in the eighteenth century came not as a result of emerging secularism but instead because "persecuted religious minorities" looked at the record of established state churches and worried about the prospect of practicing their own faith. It was fear of oppression, and the knowledge that state power corrupts faith, not a nascent agnosticism, that drove Jefferson and Madison toward the separation of church and state. But if the option of universalism is unpalatable, what is the alternative?

Here Obama turned explicitly to Rawls. If progressives would abandon their biases against religion, "we might recognize the overlapping values that both religious and secular people share when it comes to the moral and material direction of our country." His formulation of Rawls's argument about "overlapping consensus" comes close to paraphrasing the language of *Political Liberalism* quoted above: "Democracy demands that the religiously motivated translate their concerns into universal, rather than religion-specific, values. It requires that their proposals be subject to argument, and amenable to reason." Obama acknowledged that those committed to the truth of their own position will have difficulty accepting such requirements, but he concluded that "in a pluralistic democracy, we have no choice. Politics depends on our ability to persuade each other of common aims based on a common reality." It requires, in short, a willingness to deliberate, and a commitment to compromise in order to reach provisional agreement.

That willingness does not come easily to those who believe they hold the truth. Obama understands the problem. "Religion does not allow for compromise. It insists on the impossible." Sealing his Rawlsian argument with the powerful formulation familiar to every reader of Max Weber's essay "Politics as a Vocation"—which Obama had engaged multiple times since he first encountered it in Boesche's course on European thought—he concluded that basing one's life "on such uncompromising commitments may be sublime," but "to base our policy making on such commitments would be a dangerous thing." Combining arguments from the discourses of deliberative democracy as well as civil society and communitarianism, Obama offered a pragmatist version of Rawls's case for working toward an overlapping consensus. Whatever our own convictions, when we enter the realm of public debate, we must offer reasons that our fellow citizens, whatever their own beliefs may be, can find persuasive. A pluralistic society and a liberal democracy offer no alternatives.

In *Dreams from My Father*, Obama had described mid-century America as a world of certainties, even after it was exposed as impossible, a "lost Eden" whose appeal extended "beyond mere childhood." But it proved as fragile as any Eden. After the hard lessons won by exposure to the rough edges of Chicago politics and the varieties of historicism that he encountered in law school, Obama reflected in his memoir on the discordant voices echoing in his mind and the clashing images jostling to embed themselves permanently in his memories. "Each image carried its own lesson," he writes, "each was subject to differing interpretations." The inspirational words of King, speaking to the multitude from the Lincoln Memorial, and the indelible images of Freedom Riders on buses and black students staging sit-ins at lunch counters seemed to summon him toward a rock-solid ideal of justice, a bedrock conviction that would motivate heroic action. That was also the world of John L. Lewis and the CIO, the world that had inspired Alinsky and many later radicals in the 1960s. But Obama remained wary of that temptation. Aware that unities are ephemeral and often illusory, he knew too that it is a mistake to confuse private motives with public warrants.

Obama sees through the comfort that many Americans derive from such shared and cherished memories of a heroic generation and its supposedly triumphant achievement of equal rights for all. He points out that "such moments were partial, fragmentary." Even among his allies in Chicago, his fellow community organizers and activists, unity was chimerical. "With our eyes closed, we uttered the same words, but in our hearts we each prayed to our own masters; we each remained locked in our own memories; we all clung to our own foolish magic." As he reflected on the chances of political change, Obama wrestled with the consequences for political action of his own disillusionment. He observed that the men in his south side barbershop did not want the victory of Chicago's first black mayor, Harold Washington, sullied by reminders of the challenging task ahead. "They wouldn't want to hear that their problems were more complicated than a group of devious white aldermen," or be told that "their redemption" by the new mayor was likely to remain "incomplete." The more hardheaded of his associates, those who believed that all political engagement is always self-interested and all political affiliation clannish, "knew that in politics, like religion, power lay in certainty—and that one man's certainty always threatened another's." Against this advice about the strategic or political power of certainty, Obama had to weigh counterarguments about doubt.

The streets of Chicago's far south side showed the pervasiveness of self-interest, the tensions dividing groups from each other, and false certainty, but Obama had to compare that knowledge with other lessons. He had also learned about the faithfulness and forgiveness practiced by some members of the religious congregations in Chicago, Christians who sought, sometimes successfully, to act according to an ethic of love rather than enact a politics of resentment. He thought it should be possible to direct their empathy as well as their anger toward political engagement. Community organizers should pay attention to both sets of impulses instead of depending, as did some of Alinsky's followers, on channeling popular anger into cathartic but often unproductive confrontations with power.

Obama had learned different, but congruent, lessons in Michael Baron's year-long seminar on international relations as an undergraduate at Columbia. With Baron he had studied the dynamics of decision making in situations ranging from Pearl Harbor and the Cuban missile crisis to the 1973 Arab–Israeli War and the early stages of Vietnam. He had learned the dangers of "group think" and the importance of hearing all sides of a dispute before forming a judgment. He had learned that leaders in crisis situations should follow a few rules of thumb: Listen to diverse points of view. Weigh rosy projections against worst-case scenarios. Above all, put yourself in the other person's shoes. Negotiators who begin by proclaiming nonnegotiable demands end up intensifying instead of dissolving tensions. Those committed to resolving problems make progress only when they manage to see the situation from multiple perspectives, including those of their adversaries. Obama carried those lessons with him from Columbia to Chicago, and they helped him develop his own strategies as an organizer.

In law school Obama encountered, from his professors and the contributors to the *HLR*, historicist and particularist principles that made sense of the lessons he had learned before and during his time in Chicago. Knowledge is contingent and provisional. Our firmest convictions depend on assumptions that vary across cultures and change over time. If politics must be framed as a contest between rival dogmas, rival proclamations of certainty, then what happens when one has become aware—as Obama surely was by the time he returned from Harvard to Chicago in 1991—that all dogmas lack foundations, that all proclamations of certainty rest on illusions? After one has escaped the spell cast by the magic of belief in absolutes, how is it possible to inspire belief?

In the evocative final sentence of the first chapter of *Dreams from My Father*, Obama writes wistfully about his mother's and his grandparents' aspirations for themselves and their nation. When they came to realize that their dreams were unfulfilled, when they understood the gap that still separated their hopes from their experience, Obama writes that he came to occupy "the place where their dreams had been." Even after he decided that their universalist vision of human brotherhood was no more than a "useful fiction," the aspirations that his family projected on him continued to shape his own ambitions as decisively as did his own disillusionment. In the process of reaching a mature understanding of himself and the political world he would inhabit, Obama had to contend with persistent ambivalence. Although the glittering idea of a universal principle of justice retained its seductive allure, gnawing doubts, prompted by his experience and confirmed by his education, whispered that it might be no more than an illusion.

Chapter 3

Obama's American History

R EADERS ENTERING OBAMA'S BOOKS find themselves in a landscape that seems at first very different from the jagged contours and jarring conflicts between universalism and particularism, timelessness and historicism, science and hermeneutics. *Dreams from My Father* and *The Audacity of Hope* appear to occupy a different world because they are directed less toward academic philosophers or social scientists than toward the much wider audience of American citizens. But Obama has been paying attention. To a striking degree, his sensibility has been shaped by the developments in American academic culture since the 1960s outlined in chapter 2, and in this chapter I want to demonstrate that underappreciated connection. Remember that Obama was trained in two of America's leading colleges, Occidental and Columbia. He earned his law degree at one of its leading law schools, Harvard, then taught law for more than a decade at another top-flight institution, the University of Chicago Law School.

In his books Obama never explicitly addresses his education or his teaching. It isn't necessary. His writing clearly reflects his experiences as a student and as a professor in turbulent times, and his books manifest his serious engagement with the life of the mind. As anyone reading this (or any other) book can attest, reading is not the most dramatic of human practices, and Obama the writer prefers flesh-and-blood characterizations to discourses on civic republicanism, philosophical pragmatism, the discourse ethics of deliberative democracy, and antifoundationalism. Yet as I hope readers of this book will also attest, reading can alter the way a person looks at the world. Obama's worldview emerged not only from his family, his friends, and his colleagues in the sharp-elbowed worlds of community organizing and electoral politics, decisive as those surely were. His worldview was also shaped by the debates that rocked the campuses where he studied and taught, debates about ideas as well as politics. Much as he might need to mask it on the campaign trail, where he demonstrates his impressive skill as a politician, his books make clear that Barack Obama is also very much an intellectual.

Of Obama's two principal books, many people prefer *Dreams from My Father*, a meditation on Obama's personal identity and the problems of race and cultural diversity in America. Much has been written on those issues already, and for good reason. To understand Obama's ideas about American culture and politics, however, his personal story must be placed in the framework provided by *The Audacity of Hope*, a book in which one can identify the echoes of earlier and more recent voices in the traditions of American political thought. Particularly important are his discussions of the Constitution, antebellum American democracy, Lincoln and the Civil War, and the reform movements of the Progressive, New Deal, and civil rights eras. From his well-informed and sophisticated analysis of those issues emerges a particular conception of democracy.

Perhaps not surprisingly for someone who studied and taught constitutional law, Obama writes incisively about the United States Constitution. Near the end of *Dreams from My Father*, he describes the law as the record of "a long-running conversation, a nation arguing with its conscience." Given that Tribe and Dorf had attributed to Obama and Robert Fisher their conception of the Constitution as a conversation, the first part of that phrase should come as no surprise, but the second hints at the differences between Obama's writing and the wooden prose that deadens much legal discourse. In *The Audacity of Hope* Obama's argument is less lyrical but even more provocative. Against those conservatives who invoked the idea of the founders' so-called original intent, a set of determinate meanings that are said to limit what legislatures and judges can legitimately do, Obama points out—accurately—that the Constitution resulted from a series of compromises made necessary by the depth of disagreement at the Constitutional Convention and during the process of ratification. Moreover, Obama correctly observes that the decision to leave the document open to amendment testified to the framers' realization that the nation's Constitution would have to change, albeit slowly, with American culture in order to survive.

The failure to provide a mechanism for such alterations, the framers understood, had doomed earlier republics to failure—as we can see now that it doomed later republics, such as the first several republics proclaimed in France—when they proved incapable of adapting to changed circumstances. Obama quotes a crucial passage from Madison concerning the value and the necessity of open-mindedness in democracy. Reflecting on the process of reaching provisional agreement at the Constitutional Convention, Madison wrote, "No man felt himself obliged to retain his opinions any longer than he was satisfied of their propriety and truth." Everyone remained "open to the force of argument." That passage expresses Obama's understanding of democracy as deliberation.

Madison himself, although often credited with having framed the Constitution, did not get the Constitution he wanted. His own position on crucial issues such as the Senate and the authority of the executive changed not only during the convention itself but also during the debates over ratification, particularly when be became convinced by his friend Jefferson that the Anti-Federalists were right about the strategic necessity, and perhaps even the desirability, of a Bill of Rights. *The Audacity of Hope* contains no footnotes, and Obama rarely mentions the scholars whose work has shaped his ideas. It seems clear from his discussion of Madison and the Constitution, however, that he rejects claims about original intent and also sees beyond the 1950s-era obsession with Madison's so-called realist pluralism. Many scholars in the 1950s argued that Madison wisely abandoned aspirations to political ideals and settled instead for an institutional structure that would merely facilitate and accommodate the clash of competing interests. That interpretation served to justify the political moderation of the post–World War II era. Although that view still appeals to many scholars, including those on the right who praise Madison's prudence and those on the left who accuse him of selling out democratic ideals, it has become increasingly difficult to sustain. Recent historians of Madison and the Constitution, such as Jack Rakove and Lance Banning, legal scholars such as Harvard's Michelman and Tribe, Yale's Akhil Amar and Obama's longtime Chicago colleague Sunstein, and Supreme Court Justices such as Stephen Breyer, have all demonstrated why the ideal and the practice of democratic deliberation proved at least as important for the acceptance and durability of the Constitution as did the checks and balances built into the new nation's institutional architecture.

Madison's comment about remaining "open to the force of argument," for example, served as the epigraph for one of Sunstein's many books, *The Partial Constitu-*

tion (1993). Although it may be that Obama is a careful student of Madison, it seems more likely that he has been attentive to the transformation of scholarly debate concerning the Constitution. Sunstein's book offers a more ambitious, and much more fully fleshed out, version of the arguments Tribe and Dorf advanced in *On Reading the Constitution*, the argument they attributed to Obama and Robert Fisher that the Constitution is best understood as a conversation. Sunstein's book is replete with discussions of Wood and civic republicanism, Dewey and participatory democracy, and the usefulness of Putnam's philosophical pragmatism for constitutional law.

The older, conspiratorial view of the Constitution as the product of scheming elites out to dupe the unsuspecting and virtuous masses, an interpretation that originated with Charles Beard a century ago, still makes compelling drama; it persists among many historians committed to the idea that the deck was stacked against "the people" by "the interests" from the beginning. But the record of the debates in the Constitutional Convention and afterwards is much more complex. Neither the neo-Beardian conspiracy theory nor the sepia-tinted portraits of the founders trotted out by conservatives eager to preserve the status quo captures the dynamic process of writing and ratifying the Constitution.

Madison himself went into the Constitutional Convention self-consciously committed to constructing a democracy, and he came away from the ratification process convinced that the result, despite his misgivings about it, was the best that could be attained through a democratic process. In his first speech to the Constitutional Convention, Madison argued that a federal government, because it would "expand the sphere" of representatives' horizons beyond their local preoccupations to the needs of the entire nation, "was the only defense against the inconveniences of democracy consistent with the democratic form of government." Notice Madison's use of the terms "democracy" and "democratic" in that sentence. The familiar notion that Madison envisioned a republic rather than a democracy is widespread, but it is false. He did envision a representative democracy rather than a direct democracy, and the elaborate checks and balances of the federal framework appealed to him in part for that reason. But his preference for representative democracy hardly makes him an antidemocrat. Other contemporaries who shared that preference included Thomas Jefferson and Thomas Paine, two thinkers often contrasted to Madison but with whom he had much more in common from the 1770s through the 1820s than is usually recognized.

Madison aligned himself with those who opposed the idea that delegates, either to the Constitutional Convention or later to the United States Congress, should be bound by instructions from their constituents. His position derived from his faith in a particular form of representative democracy, not his distrust of its potential. He believed that the process of deliberation, if it remained open-ended, could produce results different from, and superior to, any of the ideas that representatives brought with them to an assembly. As Sunstein emphasized in *The Partial Constitution*, and as Madison's own letters after the convention confirm, Madison had experienced in Philadelphia the creative potential of deliberation, a potential short-circuited by demands that representatives must follow precisely the preexisting preferences of those who sent them. It is true that many Anti-Federalists cherished a different conception of democracy from that embraced by Madison, Jefferson, and Paine. Many Anti-Federalists distrusted the idea of delegating authority to those they elected to serve in a distant assembly. But their vision of democracy is as difficult to translate into a national framework as their critics at the time contended, and the preference for a federalist form of government did not necessarily make its champions opponents of ordinary citizens. Some Federalists, notably Alexander Hamilton and Robert Morris, did distrust the people and did seek to limit their influence. Madison's commitment to the Constitution, by contrast, like that of his chief ally in Philadelphia, James Wilson of Pennsylvania, sprang from his deep desire to see democracy survive.

In his description of the Constitution and the way it was constructed, Obama shows his familiarity with one of the most important developments in American scholarship since the 1970s, during the years since Wood and other historians sparked the republican revival and legal scholars such as Michelman and Sunstein brought it to law schools. Not only constitutional lawyers but also political theorists are now rediscovering what Madison, Jefferson, and Paine already knew: representative democracy is not a bastardized or second-best version but instead a distinctive variant of democracy that values persuasion over the rigid, unyielding defense of preferences or interests. Representative democracy is designed to substitute the dynamic process of making reasoned arguments for the simple tallying of votes dictated by constituents' preferences. In Obama's words, not only did the size of the new nation mean that "an Athenian model of democracy was out of the question" and that "the direct democracy of the New England town meeting" was "unmanageable." It was not just practicality that dictated representation.

The process of deliberation, particularly when it brought together people with diverse backgrounds, convictions, and aspirations, made possible a metamorphosis unavailable through any other form of decision making. People who saw the world through very different lenses could help each other see more clearly. Just as Madison defended the value of delegates' willingness to change their minds and yield to the force of the better argument, so Obama explicitly echoes the arguments of Madison—and, strikingly, of Alexander Hamilton in *Federalist* number 70—concerning the importance of encouraging the "jarring of parties" because such differences of opinion could "promote deliberation and circumspection." Obama does not explicitly invoke Wood's *Creation of the American Republic* or other examples of the republican synthesis he first encountered at Occidental and then again in law school. Nor does he cite the prize-winning work of historians Banning and Rakove concerning the impossibility of locating a single original meaning in the swirling debates and resulting compromises that yielded the Constitution. He does not cite the writings of his law school professors Minow, Michelman, or Tribe, nor the articles by *HLR* contributors Sunstein and Gardbaum. Obama does point out, however, that scholars now agree that the Constitution was "cobbled together" from heated debates and emerged "not as the result of principle but as the result of power and passion." The ideas of Madison were never identical to those of Hamilton, those of Morris never those of Wilson, and so on. No unitary meaning or intent can be found. Instead the Constitution shows traces of competing arguments drawn from sources including the Bible, the English common law, Scottish philosophy, civic republican traditions, and the Enlightenment idea of natural rights.

Obama the law professor concedes that such a conception of the founding appeals to him because it encourages us to emphasize the contingency of the original document and to appreciate the contingencies that lie beneath our own invocations of high principle. His constitutionalism fits neatly into the historicist framework that was displacing older verities in the academic communities of Los Angeles, New York, Cambridge, and Chicago during the 1980s and 1990s. Such historicism, he writes, might free us to "assert our own values unencumbered by fidelity to the stodgy traditions of a distant past." In other words, it might tempt us to proclaim that constitutional interpretation is a question of shifting conventions or changing paradigms. When it comes to the Constitution, we might conclude it's turtles all the way down. But Obama admits that such freedom makes him uneasy. He describes it as "the freedom of the relativist, the rule breaker," or "the apostate," and he concedes that "such apostasy leaves me unsatisfied." Caught between the pressures of Kuhn and Geertz, on the one hand, and the persistent yearning for Rawls's stable principles of justice, on the other, where can Obama turn?

He can, and he does, turn to philosophical pragmatism and to American history. What we need, he suggests, is a "shift in metaphors," a willingness to see "our democracy not as a house to be built, but as a conversation to be had." Madison did not give us a "fixed blueprint." Instead he provided a framework that cannot resolve all our differences but offers only "a way by which we argue about our future." The institutional machinery of the Constitution was intended, Obama argues, not to solve our problems once and for all but "to force us into a conversation." The Constitution gave birth to "a 'deliberative democracy' in which all citizens are required to engage in a process of testing their ideas against an external reality, persuading others of their point of view, and building shifting alliances of consent." It would be hard to find in James or Dewey, in Bernstein or Putnam, a clearer statement of the conceptual and historical connections between philosophical pragmatism and deliberative democracy in the American political tradition.

Obama's arguments about American democracy rest on a solid scholarly foundation. Sunstein argued in the *HLR* article "Interpreting Statues" that Madison envisioned the clashing of arguments in American legislatures as a uniquely productive process, a process whereby representatives found their own convictions, and those of their constituents, challenged and changed. Madison sought, as the historian Marvin Meyers argued decades ago in a brilliant essay cited by Sunstein, not merely stability but new understandings of the common good, understandings unavailable to any individual but emerging from the processes of contestation and deliberation. In Obama's formulation of this crucial point, the founders wanted above all to avoid "all forms of absolute authority," and the most perilous moments for the new nation occurred when that fallibilism was threatened by attempts to freeze the dynamic process of democratic deliberation by stifling debate. Through this process of making arguments, encountering objections, rethinking our positions, forging compromises, and testing our ideas against a resistant reality in which our schemes succeed or fail, Obama concludes, we learn "to examine our motives and our interests constantly." We learn, in short, that "both our individual and collective judgments are at once legitimate and highly fallible."

Neither Madison nor Jefferson, neither James nor Dewey, neither Putnam nor Bernstein could have said it better. Balancing the historicism of cutting-edge constitutional scholarship against his lingering desire for some-

thing more substantial than quicksand (or a tower of turtles), Obama makes use of the American tradition of
philosophical pragmatism: we should debate our differences, and test provisional interpretations of principle,
not by measuring proposals against unchanging dogmas
but through trial and error, by trying to solve problems
creatively and then democratically deliberating, yet again,
on the consequences of our experiments. "We hang on to
our values, even if they seem at times tarnished and worn,"
even if we realize that "we have betrayed them more often
than we remember." Despite everything, we affirm the
principle. Our democratic values, deliberation and truth
testing, constitute the American people as a nation developing over time. Our commitments to freedom and equality are "our inheritance, what makes us who we are as a
people." As individuals and as a nation, we are constituted by the values we cherish, the principles we seek to
realize, and the democratic process whereby we attempt to
reach those goals.

But we must not pretend that the meaning of those
shared principles has ever been anything but contested. As
the pragmatists James and Dewey insisted repeatedly, and
as more recent philosophical pragmatists have confirmed,
democratic principles should not be confused with unchanging dogmas. They must remain subject to criticism
and revision. In Obama's words, "our values must be
tested against fact and experience." Freedom and equality
had one set of meanings in the agrarian settlements of
the seventeenth century, another set in the eighteenth and

nineteenth centuries, and they are destined to have new meanings for every generation. That is the challenge of democracy, and that is the reason why the philosophy of pragmatism is uniquely suited to democratic decision making. When our understandings no longer conform to the facts of lived experience, as has been the case over and over in American history, it is time for critical inquiry and substantive change. Ritual invocations of earlier nostrums, as if such formulas could help solve problems earlier generations could not have imagined, deflect attention from the hard work of democracy.

The need for such hard work derives, at least in part, from the deeply flawed institutional structures put in place by the Constitution. Although subject to amendment, the Constitution nevertheless erected formidable barriers in the way of those who would alter the framework of American governance. Of all the flaws, the most serious was the founders' failure to address the outrageous practice of slavery. In Obama's words, the generation of Adams, Jefferson, and Madison bequeathed to their successors "a form of government unique in its genius—yet blind to the whip and the chain." A second antidemocratic feature of the "great compromise" between the North and the slaveholding South was the provision for electing two senators from each state. That arrangement has given those chosen to represent small, sparsely populated states—then Rhode Island and Delaware, now Vermont and Wyoming—equal power with the most populous. In 1790 Virginia had ten times the population of Rhode Island; California now has more than seventy times the population of Wyoming. Madison—himself a Virginian—opposed this feature of the Constitution because of its antidemocratic quality, as does Obama. From the beginning, the Senate has tended to resist change more vigorously than has the more representative House of Representatives.

The way in which the structure of the Constitution has facilitated some forms of change and blocked others remains as clear as ever in the twenty-first century. Although only slightly more than a year into his first presidential term as I write, Obama has demonstrated already the depth—and the perils—of his commitment to philosophical pragmatism and deliberative democracy, particularly in his handling of the protracted debate over health care. His flexibility and his willingness to compromise infuriated some of his supporters on the left, and the refusal of his intransigent Republican opponents caused many observers to mock the president's repeated appeals to negotiation, bipartisanship, and creative compromise. As savvy pundits left and right pointed out repeatedly, it takes two to compromise, and efforts to negotiate are futile when the other side shows no interest. But Obama's steadfast insistence that he was open to suggestions, that he was willing to meet with his adversaries and consider their ideas, and his repeated invitations to Republicans to propose alternatives served a purpose that few commentators seemed to notice as the debate wore on. He was displaying, over and over, with a patience that outraged his allies and bewildered his foes, an iron fortitude that his critics mistook for weakness. In *The Audacity of Hope* and in many of his speeches since he wrote that book, Obama has acknowledged that Americans are deeply divided on the issue of health care. Even those who agreed that our system does not work disagreed bitterly about how to fix it. Obama pointed out that calls for a single-payer plan, a comprehensive, government-run program patterned on national health care systems firmly entrenched elsewhere (such as the plan I made good use of while I was living in England in 2008–2009), had no chance in the United States. Such proposals diverged too dramatically from the traditions and practices to which Americans are accustomed. Americans happy with their doctors and their insurance plans, he promised repeatedly, should be able to keep them. In *The Audacity of Hope* he proposed trying out multiple options, notably what he called "insurance pools," taking advantage of the nation's federal structure to conduct a controlled experiment in the states. After evaluating the results, the nation could opt for the most successful solution available.

That proposal, advanced several years before Obama was elected president, suggests one way to frame the outcome of the lengthy negotiations in 2009–2010 that culminated in the passage of health care reform legislation. Thanks to Republican Mitt Romney, then governor of Massachusetts, the commonwealth had been conducting for several years an experiment in state-mandated health insurance, with encouraging results. Obama was careful not to replicate his predecessor Bill Clinton's mistake of declaring too early—and too dogmatically—what must be done to solve the problem of health care. He let the debate proceed, at times it seemed interminably, while his supporters shrieked and his foes gloated. The plan Congress eventually adopted in March 2010—the plan Obama worked tirelessly in the final months to enact—more closely resembles the Massachusetts model than any of the other options under consideration. If that model did not suit Republicans in the House or Senate in 2009–2010, not long ago it appealed to one of the most prominent Republican governors and one of the leading candidates for his party's presidential nomination in 2008.

When paroxysms of anger, even threats of violence, followed the passage of health care reform, many Americans expressed surprise. But given the intensity of public disagreement on the issue, that response might have been expected. It also suggested the reasons for, and perhaps even confirmed the wisdom of, Obama's strategy. Rather than proclaiming himself from the outset a champion of the single-payer model, Medicare for all, or at the very least the public option that I and many others considered an attractive solution, Obama instead waited patiently until the deliberative process had run its course and the House and Senate had hammered out their misshapen, unlovely bills. In his State of the Union Address, he pointedly chided Republicans for failing to offer their own ideas and invited their proposals. He later convened a much ballyhooed day-long summit to give Republicans a chance to explain their objections and present alternatives. When those overtures were greeted with even more strident refusals, it became apparent that Obama's sustained efforts to encourage, and to engage in, deliberation as a way to identify a common good had been categorically rejected. At that point he threw himself into the battle.

The result of the protracted congressional debate over health care reform resembles most of the earlier landmarks in American social legislation. Like Social Security in 1935 and voting rights, Medicare, and Medicaid in 1965, the health care reform measure of 2010 is a product of the sausage factory that we call representative democracy. Obviously far from perfect, it will need to be revised as its flaws become clear. It might also be the best bill Obama could have gotten through Congress. As a student of American history, Obama knows that the election of 2008, although historic because it put him in the White House and gave his party a majority in the House and the Senate, was hardly a landslide. The political scientist William Galston, a veteran of Clinton's White House, has pointed out that Obama's own electoral majority of 7 percent was only 1 percent greater than Clinton's in 1992, and Obama was running at the time of the worst economic calamity since the Great Depression. Democrats held sixty seats in the Senate—at least until Massachusetts, in a special election to replace Ted Kennedy after his death, bewilderingly elected an almost unknown Republican (a pickup truck owner and former model named Scott Brown) in place of the longtime champion of health care reform. By contrast, when Roosevelt began his second term in office, Democrats held seventy-nine seats in the Senate, the Republicans only sixteen. When Lyndon Johnson pushed the Voting Rights Act through Congress, Democrats held sixty-eight seats in the Senate and a 295–140 majority in the House. Moreover, in the 1930s and 1960s both parties were far less ideologically homogeneous than they are now: more than half the Republicans in the House and more than 40 percent in the Senate voted for Medicare.

People who used to complain about the lack of coherent ideology in American party politics have gotten their wish. Some, like the columnist David Broder, are not sure they like the result. More than three quarters of Americans who identify themselves as Republicans now accept the label conservative. Democrats are less unified: 40 percent identify themselves as liberals, another 40 percent as moderates, and 20 percent as conservatives. Comparing the current political situation with those of the mid-1930s and the mid-1960s makes clear, as does the difficulty Democratic congressional leaders faced in rounding up the votes to pass the final version of the bill, that Democrats were hardly in a position to dictate the terms of debate. As has happened repeatedly in American history, even a measure that incorporated many concessions to its opponents barely squeaked into law. It seems unlikely that Republicans will be able to fulfill their promise of repealing a package almost certain to win adherents as quickly as Social Security and Medicare did. Even so, as Obama noted in *The Audacity of Hope*, in a democracy "no law is ever final, no battle truly finished," which is why philosophical pragmatism and deliberative democracy go hand in hand. Principled partisans of pragmatism and democracy are committed to debate, experimentation, and the critical reassessment of results.

For that reason no straight lines run from philosophical pragmatism or deliberative democracy to Obama's positions, strategies, or policies—or any others. One of the characteristic features of pragmatism, in fact, has been the incessant disagreements among its adherents. James had been dead only a few years when his legacy was invoked by Randolph Bourne to criticize the endorsement of Wilson's foreign policy by Dewey and by James's students Lippmann, Croly, and DuBois. Every major debate in American politics in the last century has seen self-proclaimed heirs of James or Dewey lining up on opposite sides, usually on multiple sides. Getting pragmatism right does not dictate a certain political position, although the connection between philosophical pragmatism and an experimental, democratic approach to politics is hard to deny. But the forms experimentation and democracy should take are not only appropriate subjects for debate. Wrangling over such questions is what a commitment to pragmatism and democracy means. Obama has demonstrated such a commitment himself, and spirited debates about all aspects of his presidency, from its overall thrust to its tactical maneuvers, are not only bound to continue whatever he does, they are fully consistent with the conception of democracy he has outlined and embraced.

Critics of pragmatism have often faulted the philosophy because it cannot provide a formula for political action. Although the critique persists, it seems to me rooted in a misconception of what pragmatism can and cannot do. As James explained in the first book explicitly devoted to the philosophy, *Pragmatism*, it is "a method" that "stands for no particular results. It has no dogmas, and no doctrines save its method" and its "genetic theory of what is meant by truth." James and his followers have worked hard to explain that theory of truth, and they have offered different answers. James's foes caricatured his position from the start. They claimed that he was calling true whatever is "convenient" or "pleasant" to believe. To the contrary, James insisted that pragmatists—like everyone else—are constrained to believe "what fits every part of life best and combines with the collectivity of experience's demands." Thus, "our duty to agree with reality is seen to be grounded in a perfect jungle of concrete expediencies." Labeling the complaint that pragmatists endorsed wishful thinking "an impudent slander," James summed up his position in these words: "Pent in, as the pragmatist more than anyone else feels himself to be, between the whole body of funded truths squeezed from the past and the coercions of the world of sense about him, who so well as he feels the immense pressure of objective control under which our minds perform their operations?"

When even such explicit replies to his critics proved unavailing, James wrote another book, *The Meaning of Truth*, to establish that, as he put it bluntly, "an experience, perceptual or conceptual, must conform to reality in order to be true." Pragmatist philosophers have tried from the beginning to balance their opposition to dogma with their commitment to experimentation and tough-minded, sustained, critical analysis of the results of those experiments. James thought individuals should be free to conduct such experiments for themselves whenever the evidence is inconclusive, as in the domain of religious belief. But as a method for determining what experiments society should try, and how the results should be evaluated, pragmatists from James and Dewey to Bernstein and Putnam have recommended democracy.

I want to emphasize that I am not trying to establish a necessary connection between philosophical pragmatism and Obama's politics. The former does not entail the latter. I am arguing instead from Obama's writings back to the philosophy of pragmatism in order to show the congruence between antifoundationalism, historicism, experimentalism, and democracy in his way of thinking. Dissatisfied with universalism yet uneasy with particularity, Obama found fruitful methods in philosophical pragmatism and deliberative democracy. Searching for guidance about the traditions he could tap to advance his ideals of freedom and equality, he turned to American history. What did he find there?

The animating ideal of the new nation, Obama writes, was "ordered liberty." This phrase derives from the seventeenth-century founders of the New England colonies, and it can be traced forward through the American Revolution to the Whigs and then the Republicans of the

1850s. Many Americans now associate another phrase originating with the Puritans, "a city upon a hill," with Ronald Reagan, as did Republican Party vice-presidential candidate Sarah Palin during the 2008 presidential campaign. The phrase actually dates from John Winthrop's sermon onboard the ship that brought the first Puritans to Massachusetts Bay in 1630. Winthrop was referring to the settlers' vow to look after each other in the wilderness, and thereby to transform, by virtue of their exemplary Christian brotherhood, the culture of selfishness they were leaving behind them. Of course Winthrop's fellow Christians also saw fit to embrace the institution of slavery, keeping as slaves both Indians and Africans, a fact that should alert us to the distance separating their sensibilities from our own.

During the years between the Puritans' arrival in North America and the decade of the 1780s, Obama observes, Americans embraced an ideal of "ordered liberty" patterned on the Puritans' model. They pioneered a particular kind of democracy premised on what he calls "a certain humility" and "a rejection of absolute truth." Although the Puritans surely cherished the absolute truth of their Christianity, the institutions they put in place in New England towns enabled them to govern themselves. Those institutions had the unintended effect of destabilizing hierarchical authority in the public sphere and empowering the people. Instead of truth descending from on high, it would bubble up from the unruly deliberations of citizens gathering together in meeting houses to decide for themselves on issues of public concern. The early settlers of the Massachusetts Bay Colony wrestled with how they could prevent dissent from corroding their common commitments.

Growing dissatisfaction with Winthrop's coercive solution to that problem eventually burst into emigration. Renegade bands of Puritans led by Roger Williams and Thomas Hooker established communities in Rhode Island and Connecticut self-consciously organized around embryonic versions of democracy. There they institutionalized less restrictive practices oriented toward what Rawls would eventually call overlapping consensus. Those who gathered on an island in Narragansett Bay in March 1642, near today's Newport, constituted themselves as "a DEMOCRACIE, or Popular Government," and resolved to create "Just Lawes, by which they will be regulated, and to depute from among themselves such Ministers as shall see them faithfully executed between Man and Man." These New England town meetings, as Tocqueville's New England informants later explained to him, were the "cradle of democracy."

As the first generation of Puritans and equally contentious colonists up and down the Atlantic seaboard experimented with diverse forms of self-government, they gradually accumulated the experience that enabled them to forge different varieties of more or less democratic government during the 1770s and 1780s. As the colonists wrangled with each other in public forums ranging from the town and county to the state and eventually the nation, they slowly and unsteadily developed an unusual degree of competence in the tricky business of making, administering, and altering their own laws. That experience of democracy both required and bolstered the "humility" that comes from knowing that one's own convictions are not always shared by one's neighbors. Moreover, whether one is in the majority or the minority, the awareness that circumstances change and majorities are fleeting also necessitates a rejection of absolute truth—at least de facto, and at least in the political sphere. The experience of having to accept the results of elections, as unpalatable as those results might be (and were, at various times, for prominent figures ranging from Winthrop to Madison, both of whom experienced electoral defeat), can help individuals appreciate the power and, at least occasionally, the value of other points of view. From that awareness can—not must, but can—arise a degree of toleration that makes differences acceptable even when they still seem undesirable. That was the sensibility demonstrated so clearly not only in Madison's writings in the 1780s but in his behavior from the revolution through the 1820s, a long period during which he showed himself both a champion of high democratic principles and a cagey partisan operative, the architect of the political party that coalesced around Jefferson and against Hamilton.

Many Americans still prefer the comforting fable of founders who discovered unchanging Truth and distilled it into the Constitution. Others prefer the rousing tale of a noble people duped and disempowered from the start by the duplicitous architects of the Constitution. The record of Americans' squabbles in the early national period, however, shows that neither picture is accurate. Americans from different regions and states did not trust each other very much, and they were not sure their Constitution embodied any principles they should defend when their opponents were in power. They grudgingly agreed to put their faith in the possibility that provisional agreements might emerge through the unpredictable, agonistic experience of democratic contestation and compromise.

Only through that discursive process, as Madison observed, as Tocqueville confirmed in the 1830s, and as Obama clearly understands, did Americans come to know—or rather to create—what they called a common good. They understood that the ideal of a common good appeared and then receded along the horizon. It did not exist before they argued about it, and it changed shape as they tried to implement it. In Obama's words, the framers set up "a community in which a common culture, a common faith, and a well-developed set of civic virtues" enabled citizens to contain the inevitable "contention and strife" on which democracy depends. By experiencing such struggles, he concludes, Americans learned that the individual's "self-interest" is "inextricably linked to the interests of others." Although Obama does not make the point himself, that was just what Madison proposed— repeatedly—in his contributions to the Constitutional Convention and in his essays in the *Federalist*, not only in numbers 51 and 57 but also in his most often cited but too seldom read essay, *Federalist* number 10. There Madison explained why deliberation matters.

Because *Federalist* number 10 is reputed to provide evidence for Madison's hardheaded calculations and his acceptance of the inevitable role of factions, less attention has been paid to the purpose Madison thought such conflicts serve. Like the countless Americans who wrote and rewrote local and state constitutions during the 1770s and 1780s, Madison referred repeatedly to advancing "the public good" and the "good of the whole" as the aim of the Constitution and the result of debates among the people's representatives. And Madison was not alone. Because of our tendency to turn Alexander Hamilton into the champion of centralized authority he later became, it is easy to forget that he was able to ally with Madison to write the *Federalist* because the two shared enough ideas to blur their disagreements. It was Hamilton, as Obama notes, who wrote that "the jarring of parties" and diverse opinions could "promote deliberation and circumspection." Like the passage from Madison that Obama quotes in *Audacity*, this passage from Hamilton's *Federalist* number 70 figures prominently in Sunstein's *Partial Constitution*, where he uses it to illustrate, as Obama does, the potential fruitfulness of diversity and debate.

Writing several decades later, Tocqueville likewise emphasized the liveliness of disagreements as a distinguishing feature of American public life in *Democracy in America*. Tocqueville learned a lot from traveling across the new nation, but the most important of his sources were three self-conscious champions of the idea of "ordered liberty" emphasized by Obama, the New Englanders John Quincy Adams, Josiah Quincy, and Jared Sparks. At the heart of Tocqueville's *Democracy* lay a cluster of arguments about ordered liberty that he took from these informants. Tocqueville stressed Americans' willingness to participate voluntarily in community activities, not because they were uniquely virtuous but because they discerned the meaning of what he called "self-interest properly understood." From experience they learned to see their own individual interests in relation to the interests of their neighbors, and vice versa. Obama the community organizer turned professor of constitutional law has a solid grasp of the dynamics of American democracy. He knows the process whereby individual interests can become transformed into something larger. He learned the theory from Wood and the civic republican revival; he saw—and for several years helped shape—the practice in the far south side of Chicago.

Obama is bewitched by neither the chimerical consensus of Louis Hartz's projected liberal tradition of the 1950s, in which America was defined simply by the universal reverence for property, nor by the shrill originalism of some recent prominent jurists. Instead Obama prefers Tocqueville because he realizes that Americans have always sought a variety of goals consistent with their very different ideals and aspirations. Democracy means squabbling about differences, reaching tentative agreements, then immediately resuming debate. Obama understands that disagreement is more American than apple pie. The hallmarks of early national American political culture, as sketched in *The Audacity of Hope*, mirror those that appeared in the articles published in the *HLR* in the early 1990s and updated in the Saguaro seminars a few years later: civic republicanism, deliberative democracy, communitarianism, and, in the forced practice of experimentation, at least the bare outlines of the philosophical pragmatism that took another century to develop.

Obama also sees something many of his most enthusiastic supporters on the left have trouble accepting: the willingness to endure acceptable compromises instead of demanding decisive victory over one's opponents has been a recurring feature of American democratic culture. Tocqueville never tired of contrasting that characteristic to the fatal unwillingness of his fellow French citizens to reach accommodations with each other. Tocqueville explained the success of American democracy by inverting the lessons of France's failure. Whereas the French Revolution foundered on the civil wars that erupted between monarchists and republicans, between champions of the old regime and the new, and between Enlightenment fundamentalists intolerant of religion and Catholics who remained equally intolerant of atheism, Tocqueville marveled at the willingness displayed by Americans of different backgrounds to find common ground. Or at least to tolerate their differences. From a variety of experiences ranging from barn raisings to service on juries, Americans were learning to learn from each other. From the perspective of Tocqueville, born into an aristocratic family but bewitched by the magic of democratic equality, that transformation both demanded and further developed an ethical sensibility that recognized the legitimacy of difference and the productive potential of disagreement.

In a similar vein, Obama observes that he became committed to American politics, and to running for elective office, because he believes that something lies beyond the undeniable cynicism and partisanship that prompts so much unpalatable political maneuvering. His inoculation against that cynicism has been tested again and again. Almost immediately after he was elected president, it was tested by the stupefying corruption of his state's chief executive, who apparently sought to sell to the highest bidder Obama's seat in the U.S. Senate. It has been tested since his inauguration by Republicans steadfastly resisting his attempts to forge bipartisan agreements and by his fellow Democrats who want him to ram their victory—and the less than overwhelming majorities Democrats enjoy in Congress—down their opponents' throats. Obama's rejection of cynicism and his wariness of partisanship have been among the defining features of his political career, and he knows that they have become more difficult to sustain amidst what he calls the "industry of insult" that now drowns out more moderate voices. Obama accounts for his continuing allegiance to civility by invoking a "tradition that stretched from the days of the country's founding to the glory of the civil rights movement, a tradition based on the simple idea that we have a stake in one another, and that what binds us together is greater than what drives us apart."

Appropriately enough for someone who has lived and worked on the south side of Chicago, in neighborhoods not that far southeast of Jane Addams's Hull House, Obama's reference to "that which binds us together" echoes the almost identical words that Addams wrote to explain the settlement house movement in her memoir *Twenty Years at Hull House* (1910). Using a phrase she attributed to the founder of the English settlement house movement, Addams professed her belief "that the things which make men alike are finer and better than the things that keep them apart, and that these basic likenesses, if they are properly accentuated, easily transcend the less essential differences of race, language, creed, and tradition." Addams, like Tocqueville, derived her cultural cosmopolitanism from her democratic ideal. "Hull-House was soberly opened on the theory that the dependence of classes on each other is reciprocal." Because "the social relation is essentially a reciprocal relation, it gives a form of expression that has peculiar value," the value added by expanding the appreciation of individuals for those unlike themselves. Obama's fondness for this formulation has become even clearer since his election as president. He used it in his Cairo address to the Islamic world and in his Nobel acceptance speech in Oslo, and it is a staple of the message he takes to meetings around the United States. For him it captures the heart of democracy.

Hull House inspired a generation of well-to-do native-born women to live and work with recent immigrants from a wide range of different cultures. Since the 1960s critics have maligned and satirized the efforts of such progressive reformers, both men and women, because beneath their language of uplift and harmony many skeptics see schemes of cultural imperialism and social control. Some progressives did participate in efforts to enforce racial segregation, restrict immigration, and prohibit the sale of alcohol, but the progressives were a diverse coalition that also included democratic socialists and the founders of the NAACP. Some commentators sagely contrast the supposedly elitist progressives and the supposedly democratic populists, a distinction almost always made to the detriment of the former that neglects the continuity in central aspects of the groups' agendas. Finding veiled, sinister impulses beneath the efforts of those involved in settlements or in the social gospel—concerted efforts to ameliorate conditions of urban poverty—seems to me difficult to do. Settlement house workers such as Addams, whatever else they achieved, did at least begin the process of transforming middle-class attitudes toward cultural diversity and urban poverty, helping to make the former more acceptable and the latter a scandal. If Obama is right in "Why Organize," then perhaps social activists such as Alinsky's community organizers should draw as heavily on Jane Addams's empathy as they do to John L. Lewis's intransigence.

If Obama only indirectly refers to the ideas and example of Jane Addams in *The Audacity of Hope*, he much more explicitly invokes the progressives' ideas of graduated taxation and government regulation of the economy. These two ideas, embraced by Democrats from the election of Woodrow Wilson in 1912 through the presidency of Lyndon Johnson, have been largely repudiated since the election of Ronald Reagan in 1980. In recent decades a bipartisan consensus has formed about the desirability of lowering taxes and around the theory—disproved by the catastrophic recession that began in 2008—that state regulation of the economy is less efficient than reliance on free markets. There is also widespread agreement among economists, whether they applaud or deprecate the fact, concerning one of the consequences of deregulating the economy and reducing taxes on the wealthy: the gap separating the richest from the poorest Americans has grown dramatically in recent decades.

That gap separating the wealthiest Americans not only from those at the bottom but from those in the middle of the range of income distribution shrank from the New Deal until the oil crisis of 1974. It shrank not by accident or through simple economic growth but because of four deliberate strategies: (1) progressive taxation, (2) economic regulation, (3) support for unionization, and (4) massive investment in higher education. In the aftermath of Reagan's election in 1980, all those strategies have been deemed inconsistent with American principles. At least partly as a consequence, inequality has soared to levels unseen at least since the late nineteenth century and perhaps unprecedented in American history.

Like the progressives and New Dealers before him—and like the founders of the American republic before them—Obama sees such increasing economic inequality as inimical to democracy. His critique of inequality in *The Audacity of Hope* might seem to place him at the edge of twenty-first-century American political debate, but it descends from a long tradition. Although the great champions of independence John Adams and Thomas Jefferson grew to disagree with each other about many things, they never wavered from their conviction that the American experiment with self-government would succeed only if the nation's citizens remained roughly equal in their economic standing. For that reason both opposed the standard European practices of primogeniture and entail. Both saw that such techniques, which provided for passing down estates and fortunes intact to first-born sons, had enabled European aristocrats to consolidate their wealth and their power at the expense of everyone else. Adams and Jefferson agreed that democracy could survive in the United States only if the nation prevented the emergence and persistence of extremes of wealth and poverty such as those of the old world.

Both Adams and Jefferson distrusted Alexander Hamilton's schemes for consolidating the power of bankers because both valued producers of wealth—whether farmers or artisans—over those who, in Adams's phrase, only "moved money around." In a long-forgotten letter to Jefferson, Adams described banking as an "infinity of successive felonious larcenies." Given that the financial sector's share of the United States economy has increased dramatically in recent years, perhaps the time has come to resurrect this observation. Coming from the pen of contemporary conservatives' favorite founder, Adams's words ought to figure in debates about regulating the financial sector. Whatever the reasons behind investment banks' dramatic increase in revenues, ever-increasingly inequality, as Adams and Jefferson agreed, is disastrous for democracy. First steps toward Rawls's ideal of a "property-owning democracy" were taken in early America, and the new nation continued in that direction thanks to the ideas of Adams, Jefferson, and other members of their generation who ensured that the United States would never permit a hereditary aristocracy to develop. Progressives and New Dealers contributed the ideas of a minimum wage, graduated taxation, economic regulation, collective bargaining, and expanded access to higher education in order to update that original American commitment to economic equality—at least relative to the nations of Europe.

Obama also explicitly endorses the judgment of the quintessential progressive lawyer, the "people's attorney" Louis Brandeis. "In a democracy," Brandeis wrote, "the most important office is the office of citizen" because democracy requires all individuals to see beyond their narrow personal interest and attend to the common good. Obama's approach to economic and political reform essentially extends that of the progressive reformers who sought to rein in corporate power by various means.

Brandeis wanted to attack "bigness" directly, through antimonopoly measures. Others preferred the "Wisconsin idea" of nonpartisan public servants engaging in research to identify problems and mobilize public resources to address them. From that orientation emerged the independent regulatory agency. The idea of a body operating in the interest of consumers originated in the Interstate Commerce Commission in 1887. It was reborn in Wisconsin in the 1910s, then exported to other states and the federal government.

Progressive reformers adopted a wide range of strategies, but in the economic realm they built on that idea of regulation in the public interest until the retrenchment of government in the 1920s. Herbert Hoover's "associative state," which effectively empowered business and enriched businessmen at the expense of government authority, contributed to the skewed income distribution that helped cause the catastrophic Great Depression by reducing the buying power of most Americans. Franklin D. Roosevelt, after initially resisting the progressives' approach, resurrected it in the New Deal. In Obama's words, the Social Security Act of 1935 was "the centerpiece of the new welfare state, a safety net that would lift almost half of all senior citizens out of poverty, provide unemployment insurance for those who had lost their jobs, and provide modest welfare payments to the disabled and the elderly poor." Although it was full of holes, the Social Security Act represented a beginning, and as it expanded it has provided much wider coverage, particularly for senior citizens. That process of gradual expansion and consolidation might provide a model for health care reform in the coming decades.

Roosevelt proposed a more dramatic expansion of the New Deal when he laid out his plan for a more generous scheme of social provision in his second bill of rights, a program he announced in his State of the Union Address in 1944. In *The Audacity of Hope*, when Obama listed the concerns that animated citizens he met while preparing to run for the United States Senate in 2002, he outlined essentially the same program on which Roosevelt campaigned for reelection almost six decades before: a living wage, health insurance, good schools, safety from criminals at home and enemies abroad, a clean environment, "time with their kids," and "a chance to retire with some dignity and respect." Like Roosevelt, Obama judged those hopes modest and, for a nation as rich as America, achievable. Roosevelt died before he had the chance to fight for those programs at the end of World War II. Many historians doubt he would have made the effort, or that he would have succeeded had he tried. But he did achieve such goals in the GI Bill, and extending its provisions for all Americans seems to me a struggle he might have thought worth waging had he lived out his fourth term in office. Obama's friend Sunstein has recently made an ambitious and convincing case for that conjecture in his book *The Second Bill of Rights*, an account consistent with Obama's own observations in *The Audacity of Hope* concerning FDR and the New Deal.

Obama has no illusions about the mid-twentieth-century Democratic Party. He understands it harbored and humored vicious southern racists who weighed every initiative against their overriding commitment to preserving the South's regime of white supremacy. He knows that the Democratic Party coalition was held together by inspiring ideals—"a vision of fair wages and benefits"—and hard-nosed calculations—"patronage and public works"—and above all by "an ever-rising standard of living." Although Obama applauds the achievements of the New Deal, he acknowledges its limitations—and not only its failure to tackle institutionalized racism. In the 1930s Roosevelt was denounced as too timid by Dewey, Niebuhr, and their allies on the radical left, who criticized him for failing to make America socialist when he had the chance. Conservatives have denounced him ever since for doing just that. Rejecting both of those exaggerated characterizations, Obama credits the New Deal for achieving what was politically possible. His interpretation faithfully echoes and updates Carl Degler's still persuasive account, in *Out of Our Past*, which was the interpretation of the New Deal to which Boesche first exposed Obama at Occidental. According to Degler and other historians who share this judgment, including William Leuchtenburg and, more recently, David M. Kennedy, Roosevelt brought to the United States lasting measures such as the Social Security Act, unemployment insurance, assistance for the disabled, and regulation of the failed banking system, all of which prevented the nation's economy from slipping further into chaos. As Obama observes correctly, the New Deal addressed the scandal of child labor, established the forty-hour workweek and the minimum wage, and provided unprecedented support for unionization.

Such steps were intended, in the words of Roosevelt that Obama endorses, to ensure "freedom from want" and "freedom from fear." Although accomplishing all that took not just a couple of years but most of Roosevelt's four terms in office, and necessitated very skillful negotiating with adversaries within as well as outside his own party, the accomplishments of the New Deal nevertheless fell far short of Roosevelt's ultimate goals, the second bill of rights, on which he campaigned successfully for reelection in 1944. These programs, however, did establish a precedent—the legitimacy of social provision—which enabled later generations to extend those principles and expand the range of Americans covered by those programs. Obama reports in *The Audacity of Hope* that he carried with him similar aspirations as he entered the United States Senate.

Since the autumn of 2008 Obama has repeatedly emphasized the responsibility of the federal government to return to its earlier practice of regulating the American financial sector. It has become clear to many observers—although some disagree—that the bipartisan mania for deregulation during the 1990s helped usher in the worst economic crisis since the 1930s. Obama has pledged to address the problems caused by that deregulation, and he has brought Sunstein, Tribe, and others to Washington to help spearhead the effort. But it is far from clear whether Obama's words will translate into renewed and effective government oversight of the financial sector in the interest of American consumers. After all, other central figures in his administration, including Timothy Geithner and Larry Summers, helped facilitate some of the changes now considered toxic during the years they served in the Clinton administration. Neither Geithner nor Summers has indicated that he has changed his mind about the steps that were taken in the 1990s.

It is not yet clear what principles of political economy Obama deems appropriate for the United States now that the pressures of globalization have made it impossible for Americans to escape economic pressures exerted by nations and corporations around the world. How he intends to translate the endorsements of progressive and New Deal policies in *The Audacity of Hope* into a new set of Democratic policies remains murky. Has he considered the bold vision he encountered in his courses with Roberto Unger, a radically decentralized economy in which public funding of private initiatives empowers the creative potential of ordinary citizens? Or have the economic advisers Obama has brought into his administration fulfilled the prophesy of Frank Davis? Having been "trained," in other words, has he now been yanked by the chain of power back from the commitment to economic democracy proclaimed in *The Audacity of Hope* to the tepid economic centrism of Democratic Party insiders since the 1980s? It is too soon to say, but the early indications suggest there may be reason for concern. Will Obama resist, or will he succumb to a vision of political economy that places the interests of investment bankers over those of unemployed job seekers? His long-term legacy will depend on the answer.

It is even less clear what levers Obama thinks can be pulled to address the yawning gulf between the ever-richer rich and not only the poorest Americans but also the middle class that has been growing relatively poorer for the last thirty years. If Obama envisions a strategy for moving in the direction of Roosevelt's vision of a second bill of rights, or of either Rawls's or Unger's version of a property-owning democracy, or of directly addressing the problems of poverty that he described so vividly in his account of Chicago's far south side in *Dreams from My Father*, he has not yet revealed it. Merely rolling back his Republican predecessors' tax cuts for the wealthy, even though that suggestion was enough to spark controversy during the campaign of 2008, may prove inadequate unless it is accompanied by other measures such as a genuinely robust, and enormously expensive, jobs program. If the big banks were deemed too big to fail, as Obama's erstwhile ally Cornel West has observed, why shouldn't we say the same thing about unemployed American citizens floundering in the absence of work? If the founders were right to believe—as did progressives, New Dealers, and champions of the Great Society, and as Obama himself wrote in *The Audacity of Hope* that he believes as well—that democracy requires at least rough economic equality, then the United States for several decades has been slipping further and further away from one of its central animating principles. Whatever Obama's political economy proves to be, his diagnosis of the problems of financial malfeasance and his initial proposals for its solution in *The Audacity of Hope* echo those of the progressives and New Dealers who constructed the regulatory apparatus that has been largely dismantled since 1980. Whether he attempts to live up to that commitment will prove one of the defining features of his presidency.

Unlike most of his colleagues in the Democratic Party, however, Obama has also acknowledged that regulation can fail, or go too far. In one of the most striking passages in *The Audacity of Hope*, he credits the Reagan revolution with removing some constraints that had ceased to serve a purpose but persisted only because of inertia and dogma. Distinctive among Democrats in recent decades, Obama criticizes members of his own party who have allowed themselves to be boxed in by their automatic opposition to all Republican Party initiatives. As a result Democrats often resist using market principles even when they are the appropriate tool for solving some social problems. Obama concedes that even the firmest of progressive principles yield only rough guidelines, not recipes or rule books. Like many of his teachers at Occidental, Columbia, and Harvard Law School, and like his colleague Sunstein in particular, Obama sees in the philosophy of pragmatism an escape from ideological straitjackets of multiple hues and a warrant for experimenting with different policies to see what works.

As I have noted, an important conceptual difference separates philosophical pragmatism, which emphasizes experimentation on principle as a way of testing provisional truths, from a vulgar pragmatism that bends before every breeze and has no principles to compromise. Philosophical pragmatists admit uncertainty, proclaim fallibilism, and welcome diverse points of view. For that reason, it can be hard to distinguish in practice between philosophical pragmatists willing to experiment and vulgar pragmatists who compromise for the sake of compromise, who seek accommodation merely to avoid conflict rather than to achieve results. In *The Audacity of Hope*, Obama makes clear that he understands the distinction. Only the historical record will show whether it remains equally clear in the Obama presidency.

Obama's criticism of one particular feature of the growing economic inequality in the United States is also a clear echo reverberating from the Progressive Era. When he notes in *The Audacity of Hope* that the pay of chief executive officers in America skyrocketed from 42 times the pay of the average worker in 1980 to 262 times in 2005—and by the time he was elected in 2008 it had become nearly 50 percent higher than that—and when he calls for renewed attention to economic regulation in the interest of the common good, he is invoking themes from earlier in the twentieth century. He notes that the purchasing power of average American workers remained flat between 1971 and 2001, almost certainly the longest period of stagnation in American history and a fact surprisingly little known and little discussed in public debate. During that period, the income of the best-paid Americans (the top hundredth of 1 percent) soared by nearly 500 percent. Wealth distribution is far more unequal now than it was in the 1970s, Obama observes accurately, which means that "levels of inequality are now higher than at any time since the Gilded Age" of the late nineteenth century. It was that problem that populists and progressive reformers set out to address. In *The Audacity of Hope*, as he did in the 2008 electoral campaign, Obama endorses the view of the fabulously wealthy Warren Buffet, who has pointed out that when he pays a smaller fraction of his income in taxes than does his secretary, the United States faces a serious problem of fairness. Even before the current recession Obama wrote that "our safety net is broken," and when he calls for equalizing the shares paid by the rich and the not so rich to fix that problem of unfairness, he is not importing ideas of socialism. Instead he is speaking a venerable American vernacular of egalitarianism, the language of John Adams and Thomas Jefferson; of Jane Addams, Louis Brandeis, and Woodrow Wilson; and of John Dewey, Franklin Roosevelt, and Lyndon Johnson.

Obama points out bluntly that there are no economic laws driving the increase in CEO compensation in recent decades. People in those positions worked just as hard before 1980. In nations where they are paid a fraction as much, they appear to work just as hard—and just as effectively, if not more effectively—than in the United States. Obama insists instead that the change has been cultural and that it will be reversed only when we return to earlier American ideas of justice as fairness. To make the point in *The Audacity of Hope*, Obama does not invoke Rawls's difference principle, which holds that inequalities must benefit the least advantaged, even though it would provide a sturdy argument for his case. Instead he invokes his mother's insistence on empathy, her advice that he should imagine himself in the position of those he was tempted to bully as a child. From his essay "Why Organize" through the 2008 presidential campaign, Obama stressed the importance, for citizens in a democracy, of seeing the world from the perspective of those who lack privileges many Americans take for granted.

Americans who profess to be untroubled by the nation's growing inequality, Obama writes in *The Audacity of Hope*, need just such reminders about the old-fashioned and only recently unfashionable virtues of sympathy and empathy. Strikingly, when the first opportunity came for Obama to nominate a justice for the Supreme Court, he singled out the importance of empathy as an indispensable characteristic. Equally strikingly, that emphasis came under attack when it was discovered that his nominee, Justice Sonia Sotomayor, had acknowledged that her status as a Latina born in Puerto Rico gives her a particular outlook on the world. Obama has demonstrated his own awareness of the cultural particularity of all experience;

seen in that light, Sotomayor's comment seemed uncontroversial, even banal. In his books Obama contrasts his experience as a man with a white mother and a black father to the experiences of both whites and blacks. "I can't help but view the American experience through the lens of a black man of mixed heritage," he writes in *The Audacity of Hope*, "forever mindful of how generations of people who looked like me were subjugated and stigmatized, and the subtle and not so subtle ways that race and class continue to shape our lives." But to those for whom the principle of neutrality represents the royal road to Truth, the observations that all experience is particular and historical, not universal, and that all knowledge is perspectival and partial, not objective, are not only unfamiliar but deeply troubling. Fortunately for Sotomayor, her sophisticated understanding of her positionality could be hushed up because her record as a judge could be shown to demonstrate that her background and sense of self had not "skewed" her decisions. Only then could she sail through her Senate hearings and be confirmed as a Supreme Court Justice.

Obama's insistence that justice as fairness should be considered in economic terms rather than merely as equal treatment before the law is hardly a novel position. Nor is it un-American, despite charges sparked by his brief exchange during the campaign with the fleetingly famous "Joe the Plumber." Instead, as I have noted, such concerns have surfaced repeatedly in American history from the eighteenth century until the present. Insistence that successful democratic government requires not only political equality but at least rough economic equality has been a persistent feature of American political thought and practice ever since the Puritans' strictures against excessive wealth. Contemporaries who hearken back to a simpler time of firmer principles might want to ponder the Puritans' strict sumptuary laws, the rules they used to guard against excessive consumption or displays of wealth as signs of sinful indulgence.

Of course not all Americans in the seventeenth or eighteenth century commanded equal resources. A great gulf separated landowner and successful attorney John Adams from landless servants, although it might be worth noting that a large gap also separated Adams himself from his shoemaker father. An even greater gulf separated Jefferson and Madison from poor farmers in Virginia, and it is obvious that an enormous chasm separated southern planters from their slaves. But unlike more recent conservatives, who make a virtue of inequality and claim that authentic Americans should see it as a spur to industry and productivity, seventeenth-, eighteenth-, and nineteenth-century Americans worried obsessively about the problem of great wealth because they feared it was inimical to democracy. They believed that an America marked by enormous fortunes would become an America too similar to the monarchies of Europe to remain a democracy.

Challenging inequality, far from manifesting a "socialist" or otherwise un-American propensity, instead descends in a direct line from the deepest and richest traditions of American culture. From the days when John Winthrop urged his fellow Puritans to "abridge ourselves of our superfluities" so that every member of the community could have enough to survive, the impulse to ensure that wealth is shared fairly is a fundamental American value that has only recently—and in increasingly brazen terms—been decried. It is also, as Winthrop did not hesitate to point out, the central message of the Christian scriptures. To pretend otherwise, which has been one of the most shrill and insistent claims of many self-proclaimed American traditionalists in recent decades, is to ignore not only the Beatitudes but also a central feature of American political and intellectual history that dates back to the early seventeenth century. It was hatred of the privileges accompanying great wealth that motivated many Europeans to emigrate to America in the first place. Anxiety about the consequences of enormous fortunes for popular government has animated American political movements ever since the 1770s, when the first American patriots challenged the prerogatives of wealthy British merchants and aristocrats whom they sent scurrying back to Britain or north to Canada. No citizen of the United States need apologize for criticizing inequality; it is instead the defense of inequality as beneficial that betrays the traditional American ideal of equality.

Obama also speaks the language of the social gospel, one of the most vigorous of the strands in the progressive reform coalition. In *The Audacity of Hope*, he criticizes his fellow Democrats for turning away from America's rich religious traditions in terms similar to those he used in his 2006 Washington address to Jim Wallis's conference "Building a Covenant for a New America." In *The Audacity of Hope*, Obama recounts his own decision to join the Chicago congregation of the Reverend Jeremiah Wright, the fiery preacher whose stinging criticism of American racism was to cause Obama such trouble in the spring of 2008. Neither Obama's mother nor her parents were churchgoers. His years in the primarily Islamic nation of Indonesia, where he spent two years in a public school and two more in a Catholic school, did not leave any imprint of either Muslim or Christian religious traditions. His first sustained engagement with organized religion came when he worked with the Catholic-sponsored Developing Communities Project in Chicago after graduating from Columbia. Although he reports being attracted to the idea that Christ had preached a social gospel and worked with the poor, Obama himself remained cool to the idea of religious faith. In Chicago he respected the dedication of the Catholics working in neighborhoods surrounding the grim Altgeld Gardens housing project, where he learned the ropes as a community organizer, and he was more puzzled than chastened when a black Baptist pastor told him that allying with Catholics placed him "on the wrong side of the battle."

From Obama's perspective at the time, all the rival religious doctrines seemed equally and excessively dogmatic. He realized that he was "a heretic," or perhaps not even that: "for even a heretic must believe in something, if nothing more than the truth of his own doubt." In the early stages of his work in Chicago, Obama was whipsawed between the cynicism of Gerald Kellman, the secular Jewish radical who hired him as an organizer (and who later converted to Catholicism himself), and his own distaste for the rivalry between the Catholic and Protestant congregations that had trouble working together on behalf of Chicago's poor. Obama dismissed the ideal of Christian fellowship as just another illusion, another spell to be broken. But slowly he began to change his mind.

Obama describes a meeting at which a few members of the Altgeld community reflected on the deep sadness they felt when they contrasted the memories of their own childhoods, poor but joyous, to the joyless mood of the children they knew. According to Wilbur, a janitor and self-appointed lay deacon in the Catholic parish of St. Catherine's, such children never smiled. Instead they seemed "worried all the time, mad about something. They got nothing they trust." Other residents chimed in. Before the meeting a woman named Mary, one of the few whites in the neighborhood, had asked Obama what motivated him to work in the community. For her, for Wilbur, and for their fellow Catholics, the passion to take Christ's message to the poor sprang from their faith. When she asked why Obama was there, he could muster no good answer. But after the meeting closed with a simple prayer for "the courage to turn things around," something inside him clicked. In the presence of others forging community from their shared anxieties and aspirations, Obama reports that he sensed "a feeling of witness, of frustration and hope," which passed through the gathering and at the end "hovered in the air, static and palpable." He sought out Mary and told her, "I don't think our reasons are all that different." Under the pressure of changing conditions, his perspective was shifting.

If Obama's own personal experience of community in Chicago gradually altered his attitude toward religious faith, firsthand experiences of the consequences of the absence of community made an even deeper impression. The random violence of gangs and a sobering encounter with armed and trigger-happy teenagers prompted his own epiphany: whereas even as a disaffected teen he had felt tied to a social order that enabled and forced him to discipline his "unruly maleness," to internalize the empathy and the guilt that restrained his impulses, the youths of Chicago's far south side lacked just those ties. They had "shut off access to any empathy they may once have felt," and as a result they were breaking away from the rest of the community and forming another clan, "speaking a different tongue, living by a different code." He saw in their eyes the same deadness Wilbur saw: such youths "just don't care." Understanding their contempt for the norms he had taken for granted made Obama realize, for the first time, that he was now afraid and why he had reason to be.

As he struggled to connect with the communities of the far south side and deploy their resources against the gangs' nihilism, Obama was told that he might have better luck if he had a "church home" of his own. But he was not tempted. His skepticism was deeply rooted. He suspected that even the older church-going blacks by now understood, as he did, the hollowness of the dreams that had prompted them to join the civil rights movement. They thought then that they had "marched for a higher purpose." They had mobilized "for rights and for principles and for all God's children." Eventually, though, they must have "realized that power was unyielding and principles unstable." At that moment, feeling enlightened by his own certainty of their disillusionment, he thought they must have understood that nothing had changed and that nothing would change. The enduring legacies of slavery and Jim Crow, persisting in residential and educational segregation and limited economic opportunity, continued to constrain the life chances of almost all African Americans. Briefly sharing the pessimism he projected onto black Chicagoans, Obama began worrying that the only freedom available was the freedom of escape. His own frustration, coupled with a yearning for some sense of accomplishment, prompted Obama himself to begin thinking about swapping community organizing for law school. He could and would return, he told himself, equipped with the expertise he lacked. He would be in a better position to get results when he brought back the Promethean fire of the law.

During the three years he spent working as a community organizer in Chicago, Obama became acquainted with more and more ministers and priests, more and more church-based social activists. Many of them earned his grudging admiration. Some were corrupt, others laughably inept, but most seemed genuinely committed to serving their congregations. Still he remained "a reluctant skeptic," unsure of his motives, "wary of expedient conversion, having too many quarrels with God to accept a salvation too easily won." While he was thinking about law school, Obama decided to investigate Trinity United Church of Christ, the church of Jeremiah Wright, a successful pastor recommended to him by several colleagues as a possible ally and resource. Belonging to a black Protestant congregation might not only slake his thirst for purpose, as he described it to Wallis's conference in Washington in the summer of 2006, it might also strengthen his ties to the black Chicagoans he was trying to organize. When they first met, Wright told Obama that some observers considered his church too radical and others thought it too moderate, some too bourgeois and others too working class. Obama was impressed by Wright's straightforward embrace of the traditions of black Christianity and his deliberate attempt to blend Christian and African elements in his church services. Obama read the "Black Value System" adopted by the Trinity congregation and liked what he saw. Its commitment to Christian activism and its emphasis on community, family, education, the work ethic, discipline, and respect resonated with his own maturing values—and with those his mother had worked so diligently to infuse in her young son.

Obama attended services at Trinity on a Sunday when Wright preached a sermon entitled "The Audacity to Hope." The message pierced Obama's armor of uncertainty. Listening to Wright, Obama writes, he felt for the first time the desire to surrender himself to a divine power that could help him, as it seemed others in the church had been helped, to recover from the knowledge that they had reached "a spiritual dead end," that they had been "cut off from themselves," that on their own they could not escape the desperation enveloping their communities. The black church embodied centuries of struggle, Obama realized, and Trinity seemed to him "a vessel carrying the story of a people into future generations and into a larger world." As a child, Wright explained in his sermon, he had failed to understand the point of religion himself. Not until he learned about the vertical dimension of his relation to God did the horizontal dimension of social service make sense. One member of the congregation that Sunday could feel pieces of a puzzle fitting into place. As the Trinity church service concluded, through tears that surprised him Obama "felt God's spirit beckoning me."

Obama links his own odyssey as a religious seeker to those of other Americans who have embraced religious traditions as adults. He notes that nearly all Americans consider themselves in some sense religious, a fact that bewilders secular Europeans and distinguishes the United States from the nations of Western Europe perhaps more decisively than any other feature of contemporary American culture. In discussions after I delivered preliminary versions of this analysis of Obama's books to audiences in British and European universities and civic groups from late 2008 through early 2010, I almost always encountered the same assertion: Obama must have converted to Christianity simply in order to make himself more palatable to the American electorate. Although plausible, this hypothesis seems to me unconvincing. First, although it might have helped Obama to have a "church home" had he continued working in Chicago, he was already expecting to leave for law school in a few months. Second, Obama must have known that joining Jeremiah Wright's congregation would carry risks as well as potential rewards for an ambitious public servant perhaps already contemplating electoral politics. Third, given his lifelong distrust of organized religion and his contempt for expedient conversions, it seems to me likelier that Obama converted from conviction than for strategic purposes. Perhaps his motives cannot be unwrapped; perhaps one reason need not rule out others.

Obama himself makes no attempt to disentangle the various strands that led to his decision to join Wright's congregation. Instead he merely relates his experience at Trinity. In the spirit of William James's *Varieties of Religious Experience*, Obama's conversion narrative rests on no metaphysical or theological foundation but only on his own felt experience. That is enough. It may be true that many devoutly religious American voters are not yet prepared to send an atheist to the White House. Obama's books as well as his speeches, however, indicate that his faith rests on a mature, well-considered commitment to African American traditions of Christianity rather than a desire simply to please religious voters. As he expressed it for those attending Wallis's 2006 "Building a Covenant" conference, his Christian faith has guided his own values and beliefs.

It is no surprise that people without religious faith are skeptical about those who profess such faith. When Obama casually observed, at a crucial moment during the primary elections for the Democratic Party nomination in the spring of 2008, that some Americans "cling to" religion as an anchor against cultural change and economic reform, some observers saw in his remarks evidence that, beneath the veneer, he too remains an agnostic. But his explanation of his comments, like his account of own conversion in *Dreams from My Father*, instead distinguished between religious traditions as a refuge against a changing world and as an inspiration for engaging with it.

The significance of that difference may not matter—or may seem strained—to atheists and fundamentalist Christians certain of the truth of their own very different convictions. But it is hardly a trivial distinction. Obama's self description as "Christian and skeptic" grows from a hardy strain of nondogmatic Christian political and social activism. That tradition originates in the Gospels, descends through bands of medieval friars, and has persisted for centuries among religious and lay Christians who seek neither glory nor glamour but only to do God's will, as they understand it, by serving the poor in a spirit of humility. It bears a striking resemblance to the form of religiosity that Lincoln expressed in the final years of his life, as Obama himself has noted. Rather than maligning communities of faith, Obama's comment about clinging to religion expressed the bewilderment shared by most progressives that so many Americans whose economic situations continue to deteriorate direct their anger against enemies (such as defenders of the right to abortion, gay marriage, and gun control) who exercise no real power over their lives instead of mobilizing against economic arrangements sustained by a plutocracy that wields real power quietly. The New Deal coalition fractured in the 1970s not only because of cultural fissures but because the American economy began to sag, and working-class whites began seeking explanations for their declining prospects. As the culture wars dating from those years have dragged on, Democrats have been unable to build from conditions of economic stagnation an electoral coalition as hardy as Roosevelt's, a vigorous movement animated by what Obama terms "economic populism."

Obama's off-the-cuff comment about people clinging to religion, based on his shrewd understanding of his party's conundrum, was spun by pundits into a denunciation of religion inconsistent with his own Christian faith and practice and his earlier expositions of his view of the relation between politics and religion. The charge stuck because of a much deeper and more significant rift among

Americans professing religious belief. The very gulf to which Obama pointed in his Washington address now threatened to swallow his candidacy.

The gulf now separating the social and political as well as theological beliefs of liberal, often highly educated, and frequently affluent Protestants, Catholics, and Jews from their more conservative and frequently less affluent coreligionists, and especially from evangelical Protestants, has continued to widen. Because of that divide, many believers on the left now have more in common with each other than they do with other members of their own denominations, with whom they disagree on many controversial questions. To many traditionalists, such progressives—like Obama himself—hardly seem to be religious at all, because so much of what they embrace varies so starkly from those values that culturally conservative Americans cherish. Given that wider context, it was not difficult for his critics to portray Obama's frustration with his political difficulties as opposition to religion itself, at least religion as members of many American denominations understand it. American history (like every nation's history) is distinctive for many reasons, but the presence of multiple religious traditions, none of which can plausibly claim official status, is surely among the most striking features of the United States, as Obama understands. Inasmuch as the recent cross-denominational split dividing liberals from conservatives erodes that long-standing tradition of religious pluralism, it threatens to weaken Americans' toleration of diversity and reinforce the polarization that

Obama, like Robert Putnam and other students of civil society, considers so debilitating, and that impedes the operation of Rawls's overlapping consensus.

The risks attached to Obama's choice of Jeremiah Wright's church became clear later in the campaign for the Democratic presidential nomination. Had Obama not delivered his memorable speech on race in Philadelphia on March 18, 2008, his candidacy might well have gone down on the shoals of Wright's hard-edged anger. To me and to many Americans, Wright's rage over American race relations seemed understandable and entirely justified. To us, Obama's repudiation of his pastor suggested that he might be pandering to American Pollyannas who pretend the nation's race problem has been solved. But after rereading and reflecting on it, I have changed my mind about Obama's speech. It provides one of the clearest expositions of his attitude toward the contingency and partiality of cultural values. In his illuminating, blow-by-blow account of Obama's path to the presidency, his campaign manager David Plouffe confirms what others said at the time. For his Philadelphia speech Obama did not need the assistance of his speech writer Jon Favreau, and not only because Obama remained the "best writer in the campaign," in Plouffe's words. Obama told Plouffe, "I already know what I want to say in this speech. I've been thinking about it for twenty years." It shows.

Obama began his already classic address by taking a leaf from Wright's own book, noting accurately that some Americans considered him too black to run for president while others considered him not black enough. He acknowledged that he is not African American but the child of a black African father and a white American mother. He explained that he understands the difference. He also made clear that he understands the reasons why so many African Americans share Wright's anger about the continuing consequences of slavery for blacks in the United States. Blacks typically experience inferior schools, encounter greater obstacles to employment and affluence, and confront persistent racism that poisons even the lives of many blacks who manage to succeed economically. Nothing in Obama's Philadelphia speech soft-peddles those stark facts. But instead of freezing that reality and authorizing that perception, Obama contextualized it.

He shifted his focus from the lives and perceptions of African Americans, perceptions grounded in generations of painful experience, to the resentments of white Americans. He pointed out that most whites have been struggling economically for decades. As they watched a few blacks rise to positions of prominence, they resented the government programs that they had been told, ever since Reagan's election as governor of California, were responsible for their own stagnating conditions. Such whites were angry too, and they had grown accustomed to directing that anger against blacks. From their point of view, many African Americans lived irresponsibly and took unfair advantage of welfare and affirmative action programs.

In his Philadelphia speech, Obama acknowledged the

gulf dividing the experience of blacks and whites in America. He also acknowledged the reasons why they saw each other as they did. Different realities had shaped their different perceptions. In other words, he was practicing the perspectivalism and cultural interpretivism he had learned in school. But rather than preaching such principles to his audience, he characteristically personalized that cultural division and brought it to life. Although he disagreed with Jeremiah Wright's "incendiary language," he could not disown the pastor who had awakened his Christian faith, married him and baptized his children, and "been like family to me." Nor could Obama disown his white grandmother, even though she had expressed a fear of black men who passed her on the street and sometimes used "racial or ethnic stereotypes that made me cringe." She loved him "as much as she loves anything in the world," and his love for her was equally unconditional. His own bonds to his black pastor and his white grandmother, just as much as his occasional unhappiness with their ways of thinking, talking, and acting, encapsulated the complexity of American race relations. They were both right, and they were both wrong. Americans had to learn to see both sides, as decision makers in any conflict had to do. Americans had to suspend judgment, even though they wanted passionately to accuse, to hate, to renounce. They had to understand, as Obama himself had learned to understand, that resolving conflicts requires, first, resisting the temptation to state one's beliefs dogmatically; second, seeing the situation from the point of view of one's adversary; and third, empathizing across differences in order to find common ground.

Obama's sharpest criticism of Wright revealed one more dimension of his sensibility. The two agreed on the history of American race relations. Obama indicted slavery and elaborated on its enduring legacy of hatred and injustice. But he could not accept Wright's judgment that America was perpetually locked in the stranglehold of Jim Crow. Wright spoke "as if America was static," as if the tragic problems of the past would persist inevitably and indefinitely into the future. Instead the "true genius of the nation," Obama insisted, "is that America can change." From his high school days in Honolulu to his presidential campaign, Obama had wrestled with the world-weary advice of well-meaning friends and political radicals who assured him that racism would remain as bad as it had always been. He never bought it. As a teenager Obama could not share his black friends' comments about "white folks" without thinking about the love of his mother and her parents. When his education continued in college and law school, he learned another set of reasons to doubt the cynics. He learned that the United States has been changing from the moment the nation ratified its Constitution. That commitment to change is written into the nation's DNA. When Wright froze American racism into a fixed feature of the national culture, he was betraying two principles Obama embraced: democracy and historicism.

After the Philadelphia speech, some of Obama's critics on the left excoriated him for abandoning Wright. Obery

Hendricks, Jr., wrote that Obama subjected Wright to "a humiliating public betrayal." He compared the ostracizing of Wright to white supremacists' gruesome 1899 lynching of Sam Hose, as brutal and sadistic an example of human cruelty as the American historical record contains. Clarence Thomas, when he was nominated to the Supreme Court, accused those opposing his confirmation of engineering a "high-tech lynching." Thomas went on to be confirmed, but this time, according to Hendricks, the term fit: as a result of the media frenzy fed by Obama's speech, Wright suffered "social death." Others on the left accused Obama of equating blacks' and whites' resentments, as though centuries of suffering under slavery and Jim Crow were somehow balanced by the frustrations felt by whites in recent decades.

Obama's critics on the right, by contrast, charged that he had excused Wright's anti-Americanism and thrown America under the bus. From conservatives' perspective, Obama had it backwards. When he urged struggling whites to direct their resentments against "a corporate culture rife with inside dealing" and "short-term greed," a political culture "dominated by lobbyists and special interests," and "economic policies that favor the few over the many," he was blaming the free-enterprise system for problems that American conservatives thought only a capitalist system untainted by government intrusions could solve. In other words, both the Left and the Right wanted Obama to endorse their own diagnosis of America's ills; neither side was willing to give an inch. The dogmatic statement of beliefs, the rejection of opponents' perspectives, and the denial of empathy across the racial divide character-ized some of the most strident responses to Obama's speech from Left and Right alike.

Obama closed his Philadelphia speech with a little story about a young white woman named Ashley. When his South Carolina volunteers were explaining why they had joined the Obama campaign, Ashley told the story of her mother, who had to file for bankruptcy after she was diag-nosed with cancer when Ashley was nine. Ashley assured her mother she loved mustard and relish sandwiches, the cheapest food available, so they could survive until her mother could return to work. Ashley said she had volun-teered for Obama because she wanted a health care system that would help other children and their parents. Others in the room gave their reasons and endorsed their favorite causes, until finally they came to an older black man who didn't point to any particular issue or even mention Obama himself. In Obama's words, "He simply says to everyone in the room, 'I am here because of Ashley.'" Obama conceded that such human connections are not enough. They will not improve health care or the economy or education. But "that single moment of recognition be-tween that young white girl and that old black man," he concluded, "is where we start."

When Obama told Plouffe he had been working on the Philadelphia speech for twenty years, he was right. Plac-ing the speech in the context of arguments drawn from civic republicanism and communitarianism, from discourse ethics and deliberative democracy, from historicism and Rawls's overlapping consensus, from Geertz's hermeneutics and the neopragmatists' emphasis on fallibilism, it is easy to see in the speech most of the principal components of Obama's worldview. If he did not convince all his critics—and he certainly did not—the speech did enable him to express his deep-seated commitments to listening, respecting those who disagree, and valuing empathy as a necessary if not sufficient condition for democratic politics. In the poignant story of "that young white girl and that old black man," Obama encapsulated central features of his sensibility and of his campaign.

Obama's religious conversion had enabled him to put together several forms of realism, and it is not surprising that commentators have noted the Augustinian or Niebuhrian quality of his Christianity. From his Indonesian stepfather, Obama learned that the world is a cruel, unyielding place in which individuals survive by playing the cards they are dealt. From his grandfather's friend Frank Davis, he learned that for blacks the fact of racism cannot be avoided no matter how hard one tries. From his mentors and his associates in Chicago organizing, he learned that the secret to politics is power. From Wright, he learned that Christianity is a fighting faith, a source of resolution that can stiffen backbones in the face of enduring hatred. Christian love, Obama came to understand, requires more than his mother's and grandfather's gauzy, wistful dreams of human brotherhood. It requires instead a commitment to justice that is deep enough—fierce enough—to enable one to withstand resistance without abandoning hope. "I'm skinny, but I'm tough," Obama is fond of telling crowds. That toughness manifests itself in an imperturbability that some critics find eerie and others maddening. It can surely be traced to the hard knocks of his childhood, the steady diet of rebuffs and failures he experienced in Chicago organizing, and the matter-of-factness of his friends on the far south side and his relatives in Kenya, whose firsthand knowledge of the world's injustice did not break their spirit. Important as all those influences have been, *Dreams from My Father* shows that Obama's steeliness in the face of opposition comes just as powerfully from the resources of African American Christianity, a tradition that has sustained people suffering from and struggling against forms of evil far deeper than those he has had to confront in his own life.

In light of his own religious faith as well as his sense of the spirituality of the American public, Obama has stressed repeatedly his bewilderment that so many of his fellow Democrats refuse to talk about religion. That refusal, he writes in *The Audacity of Hope*, not only has left such Democrats vulnerable to cultural conservatives' charges of Godlessness, it has also robbed his party of one of the most valuable resources available in public life. "I think Democrats are wrong to run away from a debate about values," Obama writes. "It is the language of values that people use to map their world. It is what can inspire them to take action, and move them beyond their isolation." Like the overwhelming majority of Americans outside the small subculture of academic life, Obama locates the foundation of his own moral principles in his religious faith, implausible or problematical as that feature of his sensibility may be to many academics on both sides of the Atlantic.

Obama has never suggested that he thinks religion provides the only foundation for an ethical life. In his inaugural address he went out of his way, when listing the various religious traditions that attract large numbers of Americans, to include "nonbelievers." To some that seems momentous, to others a trivial gesture. To others it shows simply the cagey Obama's awareness that most of his colleagues in the academic world do not share the religious faith that he, along with most Americans, claims to embrace. But viewed within the broader framework of Obama's ideas, and particularly in light of his discussion of religion and the need to create an overlapping consensus through public debate, it is hardly surprising that Obama has repeatedly urged Americans to tolerate those with different beliefs. He believes that spirit of toleration should extend in both directions, from the religious to the nonreligious and vice versa.

Obama himself has faced head-on the challenge of discussing the implications of his beliefs for politics. He reiterates in *The Audacity of Hope* his conviction that "shared values" ought to be "at the heart of our politics." In that spirit he aggressively disputes a familiar distinction, which dates from the era of the Cold War, between what the philosopher Isaiah Berlin called negative and positive liberty.

Obama echoes instead the arguments that Dewey made repeatedly from the 1890s through the 1940s, arguments that seem less familiar in twenty-first-century American and European academic debates than they were in the United States during the first half of the twentieth century, during the years before they were banished by analytic philosophers. Obama contends that "freedom from," or negative liberty, makes no sense in the absence of "freedom to," or positive liberty, which he describes as "the ideal of opportunity and the subsidiary values that help realize opportunity." Formal freedom is meaningless unless individuals possess the resources, both economic and cultural, that enable them to make use of their freedom.

This formulation clearly hearkens back to the republican understanding of freedom shared by Adams, Jefferson, and Madison, emphasized by Tocqueville, and updated by Brandeis, Addams, and Dewey in the era of progressive reform. From this point of view, freedom has never been a matter of simply being left alone to do whatever one wants to do. It has always been a question of disciplining impulses according to ethical principles and considering the demands of the common good. Ronald Reagan opened a new era in American history when he invited Americans to ask whether they were better off, as individuals, than they were four years earlier, and to vote accordingly. Although William McKinley's "full-dinner-pail" campaign in 1896 offered a similar promise of personal prosperity, and some Republican candidates in the 1920s had followed his lead, the unvarnished appeal to economic self-interest has been somewhat rare in American politics. No eighteenth-century candidate for office would have considered such an appeal to individual self-interest; it was inconsistent with the civic virtue required for republican government, and it eroded the self-sacrifice citizens were expected to show. All the founders' appeals were couched in terms of the public good, which was understood to transcend the desires or the well-being of any single individual.

In Obama's effort to shift American public discourse away from obsessive concern with freedom *from* government, famously defined by Reagan as "the problem" of American life rather than a means to its solution, Obama knows he is trying to resuscitate a much older way of thinking about politics. His invocations of the public good have roots that stretch much more deeply into American history than do the strident appeals to individual self-interest that have become almost reflexive across the political spectrum in the last three decades. The American Revolution emerged from a constellation of ideas with religious and ethical as well as political and economic dimensions. Although Americans who flatten that rich body of ideas by emphasizing only the right to make and spend money sometimes call themselves conservatives, they show limited understanding of the complexity of their nation's founding ideals.

Also echoing that persistent American tradition of civic republicanism are the following words from *The Audacity of Hope*: "Our individualism has always been bound by a set of communal values, the glue upon which every healthy society depends." Obama insists that Americans value "community," "patriotism," "a sense of duty and sacrifice on behalf of our nation. We value a faith in something bigger than ourselves, whether that something expresses itself in formal religion or ethical precepts." Finally, he writes, "we value the constellation of behaviors that express our mutual regard for one another: honesty, fairness, humility, kindness, courtesy, and compassion." A similar litany punctuated Obama's acceptance speech the night of the election and his inaugural address, and it seems safe to predict that he will continue to repeat this message as he attempts to reorient the Democratic Party toward the values of empathy and reciprocity, two of the central animating norms of American democratic culture. The reformist traditions Obama has inherited, ranging from the antebellum crusade against slavery through the progressive, New Deal, and civil rights movements, all grounded their arguments on calls to community and the Christian ideal of brotherhood. In her brilliant study of contemporary American political culture, *Talking to Strangers*, Danielle Allen identifies self-sacrifice as an indispensable and seldom acknowledged characteristic of democratic citizenship. Like Obama's implicit argument in *Dreams from My Father*, Allen's case rests firmly on Ellison's *Invisible Man*. Only by fusing individual responsibility—the willingness to sacrifice—with the aspiration to equality can democracy's potential be realized and the principle affirmed. If contemporary Democrats hope to inspire a new wave of challenges to injustice and inequality, once again with an emphasis on economic reform as well as civil rights, they are neglecting the strongest weapons in the American cultural arsenal if they ignore the rich heritage of earlier progressive activists who called for justice on the basis of principles at the heart of America's religious as well as civic traditions.

Among the signature features of Obama's books is his self-consciousness. He realizes that the idealism of the preceding sentences, at least for some readers, might sound too much like the Boy Scout handbook. So he spices such words, drawn from the communitarian recipe file, with directness. He concedes that balancing individualism and community has never been easy. He admits that we have to keep in mind both the importance of cherished values and the potential danger of rigid ideologies. As he puts it, in a phrase that would evoke a nod of assent from James or Dewey, "Values are faithfully applied to the facts before us, while ideology overrides whatever facts call theory into question." Obama's voting record, both in Illinois and in the U.S. Senate, shows clearly that he is a man of the left. But his books make it equally clear that he is flexible in his application of his convictions to particular problems. He is a principled partisan of democracy and pragmatism in the tradition of James and Dewey. He believes in the founders' ideals of equality and liberty. But he believes that achieving those goals requires working to forge agreement about forms of democratic experimentation, and he believes that those experiments must be followed by the critical assessment of results. Instead of the rigid stands some of his ardent supporters on the left demand, he prefers the pragmatists' counsel of dynamic, flexible responses to a dynamic, recalcitrant reality.

That willingness to compromise, that commitment to fallibilism and experimentation, does not reveal a lack of conviction. Instead it evinces a particular kind of conviction, the conviction of a democrat committed to forging agreement rather than deepening disagreements. Whereas many radicals as well as many conservatives believe that they possess the truth and that their opponents are evil as well as misguided, Obama accepts different political perspectives as a normal and healthy sign of a vibrant culture. When he says, as he did in his health care address of September 13, 2009, that "I still believe we can replace acrimony with civility," and when he praises Gandhi "because he ended up doing so much and changing the world just by the power of his ethics," he is deliberately signaling a different conception of politics than that to which most Americans have grown accustomed in recent years.

Obama also embraces a more complex and nuanced conception of democracy. He understands that even virtue can veer into vice. Self-reliance and independence can morph into selfishness and license, ambition into greed, patriotism into jingoism, faith into self-righteousness, and charity into paternalism. Finding the right balance, Obama acknowledges, requires care, the courage to experiment, and the willingness to listen, a quality increasingly rare in our ever more acrimonious polity. Obama reasons that our critics can sometimes help us see our excesses more clearly than we can see them ourselves. They can show us how our plans collide with "countervailing values" cherished with equal fervor by other Americans. In *The Audacity of Hope*, Obama offers as an illustration his own experience shepherding through the Illinois legislature a modified bill on capital punishment that eventually earned unanimous approval, then he immediately concedes that such compromises often prove elusive. The first year of his presidency proved the point.

Obama is a shrewd and an unusually well-informed observer of American political life and the so-called culture wars of recent decades. He knows that many searching studies of contemporary American public life, including those written by journalist E. J. Dionne, sociologist Alan Wolfe, and political scientist Morris Fiorina, have reached a similar conclusion: Americans are much less divided on most so-called wedge issues than members of the fringes of both parties claim. In poll after poll, study after study, social scientists have found that the vast majority of Americans, over 80 percent in many instances, cluster toward the middle on questions such as abortion, gay marriage, gun control, and immigration restriction. Whereas activists in both parties have forced their candidates to embrace positions at opposite ends of the spectrum on these hot-button issues as litmus tests of their ideological purity, the bulk of the American electorate lies between the poles. To use the title of E. J. Dionne's penetrating study, that dynamic explains why Americans hate politics.

Both parties continue to feed voters false choices, stark, less nuanced positions than those held by most citizens. According to Dionne, Wolfe, Fiorina, and others who have studied recent polling data or conducted such studies themselves, Americans are willing to allow individuals a surprising degree of latitude to make their own decisions on many controversial issues, and they do not think of themselves as lacking convictions as a result. Their toleration does not mean Americans do not hold firm positions themselves; it certainly does not mean there is consensus. The disagreements are real. It means only that most Americans are more willing to accept the existence of diverse opinions, and a wider variation of practices, than journalists' shallow and sensation-driven coverage of extremists' melodramatic posturing suggests. Whereas opinion polls yield clear evidence of greater tolerance, and even a surprising degree of overlapping consensus on many divisive issues, public debate is dominated by those who are well paid to enflame passions and snuff out sparks of civility.

Obama has shown that he shares the widespread American value of toleration. He laments the developments that have prompted Left and Right to become "mirror images of each other," telling stories of "conspiracy, of America being hijacked by an evil cabal." He sees that activists' reliance on such hyperbole serves "not to persuade the other side" but only "to keep their bases agitated and assured of the rightness of their respective causes." He is willing to tolerate disagreement and diverse ways of life as a central and, on balance, enriching feature of a pluralistic culture of democracy. He is not naive about the reasons for the coarsening of public discourse. To the press, "civility is boring." He also understands the costs of that coarsening. The "amplification of conflict" exaggerates differences to such a degree that one's opponents appear not merely wrongheaded but demonic, which renders all their positions illegitimate and all their preferences contemptible. That downward spiral steadily erodes the potential for overlapping consensus, "the basis for thoughtful compromise," and even threatens "an agreed-upon standard for judging the truth." Among the most unsettling consequences of antifoundationalist particularism, perspectivalism, and historicism has been the embrace by some conservatives (and some liberals) of the belief that all facts can be spun to fit the desired conclusion. If all evidence is tainted, then perspectivalism provides a warrant for doubting any results of scientific inquiry inconsistent with one's political or social ideology. Obama remains committed to treating his adversaries with a degree of respect that his supporters find worrisome and his foes spineless. But he also insists, as did New York senator Daniel Patrick Moynihan, that although everyone is entitled to his or her own opinion, no one is entitled to his or her own facts.

There are limits to Obama's broad-mindedness, but they are not always what either his allies or his foes expect. To cite one example, he adopts an unusual position concerning urban black culture. On the one hand, like most

Democrats he emphasizes attacking the problem of poverty directly. But he insists that as valuable as an increase in the earned income tax credit and a higher minimum wage might be, empowerment also requires responsibility, honesty, and a willingness to work. Words that some Democratic politicians have been wary of pronouncing in recent decades, words such as faithfulness and integrity, words that I and other commentators such as William Galston have identified with the virtues of liberalism, recur in Obama's writings and his speeches. In his stark portrait of teenagers with nothing to lose because they care about nothing, he shows that the absence of community can be as devastating and dangerous as the presence of community can be enriching. Obama's emphasis on community grew from his education, but it also grew from his harrowing experiences in Chicago housing projects and from the inspiration he derived from the religious congregations he came to know. He can face the fact that gang members' nihilism has devastating consequences, a conviction shared by urban black civic and religious leaders and by southern and southwestern evangelicals, without being paralyzed by fear that such criticism will be denounced as racist.

Obama's approach to the problems facing impoverished women, white and black, is also distinctive. On the one hand, Obama advocates the full agenda of second-wave feminism: better job training, universal access to affordable and high-quality child care, and, perhaps above all, flexible work schedules. This is the program laid out by many feminists, including pragmatist scholars Joan Williams and Nancy Fraser. Obama uses the work of Amelia Tyagi and Elizabeth Warren (the latter of whom he brought into his administration to oversee the Troubled Assets Recovery Program) to demonstrate that women are working not to increase their families' discretionary incomes but to invest in their children's future. With more than 70 percent of mothers working outside the home, and members of the middle as well as working classes squeezed by flat incomes and quadrupling health care bills, it is time to stop pretending that Ward and June Cleaver remain the norm for American family life. More often now in the realm of myth than in reality do American women tend the home while most men, even though they are working ever longer hours, bring home with a single paycheck what used to be called, in a phrase that now seems quaint, "a family wage."

On the other hand, Obama also issues a bold call for reorienting male sensibilities and reinvigorating family life, a summons he bolsters by explaining why he has found his wife Michelle's rock-solid family such an inspiration. Her father suffered from multiple sclerosis from age thirty. Despite the enormous effort required by everyone involved, he kept working as he and his family struggled through the thirty-five years of steady deterioration that marked the rest of his life. After decades of criticism leveled by black and white radicals against prominent members of the black bourgeoisie who have lamented the instability of black family life, positions such as Obama's have been unpopular on the left. In the face of defenses of free expression made by cynical entrepreneurs who exploit that freedom to stoke a culture of violence and misogyny, adopting the stance on the importance of intact families that Obama has taken in both of his books appears to some commentators to be conservative.

Perhaps that response explains why it has become difficult for many Democrats, black as well as white, to take a stand against the hip culture of celebrity, money, guns, drugs, and hypersexuality that Obama considers so destructive, particularly, if hardly exclusively, of African American urban life. Obama's words have antagonized some Americans who think of themselves as being on the left, whites as well as blacks, who see in his critiques proof that he is too middle class, or not black enough, or too much "the town scold," as he puts it himself, to speak for African Americans. In his books Obama acknowledges that criticism but defies it. Instead he insists that Democrats are making a fatal error if they allow the importance of family life, like the role of religion, to be considered the issue of a single party. Both black and white working-class voters have been put off by the failure of Democratic Party politicians to acknowledge the cultural cost of America's unraveling families. Perhaps because Obama lacked the stability he cherishes in his wife's family, and perhaps because he saw firsthand the consequences of fractured families in Chicago's far south side, he speaks and writes passionately about the importance of family life.

That observation brings me to the final issue I want to address, race and ethnicity. Obama admits that many people see his prominence as an indication the United States has become, as he puts it in *The Audacity of Hope*, a "postracial" society. He notes that demographic projections indicate how quickly the rest of the nation is likely to follow California in becoming "majority minority." The predominance of Americans who claim European ancestry is rapidly becoming a thing of the past. Incisive scholars have been writing about this phenomenon for a couple of decades now. Literary scholars such as Werner Sollors and Henry Louis Gates, Jr., sociologists such as Mary Waters, political scientists such as Michael Walzer and Jennifer Hochschild, philosophers such as Kwame Anthony Appiah, and historians such as David Hollinger and Ronald Takaki are just a few of the many writers who have probed the significance of these demographic and cultural changes.

In my own teaching of American history, I have found particularly valuable Hollinger's book *Postethnic America*, not only because it captures the changes of recent decades but because it places those changes in the much longer trajectory running from the late nineteenth-century imposition of Jim Crow through the immigration restriction of the 1920s to the recent emergence of the ideals of color blindness and multiculturalism. Hollinger holds out an ideal that he calls "affiliation by revocable assent," by which he means that individuals should enjoy the freedom to embrace or renounce any aspects of their biological and cultural inheritance that they choose. Gates and Sollors have advanced their own versions of this idea. But these scholars contrast white ethnics' power to highlight or downplay any part of their increasingly complicated lineage, if they choose to do so, to the unfreedom of ascribed or imposed identity forced on blacks by America's "one-drop rule," which stipulates that any African blood makes a person legally black.

Although demography may be destiny, and the rates of intermarriage among members of most ethnic groups continue to accelerate, the black–white divide in the United States remains sharp. In most parts of the world, Barack Obama is considered to be mixed race. In America, he is black, and he cannot escape everything that others ascribe to him or impose on him as a result of that simple fact and all it implies. Although Obama acknowledges and celebrates the changes that the United States has experienced since the civil rights movement, he is justifiably cautious about declaring the battle won. Obama resists the strategic racial solidarity so persuasively championed by Tommie Shelby in *We Who Are Dark* in favor of a position closer to Eddie Glaude's explicit embrace of philosophical pragmatism in his book *In a Shade of Blue*. Glaude finds inspiration in the writings of James and Dewey for his antiessentialist politics, which is oriented toward affirming the varieties of African American religious experiences for purposes of democratic reconstruction. According to both Shelby and Glaude, racial and cultural identities are not something fixed, a treasure to be uncovered through archaeology, but a set of resources to be deployed pragmatically. Sharing that insight, they differ in their judgments concerning the most fruitful strategic choices.

A controversy that erupted in the summer of 2009 illustrates just how volatile such issues remain. When Gates returned to his home in Cambridge, Massachusetts, from a trip to China, he found himself confronted by a white police officer sent to investigate a reported break-in. After showing identification to prove he was standing in his own home, the African American Gates objected to the officer's manner, the officer objected to Gates's, and the distinguished and famously personable scholar found himself hauled off in handcuffs. When Obama used the word "stupidly" to describe the way the Cambridge police responded—a word that I and most people who know Gates consider appropriate (if ill-considered) in the circumstances—he ignited a firestorm. No matter what Obama said or did, including inviting both men to the White House for a beer, the furor would not die. The president's campaign to "lower the temperature" in America—not only on the issue of race but on the other issues of the culture wars—crashed against a wall of prejudice that had been obscured but not destroyed by his election. Whatever progress has been made, Americans continue to interpret such highly charged interactions through filters that predispose them reflexively to blame blacks—or whites—whenever things get out of hand. The reverberations of the Gates affair indicate how very far the United States remains from being a postracial society: polls indicate that a poorly chosen adverb, uttered at the end of a long press conference, ignited brush fires of racist invective that might have long-term consequences for Obama's presidency. Racial discrimination may be illegal, but racism persists.

The issue of race remains uniquely volcanic in American history, and that fact reminds Obama that pragmatism and democracy are sometimes not enough. In *The Audacity of Hope* he points out that slavery was the one question in American history on which there could be, finally, no compromise. Indeed, from the very beginning, when the first enslaved Africans arrived in Virginia almost four centuries ago, slavery and its legacy have provided the overwhelming, undeniable proof of the limitations of the American democratic project. Notwithstanding the "genius" of the amendable Constitution, its architects were, to repeat Obama's apt phrase, "blind to the whip and the chain." The persistence of slavery mocked the ideals of freedom and equality and the ethic of reciprocity. It cast a shadow over Americans' boasts about the comparatively small gaps between their rich and their poor. Obama refers to the heroic struggles fought by slaves and abolitionists, who learned from experience that on the question of slavery, "power would concede nothing without a fight." The intransigence of Frederick Douglass and the moral integrity of those who demanded the immediate end of slavery—not the moderation urged by their antislavery allies—changed the climate of debate. Tellingly, Obama draws from the Civil War the lesson that "it has not always been the pragmatist, the voice of reason, or the force of compromise, that has created the conditions for liberty."

Yet from his realization that the battle to end slavery was ultimately won by those who refused to compromise, Obama draws a lesson both unexpected and unconventional, especially for an African American on the left. He writes that he is chastened by the example of such antislavery absolutists whenever he encounters zealots today. Although he deprecates the extremism of some contemporary activists, he finds himself wondering if they might someday be thought right and the rest of us wrong. He is very careful not to extend that observation to any particular contemporary controversy, but readers cannot help making that leap themselves. Nothing in Obama's books suggests that he has second thoughts about his stances on hot-button issues such as abortion, capital punishment, gun control, or gay rights. Yet his measured comments concerning the implications of our contemporary admiration for radical abolitionists shows yet again the sophistication of his historicism. "I'm reminded," he writes, "that deliberation and the constitutional order may sometimes be the luxury of the powerful, and that it has sometimes been the cranks, the zealots, the prophets, the agitators, and the unreasonable—in other words, the absolutists—that have fought for a new order." It was Frederick Douglass, William Lloyd Garrison, and John Brown, not their moderate opponents, who forced the issue of abolition. With that awareness, Obama continues, "I can't summarily dismiss those possessed of similar certainty today—the antiabortion activist who pickets my town hall meeting, or the animal rights activist who raids a laboratory—no matter how deeply I disagree with their views." It is one thing to acknowledge that we have come a long way from slavery and from other cruelties of the past. All politicians can play that tune. It is quite another to extend that logic to one's own convictions, which Obama does by raising the open-ended question about how posterity will judge our own moderation—and our own forms of zealotry. In that brief, remarkable, and little noticed passage about his reaction to contemporary extremists in *The Audacity of Hope*, Obama again demonstrates his acute self-consciousness.

Obama acknowledges, perhaps more fully than any prominent figure in twenty-first-century American public life, the undeniable undertow exerted by historicism and antifoundationalism on all our most deeply held convictions. Yet he is not paralyzed by that understanding. Obama is able to interrogate his own convictions—to place them in a broader cultural and historical context by imaginatively scrutinizing them from a position centuries in the future—without abandoning them, much as William James did. Speaking at the dedication of the memorial erected on the Boston Common to honor the black and white members of the Massachusetts 54th Regiment in the Civil War, James passionately praised their heroic sacrifice. James understood, more clearly than some critics who have characterized his philosophy of pragmatism as lacking backbone, that one can be willing to die for a principle even though he understands that it may be contingent. For James, that was the meaning of "civic courage" in a democracy. Obama's awareness of the precariousness of even our most deeply held beliefs seems to me among the most unusual features of his sensibility. Some critics think it makes his convictions less solid. They may be proven right. But his heartfelt comments about American soldiers (including his own maternal grandfather, who fought in World War II) indicate the depth of, and the reasons for, his admiration for those who have shown themselves willing not only to affirm but to die in defense of their nation's principles of freedom, equality, and democracy.

Will Obama's exceptional self-consciousness make him less willing to kill for those principles than some other presidents have been? The strident tone of his inaugural address and the startling speed and extent of his expansion of the American military's role in Afghanistan suggest the opposite. In the sphere of international relations, Obama may prove no more successful in using philosophical pragmatism to harness his ambitions than was Woodrow Wilson. Dewey cheered the pragmatist strand he discerned in Wilson's decision to enter World War I; he accepted Wilson's explanation that the nation was going to war to create an international organization that would end war. But as wars so often do, that war had a way of transforming even the most scrupulously principled philosophical pragmatists into zealots. Dewey later accepted

Bourne's criticism and regretted his support for Wilson's failed crusade.

Obama seems convinced that the United States can control the threat of terrorism only by transforming a nation that for centuries has consisted of a loose confederation of largely autonomous and often cantankerous clans into a united, stable, law-abiding constitutional democracy. He has not always been so sure of America's power to perform such alchemy. In *The Audacity of Hope* he quotes from his October 2002, speech against the Iraq War. He predicted, accurately, that even "a successful war against Iraq will require a U. S. occupation of undetermined length, at undetermined cost, with undetermined consequences." Invading Iraq "without a clear rationale and without strong international support" would risk strengthening the appeal of Al Qaeda, which can be defeated only if the United States can win the long battle for the hearts and minds of Muslim dissidents worldwide. Many Americans skeptical about Obama's decision to commit more U.S. troops in Afghanistan—as I am—wonder whether he has read that speech since becoming commander in chief.

A string of self-confident world powers, beginning with Alexander the Great and continuing through Great Britain in the nineteenth century and the Soviet Union in the twentieth, have failed to remake Afghanistan in their image. If the United States follows their lead, we will see whether Obama's stated commitment to the critical assessment of results—and the resolution to change course when necessary rather than follow dogma blindly—extends from the domain of domestic politics to that of foreign affairs. Time will tell whether he has the courage to admit a mistake. Obama wrote, concerning Iraq, that he does not oppose every war, only "a dumb war, a rash war, a war based not on reason but on passion, not on principle but on politics." Because he understands that democracy requires deliberation, an ethic of reciprocity, and a culture committed to the peaceful resolution of conflicts, he knows that the United States "cannot impose democracy with the barrel of a gun." But with Al Qaeda now thought to be headquartered somewhere in the mountains of Pakistan, and with corruption apparently as pervasive as ever in Afghan public affairs, many Americans will continue to ask whether war in Afghanistan makes any more sense than did the war in Iraq that Obama eloquently opposed. As was true of Wilson's campaign on behalf of democracy, the stakes are high, the outcome impossible to predict.

Only weeks after committing more United States troops to Afghanistan, Obama accepted the Nobel Peace Prize in Oslo, Norway. Like some of his other major addresses, which he chose not to trust to staffers or his speech writers, Obama crafted his Oslo speech himself. It merits analysis, because it encapsulates many of his signature themes. He began by distinguishing between the war in Afghanistan, which he deemed a just war with the support of forty-two nations because of the 9/11 attacks, and other wars he judged unjustifiable. He did not have to specify the Iraq War, launched without provocation by his predecessor. The reference was clear. Obama then invoked the universal ideals embraced by the international community since Wilson first proposed the League of Nations and the United Nations was established, ideals including liberty and self-determination, equality and the rule of law. Cognizant of the criticism directed against these lofty principles since the advent of antifoundationalism, Obama acknowledged that some observers dismiss them as lovely but hollow rationalizations trotted out to justify the West's effort to remake the world in its image. He acknowledged too the anxieties of those who worry that many of the world's distinct, particular cultures will be annihilated as the West proceeds with its own projects. It is as difficult to imagine another American president raising those objections in an international forum as it is revealing that Obama felt compelled to address them directly.

Responding to such critics, Obama explained that he considers the UN's Universal Declaration of Human Rights a statement of principles not masking the "enlightened self-interest" of the United States or the developed world but expressing genuinely "universal aspirations." He justified the UN's commitment to enforce those principles when they are violated, however, not because they embody the West's greater wisdom but instead because such power is made necessary by "the imperfections of man and the limits of reason." Knowing our weaknesses as well as our strengths, Obama continued, enables us to wrestle with the persistent challenge of international affairs, "reconciling these two seemingly irreconcilable truths—that war is sometimes necessary, and that war at some level is an expression of human folly." To that end, Obama proclaimed, he intends to hold the United States accountable in its conduct of war, although he did not address the use of drones to hunt Al Qaeda in Pakistan. He also pledged to prevent the spread of nuclear weapons and diminish the stockpiles of the nations that already possess them, a promise he has taken a first step toward keeping through an arms-reduction treaty with Russia. Finally, he vowed to combat outrages such as "genocide in Darfur, systematic rape in Congo, repression in Burma." He did not mention Guantanamo.

Although Obama acknowledged that such lofty aims evoke suspicion from self-styled "realists," he replied bluntly that he rejects the notion that we are faced with "a stark choice between the narrow pursuit of interests or an endless campaign to impose our values around the world." Choosing his words with care, he sketched out a path between two very different contrasts, the first between Theodore Roosevelt's "big stick" and Woodrow Wilson's internationalism, the second between blanket condemnations of American foreign policy (such as that of his least favorite Columbia professor, Edward Said) and George W. Bush's blanket defense. As he had done in his essay as a Columbia undergraduate, Obama recommended engaging the leaders of nations charged with oppressing their own people through "painstaking diplomacy," and he invoked the examples of Richard Nixon in China, Pope John Paul in Poland, and Ronald Reagan in Berlin to illustrate the value of such efforts. He addressed directly the nagging conflict between the lure of universalism and the hard facts of particularism. Strikingly, he sought to resolve it by subjecting his own nation's commitments to critical scrutiny. "No matter how callously defined, neither America's interests—nor the world's—are served by the denial of human aspirations. So even as we respect the unique culture and traditions of different countries, America will always be a voice for those aspirations that are universal." Unlike some Americans, Obama rejected the notion that every American cause is just. But unlike some of America's critics, he insisted that no cause is to be deemed unjust simply because the United States has adopted it.

As he did in his 2006 Washington speech on religion and politics and in his discussion of those issues in *The Audacity of Hope*, Obama faced directly the thorny question of religion. He directed his argument both to his Oslo audience of overwhelmingly secular Europeans and his religious and secular fellow citizens back home. In stark contrast to the language used by his predecessor, he balanced the common charge that "religion is used to justify the murder of innocents by those who have distorted and defiled the great religion of Islam" against the "amply recorded" injustice and cruelty of the Crusades launched by Christians. Holy wars, he observed, reframing the formulation he used for Wallis's conference, obliterate the proportionality that should govern all combat. If you think you are doing God's will, "then there is no need for restraint." Again Obama was relying on the idea of finding, or building, an overlapping consensus, but this time it extended beyond his own nation to the world. The self-righteous recourse to violence as a first resort mocks "the very purpose of faith—for the one rule that lies at the heart of every major religion is that we do unto others as we would have them do unto us."

Obama deliberately tied the principles undergirding the peacekeeping efforts of the United Nations to the "law of love" that has "always been the core struggle of human nature." Once again he couched that struggle not in terms of triumphant proclamations of the justice of our cause but in strikingly different terms: "we are fallible. We make mistakes, and fall victim to the temptations of pride, and power, and sometimes evil." Note Obama's use of the first- rather than second-person pronoun, a formulation that places the United States, and the United Nations, within the circle of the irrational, the blind, the fallen, and the fallible rather than outside it, in a privileged space from which it can self-righteously judge other nations and punish them with impunity. From our multiple religious and ethical traditions we Americans should not only draw the inspiration of a shared ideal, such as the golden rule or the Christian law of love. We should also draw the lesson of humility concerning our capacity to understand as well as adhere to such maxims. Just as no individual, and no culture, holds a monopoly on truth, so no nation should take for granted that it acts for the benefit of mankind. Continuing scrutiny of one's motives and one's behavior is made necessary by the limits of reason and the temptation of pride. In the international as well as the domestic arena, deliberative engagement with one's adversaries provides the best means to test the viability and persuasiveness of one's cause. Unobjectionable, perhaps even noble, as a motive, invocations of high ideals cannot serve as a warrant in foreign affairs any more than in American politics. We cannot claim certainty; we must aim toward creating provisional, and fragile, conditions for overlapping consensus.

Finally, in his Nobel acceptance speech Obama linked two other themes that have marked his distinctive writings on justice. First, he invoked Roosevelt's phrase "freedom from want" as an essential element of "a just peace." Not only should the international community work to secure civil and political rights, crucial as those are. As Dewey insisted repeatedly, and as Roosevelt came to see in the closing stages of World War II, an adequate conception of human freedom must extend from the political to the realms of the social and economic. In Obama's words, "it must encompass economic security and opportunity," freedom from want as well as freedom from fear, for "security does not exist where human beings do not have access to enough food, or clean water, or the medicine and shelter they need to survive." Individual liberty, self-government, and the rule of law are indispensable and insufficient. Like Roosevelt—and unlike every president since his death—Obama understands that liberal democracy reaches fruition only when all citizens possess the resources enabling them to exercise their rights. Whether he intends to work actively to extend that ambitious idea of freedom from the international to the domestic sphere is not yet clear.

Second, Obama called on the international community, as he has called on Americans, to keep in mind visionaries such as Gandhi and King even as he distanced himself from pacifism and insisted that force is sometimes tragically necessary. Gandhi's and King's strategies of nonresistance "may not have been practical or possible in every circumstance." Although Obama did not make the point, neither Gandhi nor King condemned war in all circumstances. One need not oppose all wars to doubt the necessity—or the wisdom—of a particular war, as King did in the case of Vietnam and as Obama did in the case of Iraq, and as many of us Americans do in the case of Afghanistan. But, Obama continued, with reference to Gandhi and King, "the love they preached—their fundamental faith in human progress—must always be the North Star that guides us." It cannot be a blind faith, because we are too well aware of our limitations. But it should be a faith that inspires us to surpass what exists and to strive for what we believe should exist. In a passage that evoked sustained applause from his secular audience in Oslo, Obama wrapped up his speech in explicitly religious language: "Let us strive for the world that ought to be—that spark of the divine that still stirs within each of our souls." Some commentators understood Obama's Nobel speech as a species of Niebuhr's Christian realism, others as a Deweyan pragmatist's chastened idealism. However it is interpreted, the speech provided Obama the chance to showcase for the world community the unusual combination of doubt and faith characteristic of his philosophical pragmatism and his own religious faith, a combination characteristically manifested in his writing.

Self-scrutiny of the sort that Obama showed in Oslo, in his speeches on politics and religion, and in his books remains rare in American public life. So is this striking admission in *The Audacity of Hope*: "I am robbed even of the certainty of uncertainty—for sometimes absolute truths may well be absolute." Primarily for the reasons embedded in that arresting sentence, Obama finds himself, in his words, "left then with Lincoln." Obama's discussion of Lincoln reveals the reasons why he so often invokes the words of the sixteenth president, the one of his predecessors he most admires, and it reveals Obama's most profound political commitments. His account of Lincoln in *The Audacity of Hope* engages the controversies that have swirled around Lincoln's political career and his legacy ever since he emerged as a prominent national figure in the 1850s. After the Kansas–Nebraska Act of 1854, Lincoln insisted that the question of allowing slavery in the territories should not be submitted to popular vote. His Illinois adversary Stephen A. Douglas invoked the principle of popular sovereignty to justify allowing the people of the territories to choose for themselves whether or not to permit the extension of slavery. In speeches stretching from his 1854 Peoria address through his election to the presidency in 1860, Lincoln stood firm against Douglas's interpretation of American democracy. It is true, as Lincoln's critics correctly observe, that during those years Lincoln never allied himself with abolitionists who insisted on the immediate end of slavery everywhere. Yet his characterizations of slavery as "a great moral wrong" nevertheless cost him crucial support in 1858, when whites in southern Illinois swung the legislature to select Douglas for the United States Senate. After the election of 1860, even though Lincoln deliberately muted his earlier criticism of slavery in an effort to prevent secession, it was the South's perception of the promise implicit in Lincoln's earlier denunciations of slavery that sparked the Civil War.

No one before or since, Obama writes, has understood as well as Lincoln "both the deliberative function of our democracy and the limits of such deliberation." Lincoln wrestled with competing impulses. On the one hand, he was convinced that slavery was an unmitigated evil. On the other, he knew that it would end only if Americans reached a common understanding about the need to eradicate it. The result of that struggle was Lincoln's tortured decision to go to war to preserve the Union. But throughout the war he insisted that the guilt for its necessity had to be shared, by both the South that had embraced slavery and the North that had allowed slavery to survive. The power of Lincoln's sublime second inaugural address depends on that insistence. Less a declaration of victory than an act of contrition, it pledged the nation to redeem the bloody sacrifice of war by redeeming its promise of equality for all. Yet only a few years after Lincoln's death, northern and southern whites began stitching the nation back together with the doctrine of white supremacy.

Obama's paragraphs on Lincoln, among the most powerful in *The Audacity of Hope*, reveal an incisive understanding of both the advantages and the tragic disadvantages of democracy. Unless the commitment to majority rule is balanced against an equally firm commitment to realizing the ideals of individual liberty and social equality, democracy can produce—indeed, it has produced—horrible forms of injustice. Without an ethic of reciprocity that requires individuals to look beyond their own self-interest and to sacrifice for the sake of the common good, any group of three can yield a majority of two committed to enslaving the minority of one. As Lincoln came to realize, weighing the evil of such injustice against the cost of ending it by waging war is the among most serious challenges a president can face. Obama has learned, from history and from his own experience, that deliberation can improve decision making. Multiplying perspectives can improve the odds of reaching a resolution that no individual might have seen. Yet the experience of Lincoln's generation also shows that not every decision can be put to a vote. Sometimes it is necessary to change the terms of the debate, as Frederick Douglass and the abolitionists did. Although formidable challenges of war, racism, and inequality remain in twenty-first-century America, moral clarity of the sort we now assign so easily to the issue of slavery is harder to find.

In Oslo Obama reaffirmed the principles of peace and justice he extolled in *The Audacity of Hope*. In the international sphere the law of love must remain our guide. At home freedom means economic security and opportunity. But interpreting the implications of those principles provokes passionate disagreement. Americans on the left think that no war should be thought too big to end. They also think that every American who is willing to work should be regarded as too big to fail. Americans on the right believe that evil must be crushed at all costs and that the state must be restrained. Partisans on either side think only their own sharply honed principles can slice through such disagreements. But American history is more sobering. Obama's Christian humility, his pragmatist antifoundationalism, and his nuanced appreciation for the complexities of the American past all point toward the disconcerting but inescapable truth of human fallibility. The necessary war that ended slavery also ended half a million lives, after which the nation abandoned the slaves it had freed to a century-long ordeal. Obama understands that Lincoln's heroic convictions cannot be separated from the tragedies of the battlefield and the lynch mob. As the case of slavery shows, democratic compromise is not always possible. But Americans, including those who malign Obama's efforts to resolve rather than intensify conflict, should never forget the cost of its failure.

Conclusion

Dreams, Hope, and the American Political Tradition

ARACK OBAMA UNDERSTANDS the limits of certainty and the limits of compromise. He knows that democratic politics is the art of the possible, in which results are achieved through persuasion and conciliation rather than force. He knows too that religion "insists on the impossible," and for that reason people of faith often bristle at compromise. But that conflict explains why, in a culture of many religions, preserving the separation of church and state remains as crucial now as it was when Jefferson and Madison first proposed the principle in their native Virginia. Obama's skepticism has limits: he declares that he is "absolutely sure" about "the Golden Rule, the need to battle cruelty in all its forms," and "the value of love and charity, humility and grace."

But he admits that he is much less sure about the implications of those principles for particular political or legal issues. That uncertainty aligns him with Lincoln, James, Niebuhr, and contemporary American pragmatists such as Putnam and Bernstein, and it distinguishes him from Americans who believe that a bright line connects their moral commitments to their political judgments. Obama, like James and Niebuhr in particular, believes that some conflicts exact a tragic price. When values conflict, there is not always a resolution.

The most terrible example of such a conflict was the Civil War. At some level everyone now knows—just as, to quote Lincoln's second inaugural address, everyone knew then—that slavery "was, somehow, the cause of the war." Obama's most sustained analysis of the still wrenching issue of race, of course, comes in his *Dreams from My Father*. Among the most compelling dimensions of his discussion, at least from my perspective as an American intellectual historian, is the imaginative way in which Obama deploys so many of the tropes of African American male writers—but in new ways, and for his own purposes. Elements of slave narratives, especially the *Narrative of the Life of Frederick Douglass*, surface in Obama's account of the struggles that first his African father, then he himself, had to undergo as they made their ways in the different worlds of Africa, Asia, and the United States. But he knows neither of them was ever enslaved, so he is careful not to exaggerate the obstacles they faced. Elements of W. E. B. DuBois's seminal *Souls of Black*

Folk surface both in Obama's discussions of his divided consciousness concerning race (DuBois's concept of double consciousness) and in his penetrating analysis of the tragic inevitability of slavery's poisonous legacy, the inherited prejudices and social practices that doomed radical Reconstruction.

Elements of the novels of Richard Wright, James Baldwin, and especially Ralph Ellison, all of whom Obama reports having first read as an adolescent in Hawaii, surface in Obama's account of his wrestling to embrace his blackness and the resistance he encountered from others, and ultimately from himself, during his brief period of self-discovery as an angry young black man. As noted above, Obama's debts to Ellison run particularly deep. Many borrowed images from *Invisible Man*—visibility and invisibility, blindness and sight, isolation and engagement, responsibility and destiny, madness as sanity, the traces of the past in the present, the dialectic of identity in recognition and anonymity, the magic of music and names, and of course the transformative power of public speaking—pop up in passages in *Dreams from My Father*. Yet Obama acknowledges that no matter how attractive the pose of anger and alienation seemed to him as a young man, it was a poor fit, both because of his even-tempered personality and because of his very different circumstances. For all those reasons *Invisible Man*, with its desperate refusal to surrender, its determination to affirm the principle, and its resolutely indeterminate ending, left a particularly clear imprint on Obama's sensibility.

Elements of *The Autobiography of Malcolm X* and the writings of Martin Luther King, Jr., surface in Obama's attempt to weigh the advantages and disadvantages of militancy and mainstream political action and in his self-critical and sometimes tragicomic account of his early missteps as a fledgling community organizer in Chicago. Yet he knows that he lives on the privileged other side of the civil rights movement, and that it opened doors for him to enjoy opportunities previously unavailable to African Americans, so he never allows himself to draw parallels between the struggles of earlier generations and those of his own. The question of Obama's debts to earlier African American writers, and his self-consciously delicate manipulation of his own doubled status as outside/insider, has already attracted scholars' attention. An adequate analysis of that theme will require a text longer than this one. Much as Obama has learned—and drawn from— African American intellectual traditions, he never confuses the challenges he faces, or those facing African Americans now, with those faced by his predecessors, particularly those who lived before emancipation but also those who lived before the legislation of the 1960s. Although I do not dispute the crucial influence of African American texts and traditions on Obama's ideas, I resist the suggestion, which I have heard repeatedly since I began this project, that all other influences pale in comparison. I think we should stop trying to differentiate the black from the white strands in American intellectual history. Obama's writings demonstrate conclusively that his ideas, like the ideas of all American thinkers worth studying, have been woven from many different sources.

Obama writes brilliantly and poignantly about the distinct phases of his life. As a boy in Indonesia, he possessed little consciousness of race. As a teenager in Hawaii, he attempted to escape into his blackness, but thanks to the example of his hip, mixed-race friend Ray and his grandfather's black friend Frank Davis, he found that he could not. As a college student, first at Occidental and then at Columbia, he tried to own—or at least to come to terms with—his blackness, but with equally inconclusive results. In Chicago, he sought to become part of a black community, but not until later, until he married Michelle Robinson, could he find a way to make that community his own.

Only when Obama traveled back to his father's native Kenya, before beginning Harvard Law School, did the peculiarity of his own life story at last come into focus. There he became entangled in the threads that tied him to his African ancestors as well as his Kansas grandparents, and that tied him to his own youth in Indonesia and Hawaii. But that enlightenment did not happen in the way he anticipated or in a way that I have encountered in the recounting of any other American odyssey.

Obama learned from his explorations that all cultural traditions now are always in a process of mutation. He discovered that if there is any really universal quality of human culture in our day, it is hodgepodge. In Nairobi or in the smallest villages of rural Kenya, as in Chicago or in the smallest towns of rural Illinois, Obama kept finding pieces of himself, not only pieces of his ancestry but also, and even more confoundingly, pieces of his present. Yet those pieces stubbornly refused to cohere into a unified pattern. Each of them was always in the process of becoming something else. Nothing remained stable. That knowledge, I think, is what he means in the closing pages of *Dreams from My Father* when he says his visit to Africa enabled him to close a circle. It's a circle of a particular kind, drawn at a particular historical moment, which deserves our attention.

When he was a child, Obama notes at the beginning of *Dreams from My Father*, his mother gave him a book called *Origins*. He describes himself puzzling over the different explanations offered by different cultures to explain how they began. Not surprisingly, perhaps inevitably, one of the stories is the Hindu tale of the world resting on the back of a turtle. Obama reports that he asked himself the question posed by Geertz's anthropologist. But at that age he was stumped, unable to come up with the answer that it's turtles all the way down. That knowledge came later, as Obama grew up while American culture was undergoing a profoundly unsettling transformation. Born in 1961, he came to consciousness with the foundations of American culture already under scrutiny, already unstable. He grew up with an absent African economist father he admired but barely knew and a present but spiritually wandering anthropologist mother, a seeker whom he loved, but whose romantic yearnings for the exotic eventually left him uneasy.

From his mother, Stanley Ann Dunham Soetoro, Obama learned about the similarities as well as the differences among cultures. She was trained as an anthropologist at the University of Hawaii. There her adviser was, coincidentally, Alice Dewey, the granddaughter of John Dewey. Soetoro was captivated by the cultures of Pakistan and Indonesia that also intrigued Geertz. After years of extensive fieldwork in local communities in Indonesia, she completed a 1,043-page doctoral dissertation entitled "Peasant Blacksmithing in Indonesia: Surviving against the Odds." Dr. Soetoro challenged romantic leftist assumptions that Indonesian poverty resulted from the culture's predisposition against profit-making. She argued instead that it was the scarcity of capital, not aversion to capitalism, that had left rural Javanese communities unable to develop economically. She became active in early efforts to establish microcredit programs, and she criticized aid plans that distributed funds through government officials more interested in consolidating their authority and padding their bank accounts than jump-starting local enterprises. Dr. Soetoro learned from Alice Dewey, from the controversies surrounding Geertz's writings, and from her own experiences that acknowledging cultural differences need not mean projecting onto other people one's own preferences or aversions, ideals or illusions. Although his mother never tired of trying to convince Obama that he inherited a precious destiny from his father, only after her death did he come to realize, as he put it, that "she was the kindest, most generous spirit I have ever known, and that what is best in me I owe to her."

From his father Barack Obama, Sr., who left him and his mother when he was two, Obama learned different lessons. He learned about the lure of advanced degrees—his father disappeared from Hawaii to pursue graduate studies in economics—and about the lure of Africa, where his father returned to work after he completed his graduate training. Except for that month-long visit to Hawaii when he was ten years old, his father never did return to see his first American wife and his son and namesake. Although Obama resented feeling abandoned, he long cherished an image of his father as the embodiment of a cosmopolitan ideal, a shimmering, glamorous, and successful black man who beat the odds. The chapter in *Dreams from My Father* in which Obama discusses his father's visit to Hawaii displays his self-awareness and the recesses of his ambivalence. The chapter closes with a vivid image of his father playing recordings of African music and teaching his young son to dance. "I took my first tentative steps with my eyes closed, down, up, my arms swinging, the voices lifting. And I hear him still: As I follow my father into the sound, he lets out a quick shout, bright and high, a shout that leaves much behind and reaches out for more, a shout that cries for laughter." If Obama abandoned his dream of becoming a writer of fiction, such sentences from his memoir show why he had reason to entertain that ambition.

Not until Obama traveled to Africa himself, after his father's death, did he learn the details of his father's life. He learned that his father had chosen to attend Harvard alone rather than accept another fellowship that would have enabled him to bring Obama and his mother with him to graduate school in New York City. Only then did Obama learn that because of his integrity, his stubbornness—or, more likely, some combination of both—his once-successful father had been harried out of public life in Kenya and had fallen into poverty, alcoholism, and obscurity. His father died in an automobile accident before he could fully recover from the loneliness and frustration he had endured. For much of his life, Obama came to realize, his father felt no more at home in his native Kenya than in Hawaii or Massachusetts. In Africa Obama encountered a sprawling constellation of family connections. If his American family had seemed less than complete, in Africa he found family everywhere. For the first time in his life, people not only recognized his name but knew his family. Yet his extensive explorations into his own background demonstrated the lack of cultural clarity that, as he learned, often frustrates African Americans who go looking for an Eden and find only a different fallen world, equally confused and confusing. All his ancestors, and now all his living relatives, from the oldest to the youngest, "were making it up as we went along." There was no map to consult; if it had ever existed, it had been "lost long ago." Contrasting sharply to Obama's consternation is the breezy self-assurance of his Stanford-educated cousin Mark, who reports no sense of belonging in his native Kenya and no sense of loss, only "numbness," from his own African father's abandonment of his mother.

Obama's visit to his ancestral home of Alego, which the family calls "Home Squared," meaning home intensified, or "home twice-over," sparked his anticipation that he would find there, at last, the sense of wholeness, and of stable identity, that he had been seeking. Instead he found the same conflicts he had faced in America, squared. Conflicts between Kenyans from rival tribes. Conflicts between Christians and Muslims and animists. Conflicts between Africans and Asians and Europeans. Conflicts between Kenyans on schedules and those who considered schedules treason to family obligations. Conflicts between those who thought salvation lay in hard work and listless drifters with the same guarded, wounded eyes Obama had seen on the faces of Chicago gang members. Conflicts between women who demanded equality and those who found security, even comfort, in the old traditions of patriarchy and polygamy. "I'd come to Kenya thinking that I could somehow force my many worlds into a single, harmonious whole." Instead the divisions deepened; the differences only multiplied.

Obama found his own experience with conflicting cultural tendencies mirrored in Kenya. In *Dreams from My Father*, he recounts a conversation he had with a Kenyan historian, whom he calls Rukia Odero. Whether this exchange occurred or is one of Obama's creations, it yields

arresting insights that demonstrate his supple understanding of the particularity as well as the historicity of culture.
The historian told Obama that many of the visitors who
come to Africa seeking "the authentic" return home disillusioned because the very idea of authenticity has become
an illusion. For over a century all African cultures have
been mixing old and new, not only African and European
and Asian but also different and (initially if no longer)
distinctive African tribal cultures. Odero's parting words
to Obama confirm William James's original claim that
American pragmatism is merely a new name for an old
way of thinking, a disposition present in various thinkers
and traditions since the ancient world. As Odero points
out to him, Africans now confront a challenge quite different from colonialism: they must choose between competing traditions and between rival visions of the future.
As her cultural analysis confirmed Obama's own maturing historicism and perspectivalism, so Odero's parting
wisdom was that of a good philosophical pragmatist: "If
you make the wrong choice," Odero concluded, "then you
learn from your mistakes" and "see what works."

That approach to problem solving, rooted in experience
and ever mutating in response to new problems, requires a
willingness both to discard traditions that have become
unhelpful and to continue taking instruction from those
that remain vibrant and productive. Critics of philosophical pragmatism have charged from the beginning that
pragmatists lack convictions because they refuse to embrace unchanging principles. To use Weber's typology,

pragmatists have been accused of discarding the forms of traditional rationality and value rationality and relying exclusively on instrumental rationality. James's respect for individuals' choices about religion and Dewey's reverence for democratic participation both show the inaccuracy of that critique. So does Obama's appreciation for the tenacity with which individuals adhere to their cultural heritage, including not only religious faith but also other traditions that imbue their lives with meaning. Obama—like Odero, James, Dewey, Addams, DuBois, and Niebuhr, and like their predecessors Madison and Lincoln and their successors Rorty, Bernstein, and Putnam—demonstrates a nuanced understanding of the difference between sticking to dogmas regardless of the consequences and the flexibility to see when genuine loyalty to principles such as Christian love or democratic procedures requires making adjustments in their application to new realities. James's conception of an "open universe" shows his awareness that the world is ever changing. Obama's tenacious hope reflects his own awareness that such changes are not entirely beyond the reach of human direction, even though no individual in a democracy can dictate change.

In the address he delivered when accepting the Nobel Peace Prize, Obama borrowed the eloquent image used by Martin Luther King, Jr.: "Our actions matter, and can bend history in the direction of justice." But lasting reform occurs only slowly, and it can be consolidated only through patient and persistent persuasion, a willingness to admit mistakes, and a tireless commitment to taking one step at a time. A thoroughly democratic culture is not characterized, nor is democratic change achieved, by swaggering certainty but only by a deeper humility, the Christian virtue that reminds Obama that all humans on all sides of every controversy, including himself, are inevitably flawed. Democratic change requires a more enduring toughness than our impatient culture of the present, ever in search of quick fixes, is likely either to recognize or respect. In the preface to the second edition of *Dreams*, Obama contrasted those who seek "a certainty and simplification that justifies cruelty toward those not like us," those whose dogmatism undermines democratic deliberation, against those who "embrace our teeming, colliding, irksome diversity, while still insisting on a set of values that binds us together." Along with freedom and equality, those democratic values include a steadfast willingness to tolerate differences and a commitment to the fruitfulness of compromise.

Indonesia and Hawaii. Occidental and Columbia. The far south side of Chicago and the villages of rural Kenya. The law schools of Harvard and the University of Chicago. The Illinois state legislature and the practice of civil rights law. Why should we choose among these options as we try to make sense of Obama's development? As his books make clear, his experiences wrestling with all these diverse cultures and institutions shaped his sensibility. His multiple commitments—to grass-roots organizing, church-based social networks of Christian activists, law conceived as an instrument of democratic deliberation and community building, James's and Dewey's pragmatist philosophy, economic populism, and the resolution shared by Ellison, King, and Malcolm X to affirm the principle in the face of racism—may seem incompatible to some people today. Yet I see no reason why they should prove any more inconsistent now than they were decades ago, when numerous and influential progressive reformers shared just such experiences, ideas, and aspirations and effected important if incomplete change.

Obama learned throughout his life, first from his own parents and grandparents, from his reading and research guided by professors in some of America's leading universities, from his own experiences as a community organizer, and as a visitor to his extended family in Kenya, that cultures are dynamic. The values people cherish do not descend from the sky but emerge from their past and their present, and they must adapt those values creatively to solve the problems they encounter in the future.

Although it is customary in American academic life to contrast the importance of community to the importance of the individual, Obama's writing and his political career make clear that the contrast is overdrawn in his case. His democratic commitment to the importance of community was forged by his own feelings of isolation as a youth, by the anger and violence of Chicago's gangs, by the lure of St. Catherine's and Wright's Trinity congregation, and by his exposure to the debates over historicism, particularism, civic republicanism, democratic deliberation, and civil society that he encountered as a student and as a member of the Saguaro seminars. His equally firm commitment to equal rights stems from admiring his ambitious father's rise and from understanding that oppression can wear the mask of a benign but stultifying paternalism. Both intellectually and politically, Obama has amalgamated American traditions usually—but incorrectly—thought to be distinct. He has learned congruent lessons from multiple sources. Democracy works best when rights are balanced against responsibilities. Democracy requires compromise, not because it is the path of least resistance but because people can learn from each other, and because lasting change demands widespread popular assent. Change in a democracy is a work of decades, not months or even years. Obama also learned, from absorbing all these lessons, that a culture's only home is to be found in its often tortured history.

Thus it was Africa's baobab trees, with their odd, almost cartoonish shapes and their unpredictable patterns of dormancy and flowering, that provided Obama with the peculiar image of rootedness he needed—or at least the only one available to him. "They both disturbed and comforted me," he writes near the end of his memoir, "those trees that looked as if they might uproot themselves and simply walk away, were it not for the knowledge that on this earth one place is not so different from another—the knowledge that one moment carries within it all that's gone on before." That provocative image, and Obama's realization that the present carries the past within itself, brings me to my conclusion.

Barack Obama embodies a surprising number of the central themes in the American political tradition, particularly as it has come to be understood in the last half century. But he does not—he cannot—neatly reconcile all the diverse strands of the American past or the American present. As he knows, democracy thrives on difference, even as it must try to resolve disagreements, at least provisionally, through empathy, deliberation, and experimentation. Equipped with an understanding of the multiple dimensions and the dynamic history of American social and political thought and practice, Americans should be able to hear in Obama's words many echoes from the American past, both its origins and its recent decades of intellectual and cultural upheaval. Obama embraces a version of American political ideals, more egalitarian in its goals and more moderate in its means, that has fallen from favor in recent decades, as both parties have become more partisan, and as shouted invective has replaced respectful disagreements. Americans who prefer their principles stated with dogmatic certainty rather than with the humility and tentativeness appropriate for democratic deliberation might find Obama's conception of politics unpalatable. In part for that reason, and in part because he flavors his universalist aspirations with healthy doses of historicism and pragmatism still unfamiliar to large segments of the culture, many Americans have not noticed how firmly Obama is rooted in older national political traditions. Even so, if we pay careful attention to those echoes from our democratic past, we should be able to hear reverberating "the enduring power of our ideals," the force that the newly elected president invoked on the night the campaign ended. The meanings of those ideals, however, are complex, contested, and changing. They are not now, and they never have been, simple, self-evident, and fixed. Obama understands that the power of our principles of liberty and equality depends not on the fervor with which they are proclaimed but on the deliberative process from which they have developed. That process requires us to debate, test, and revise the meaning of our ideals in practice rather than genuflecting reverentially before them. Only when we affirm the process of continuous and open-ended experimentation do we affirm the principle of democracy.

Essay on Sources

R EADERS INTERESTED IN PURSUING the issues discussed in this book will find suggestions in the pages that follow. Almost all the quotations in the text come from the writings and speeches of Barack Obama, which are readily accessible. My interpretations of American history in general, and of late twentieth-century American culture in particular, derive from sources that I have arranged here according to the order in which specific questions are addressed in *Reading Obama*.

This study began with my reading of Obama's own books, which remain the best point of entry for understanding his ideas. In addition to *Dreams from My Father: A Story of Race and Inheritance*, 2nd ed. (1995; New York: Three Rivers Press, 2004); *The Audacity of Hope: Thoughts on Reclaiming the American Dream* (New York: Random House, 2006); and *Change We Can Believe In: Barack Obama's Plan to Renew America's Promise* (New York: Three Rivers Press, 2008), readers interested in Obama's ideas should consult *The Speech: Race and Barack Obama's "A More Perfect Union,"* ed. T. Denean Sharpley-Whiting (New York: Bloomsbury, 2009), which includes his March 18, 2008, Philadelphia speech on the Reverend Jeremiah Wright. The other major speeches by Obama discussed in the text, including his June 28, 2006, speech in Washington, D.C., before Jim Wallis's Sojourners' conference "Building a Covenant for a New America"; his November 4, 2008, acceptance speech in Chicago the night of the election; his January 20, 2009, inaugural address; his June 4, 2009, speech to the Islamic World in Cairo; his December 1, 2009, speech on Afghanistan at West Point; and his December 9, 2009, Nobel acceptance speech in Oslo, are easily accessible on the Internet. Obama's article "Why Organize? Problems and Promise in the Inner City," originally published in *Illinois Issues*, September, 1988, pp. 27–29, was reprinted in *After Alinsky: Organizing in the 1990s*, ed. Peg Knoepfle (Springfield, IL: Sangamon State University, 1990), pp. 35–40. The syllabus for Obama's seminar on race and the law, offered at the University of Chicago Law School in the spring term of 1994, was put on the *New York Times* website on July 30, 2008. A condensed version of the dissertation written by Obama's mother has been published: Stanley Ann Dunham Soetoro, *Surviving against the Odds: Village Industry in Indonesia*, ed. Alice G. Dewey et al. (Durham: Duke University Press, 2009).

Readers interested in more detailed elaboration of my arguments concerning philosophical pragmatism, progressive reform, civic republicanism, deliberative democracy, civil society, communitarianism, individual thinkers such as William James, John Dewey, Max Weber, Jürgen Habermas, and Richard Rorty, and the relation between these issues and the history of American democracy from the seventeenth century to the present should consult James T. Kloppenberg, *Uncertain Victory: Social Democracy and Progressivism in European and American Thought, 1870–1920* (New York: Oxford University Press, 1986); Kloppenberg, *The Virtues of Liberalism* (New York: Oxford University Press, 1998); and Kloppenberg, *Tragic Irony: Democracy in European and American Thought* (New York: Oxford University Press, forthcoming).

Among the many biographies and specialized studies of Obama that have already been published, the most detailed is David Remnick, *The Bridge: The Life and Rise of Barack Obama* (New York: Knopf, 2010). David Plouffe, *The Audacity to Win: The Inside Story and Lessons of Barack Obama's Historic Victory* (New York: Viking, 2009), provides his campaign manager's perspective. Gwen Ifill, *The Breakthrough: Politics and Race in the Age of Obama* (New York: Anchor Books, 2009); Peniel E. Joseph, *Dark Days, Bright Nights: From Black Power to Barack Obama* (Philadelphia: Basic Civitas, 2010); and Kareem Crayton, "'You May Not Get There with Me': Obama and the Black Establishment," in *Barack Obama and African American Empowerment: The Rise of Black America's New Leadership*, ed. Manning Marable and Kristen Clarke (New York: Palgrave Macmillan, 2009), pp. 195–208, illuminate the role of race in Obama's rise to prominence. Thomas J. Sugrue, *Not Even Past: Barack Obama and the Burden of Race* (Princeton: Princeton University Press, 2010), emphasizes the radical dimension of the civil rights movement and the persistence of racism in contemporary America.

On Frank Marshall Davis, the poet whom Obama credits for helping him understand black life in white America, see Frank Marshall Davis, *Livin' the Blues: Memoirs of a Black Journalist and Poet* (Madison: University of Wisconsin Press, 2003). On Frantz Fanon's classic *Wretched of the Earth* and Fanon's influence, see *Fanon: A Critical Reader*, ed. Lewis R. Gordon et al. (Oxford: Blackwell, 1996). For insight into Obama's guide to American and European history and philosophy while an undergraduate at Occidental, see Roger Boesche, *The Strange Liberalism of Alexis de Tocqueville* (Ithaca: Cornell University Press, 1987); and Boesche, *Tocqueville's Road Map* (Lanham, MD: Lexington Books, 2006). For an overview of the scholarly literature on Tocqueville, see Kloppenberg, "The Canvas and the Color: Tocqueville's 'Philosophical History' and Why It Matters Now," *Modern Intellectual History* 3, 3 (2006): 495–521.

On the ideas and continuing influence of the American philosopher William James, see Kloppenberg, "James's *Pragmatism* and American Culture, 1907–2007," in *100 Years of Pragmatism: William James's Revolutionary Philosophy*, ed. John Stuhr (Bloomington: Indiana University Press, 2010). On John Dewey, see Robert B. Westbrook, *John Dewey and American Democracy* (Ithaca: Cornell University Press, 1991); Westbrook, *Democratic Hope: Pragmatism and the Politics of Truth* (Ithaca: Cornell University Press, 2005); and Alan Ryan, *John Dewey and the High Tide of American Liberalism* (New York: Norton, 1995).

The scholarly literature on African American thought is growing rapidly; a fine collection of recent essays is Adolf Reed, Jr., and Kenneth W. Warren, eds., *Renewing Black Intellectual History: The Ideological and Material Foundations of African American Thought* (Boulder: Paradigm, 2010). Reed has been one of Obama's severest critics. In "The Curse of Community," *Village Voice*, January 16, 1996, he dismissed Obama as part of "the new breed of foundation-hatched black communitarian voices with impeccable do-good credentials and vacuous to repressive neoliberal politics." On Ellison and *Invisible Man*, see Arnold Rampersad, *Ralph Ellison: A Biography* (New York: Random House, 2007); and the diverse perspectives available in *The Cambridge Companion to Ralph Ellison*, ed. Ross Posnock (Cambridge: Cambridge University Press, 2005); *Ralph Ellison and the Raft of Hope: A Political Companion to "Invisible Man,"* ed. Lucas Morel (Lexington: University Press of Kentucky, 2004); and Kenneth W. Warren, *So Black and Blue: Ralph Ellison and the Occasion of Criticism* (Chicago: University of Chicago Press, 2003).

On the relation between community organizing and the labor movement, see Saul D. Alinsky, *John L. Lewis: An Unauthorized Biography* (New York: G. P. Putnam's Sons, 1949). The classic manifesto is Saul D. Alinsky, *Rules for Radicals: A Pragmatic Primer for Realistic Radi-*

cals (New York: Random House, 1971); see also Sanford D. Horwit, *Let Them Call Me Rebel: Saul Alinsky—His Life and Legacy* (New York: Knopf, 1989). The most widely read of Howard Zinn's many books is *A People's History of the United States: 1492 to Present*, rev. ed. (1980; New York: Perennial, 2005). In his essay "Why Organize," Obama emphasized the work of William Julius Wilson, whose controversial books include *The Declining Significance of Race: Blacks and Changing American Institutions* (Chicago: University of Chicago Press, 1978); and *When Work Disappears: The World of the New Urban Poor* (New York: Random House, 1996). For detailed analysis of Wilson and Obama, see Sugrue, *Not Even Past*, pp. 70–85. For the perspective on organizing that helped shape Obama's perspective while he was in Chicago, see John L. McKnight, *The Careless Society: Community and Its Counterfeits* (New York: Basic Books, 1996).

The best guide to the ideas shaping legal education at the time Obama was at Harvard Law School is the splendid study by Laura Kalman, *The Strange Career of Legal Liberalism* (New Haven: Yale University Press, 1996). See also Richard D. Kahlenberg, *Broken Contract: A Memoir of Harvard Law School* (New York: Hill and Wang, 1992); and Kenneth Mack, "Barack Obama before He Was a Rising Political Star," *Journal of Blacks in Higher Education* 45 (2004): 98–101, which describes Mack's and Obama's path through Harvard Law School. For concise overviews of contentious developments written in the early 1990s by members of the Harvard Law School community, see the articles by William W. Fisher III, "Critical Legal Studies," Anthony Cook, "Critical Race Theory," Joan Williams, "Feminist Jurisprudence," and William W. Fisher III, "Law and Economics," in *A Companion to American Thought*, ed. Richard Wightman Fox and James T. Kloppenberg (Oxford: Blackwell, 1995), pp. 151–56, 235–37, and 390–91. For further discussion of these issues, including particularly the relation between philosophical pragmatism and the rise of legal realism, see Morton Horwitz, *The Transformation of the American Law, 1870–1960* (New York: Oxford University Press, 1992); Kloppenberg, "The Theory and Practice of Legal History," *Harvard Law Review* 106, 6 (April 1993): 1332–51; and Kloppenberg, "Deliberative Democracy and Judicial Supremacy: A Review of Robert A. Burt, *The Constitution in Conflict* and Cass R. Sunstein, *The Partial Constitution*," *Law and History Review* 13 (1995): 393–411.

The rise, impact, and transformation of civic republicanism is a central theme in Kloppenberg, *The Virtues of Liberalism*. Gordon S. Wood, *The Creation of the American Republic, 1776–1787*, originally published in 1969, attracted enormous attention and sparked scholarly controversies that persist into the present. Wood addressed his critics in a preface to the second edition of *The Creation of the American Republic, 1776–1787* (Chapel Hill: University of North Carolina Press, 1998) and in many of the essays collected in Wood, *Revolutionary Characters: What Made the Founders Different* (New York: Penguin, 2006).

Wood's other major works include *The Radicalism of the American Revolution* (New York: Knopf, 1992); and *The Empire of Liberty: A History of the Early Republic, 1789–1815* (Oxford: Oxford University Press, 2009), both of which underscore the long-term democratic consequences of the revolution. Recent accounts interpreting the American Revolution as a popular uprising and the Constitution as a betrayal of the people include Gary B. Nash, *The Unknown American Revolution: The Unruly Birth of Democracy and the Struggle to Create America* (New York: Viking, 2005); Woody Holton, *Unruly Americans and the Origins of the Constitution* (New York: Hill and Wang, 2007); and Terry Bouton, *Taming Democracy: "The People," the Founders, and the Troubled Ending of the American Revolution* (New York: Oxford University Press, 2007).

On the influence of the Chicago traditions of democracy and pragmatism, a spirited and provocative (if perhaps overstated) article is Bart Schultz, "Obama's Political Philosophy: Pragmatism, Politics, and the University of Chicago," *Philosophy of the Social Sciences* 39 (2009): 127–73. Tracing a related tradition more explicitly back to Lincoln is Susan Schulten, "Barack Obama, Abraham Lincoln, and John Dewey," *Denver University Law Review* 86 (2009): 807–18. Robert Putnam expanded the argument from his influential article into a book with the same title, *Bowling Alone* (New York: Simon and Schuster, 2000). The classic statement of the communitarian perspective was Robert Bellah et al., *Habits of the Heart:*

Individualism and Commitment in American Life (Berkeley: University of California Press, 1985). On deliberative democracy, the central text is *Democracy and Disagreement*, ed. Amy Gutmann and Dennis Thompson (Cambridge: Belknap Press of Harvard University Press, 1996).

For the shift in American culture away from varieties of universalism toward varieties of particularism, the best source is Daniel T. Rodgers, *Age of Fracture* (Cambridge: Belknap Press of Harvard University Press, 2010), which provides a comprehensive analysis of the multidimensional transformation I discuss in chapter 2. Other overviews of American thought during these crucial years include Howard Brick, *Age of Contradiction: American Thought and Culture in the 1960s* (Ithaca: Cornell University Press, 1998); and on the political repercussions, *Liberalism for a New Century*, ed. Neil Jumonville and Kevin Mattson (Berkeley: University of California Press, 2007); and *Rightward Bound*, ed. Bruce J. Schulman and Julian E. Zelizer (Cambridge: Harvard University Press, 2008).

For John Rawls, in addition to *A Theory of Justice* and *Political Liberalism*, readers should consult Rawls, *Collected Papers*, ed Samuel Freeman (Cambridge: Harvard University Press, 1999), which includes papers published from 1955 through the 1990s, including the preface to the French edition of *A Theory of Justice* and Rawls's illuminating 1998 interview published in *Commonweal*. Also of interest is Rawls, *A Brief Inquiry into the Meaning of Sin and Faith: With "On My Religion"* (Cambridge: Harvard University Press, 2010), a volume including Rawls's 1942

Princeton thesis, his 1997 essay on his changing attitudes toward religion, and commentaries by Thomas Nagel, Joshua Cohen, and Robert Merrihew Adams. Valuable studies of Rawls include Thomas Pogge and Michelle Kosch, *John Rawls: His Life and Theory of Justice* (New York: Oxford University Press, 2007); Percy B. Lehning, *John Rawls: An Introduction* (Cambridge: Cambridge University Press, 2009); and *The Cambridge Companion to Rawls*, ed. Samuel Freeman (Cambridge: Cambridge University Press, 2002). For discussion of Max Weber's ideas of rationality and political action in relation to philosophical pragmatism, see Kloppenberg, *Uncertain Victory*, pp. 321–415; and Kloppenberg, *Virtues of Liberalism*, pp. 82–99.

Michael Sandel has published, in addition to *Liberalism and the Limits of Justice* and *Democracy's Discontent*, a book based on his popular undergraduate course at Harvard, *Justice: What's the Right Thing to Do* (New York: Farrar, Straus, and Giroux, 2009). For a sample of feminist responses to Rawls published in the late 1980s and early 1990s, see Susan Okin, *Justice, Gender, and the Family* (New York: Basic Books, 1989); Joan C. Tronto, *Moral Boundaries: A Political Argument for an Ethic of Care* (New York: Routledge, 1993); and Seyla Benhabib, *Situating the Self: Gender, Community, and Postmodernism in Contemporary Ethics* (New York: Routledge, 1992). On the lure of Habermas during these years, see *The Communicative Ethics Controversy*, ed. Seyla Benhabib and Fred Dallmayr (Cambridge: MIT Press, 1990), and *Habermas and the Public Sphere*, ed. Craig Calhoun (Cambridge: MIT Press, 1992). Collections offering perspectives on these issues from multiple viewpoints are *Liberalism and Its Critics*, ed. Michael Sandel (Oxford: Blackwell, 1984); and *Pragmatism and Feminism*, ed. Cass R. Sunstein (Chicago: University of Chicago Press, 1992).

For more detailed accounts of a process schematized in my presentation here, the multidimensional transformation of academic disciplines and American culture in the middle of the twentieth century, see *American Academic Culture in Transformation: Fifty Years, Four Disciplines*, ed. Thomas Bender and Carl Schorske (Princeton: Princeton University Press, 1997); *The Cambridge History of Science*, vol. 7, *The Modern Social Sciences*, ed. Theodore M. Porter and Dorothy Ross (Cambridge: Cambridge University Press, 2003); *The Humanities and the Dynamics of Inclusion since World War II*, ed. David A. Hollinger (Baltimore: Johns Hopkins University Press, 2006); David A. Hollinger, *Cosmopolitanism and Solidarity: Studies in Ethnoracial, Religious, and Professional Affiliation in the United States* (Madison: University of Wisconsin Press, 2006); S. M. Amadae, *Rationalizing Capitalist Democracy: The Cold War Origins of Rational Choice Liberalism* (Chicago: University of Chicago Press, 2003); Richard Tuck, *Free Riding* (Cambridge: Harvard University Press, 2008); Scott Soames, *Philosophical Analysis in the Twentieth Century*, 2 vols. (Princeton: Princeton University Press, 2005); Elizabeth Borgwardt, *A New Deal for the World: America's Vision for Human Rights* (Cambridge: Belknap

Press of Harvard University Press, 2005); and Wendy L. Wall, *Inventing "The American Way": The Politics of Consensus from the New Deal to the Civil Rights Movement* (New York: Oxford University Press, 2008).

On Reinhold Niebuhr, see Richard Wightman Fox, *Reinhold Niebuhr: A Biography* (New York: Pantheon, 1985); on Thomas J. Kuhn, see Alexander Bird, *Thomas Kuhn* (Princeton: Princeton University Press, 2000); and on Clifford Geertz, see Fred Inglis, *Clifford Geertz: Culture, Custom and Ethics* (Cambridge: Blackwell, 2000). For the resurgence of pragmatism in American thought, see Kloppenberg, "Pragmatism: An Old Name for Some New Ways of Thinking?" in *The Revival of Pragmatism*, ed. Morris Dickstein (Durham: Duke University Press, 1998), pp. 83–127, a comprehensive collection that includes essays by Rorty, Bernstein, Putnam, and many of the other contributors to the pragmatist revival that has continued into the present. Recent examples include Hilary Putnam, *Ethics without Ontology* (Cambridge: Harvard University Press, 2004); Richard J. Bernstein, *The Pragmatic Turn* (Cambridge: Polity Press, 2010); and a splendid reference work, *A Companion to Pragmatism*, ed. John R. Shook and Joseph Margolis (Oxford: Blackwell, 2009).

On the United States Constitution, a judicious and accessible recent study is Akhil Reed Amar, *America's Constitution: A Biography* (New York: Random House, 2005). James Madison, *Writings* (New York, Library of America, 1999), provides an excellent introduction to the writ-

ings of the most important figure in the framing and ratification of the Constitution. Lance Banning, *The Sacred
Fire of Liberty: James Madison and the Founding of the
Federal Republic* (Ithaca: Cornell University Press, 1995),
remains unsurpassed on Madison's ideas. On the impos-
sibility of identifying a unitary and unchanging meaning
in the Constitution, see, in addition to Sunstein's *Partial
Constitution* and Tribe and Dorf's *On Reading the Consti-
tution*, the fuller account in Jack N. Rakove, *Original
Meanings: Politics and Ideas in the Making of the Consti-
tution* (New York: Knopf, 1996). The classic essay by
Marvin Meyers is "Reflection and Choice: Beyond the
Sum of the Differences," in *The Mind of the Founder:
Sources of the Political Thought of James Madison*, ed.
Marvin Meyers (1973; Hanover: University Press of New
England, 1981), pp. xi–xlix. For up-to-date guidance into
the founding documents themselves, see *The Annotated
U. S. Constitution and Declaration of Independence*, ed.
Jack N. Rakove (Cambridge: Belknap Press of Harvard
University Press, 2009). On representative democracy
more generally, see Nadia Urbinati, *Representative De-
mocracy* (Chicago: University of Chicago Press, 2006).

On the relation between the idea of ordered liberty and
democracy in early America, see J. S. Maloy, *The Colonial
Origins of Modern Democratic Thought* (Cambridge: Cambridge University Press, 2008); and Kloppenberg, "Tocqueville, Mill, and the American Gentry," in the bicentennial
issue of *La Revue Tocqueville/The Tocqueville Review* 27, 2
(2006): 351–80. The February 24, 1819 letter from John

Adams to Thomas Jefferson is in *The Adams-Jefferson Letters*, ed. Lester J. Cappon (Chapel Hill: University of North Carolina Press, 1987), pp. 534–35. On the demise of the 1950s-era concept of American consensus, see Kloppenberg, "*Requiescat in Pacem*: The Liberal Tradition of Louis Hartz," in *The American Liberal Tradition Reconsidered: The Contested Legacy of Louis Hartz*, ed. Mark Hulliung (Lawrence: University Press of Kansas, 2010). A two-volume study of Jane Addams that captures the democratic sensibility of Chicago progressives is Louise W. Knight, *Citizen: Jane Addams and the Struggle for Democracy* (Chicago: University of Chicago Press, 2005); and Knight, *Jane Addams: Spirit in Action* (New York: Norton, 2010). On notable progressives, see Trygve Throntveit, "'Common Counsel': Woodrow Wilson's Pragmatic Progressivism, 1885–1913," in *Reconsidering Woodrow Wilson*, ed. John Milton Cooper, Jr. (Washington D.C.: Woodrow Wilson Center Press, 2008); John Milton Cooper, Jr., *Woodrow Wilson: A Biography* (New York: Knopf, 2009); and Melvin I. Urofsky, *Louis D. Brandeis: A Life* (New York: Pantheon, 2009).

On the New Deal, compare the classic accounts of Carl N. Degler, *Out of Our Past: The Forces That Shaped Modern America*, 3rd ed. (1959; New York: Harper and Row, 1984); and William E. Leuchtenburg, *Franklin D. Roosevelt and the New Deal, 1932–1940* (New York: Harper and Row, 1963); with David M. Kennedy, *Freedom from Fear: The American People in Depression and War, 1929–1945* (New York: Oxford University Press, 1999); and

Cass R. Sunstein, *The Second Bill of Rights: FDR's Unfinished Revolution and Why We Need It More Than Ever* (New York: Basic Books, 2004).

On the traditions that Jeremiah Wright inherited, see Ralph Luker, *The Social Gospel in Black and White: American Racial Reform, 1885–1912* (Chapel Hill: University of North Carolina Press, 1991); and Fred C. Harris, *Something Within: Religion in African American Political Activism* (New York: Oxford University Press, 2001). On Wright himself, see *What Makes You So Strong? Sermons of Joy and Strength by Jeremiah A. Wright, Jr.*, ed. Jini Gilgore Ross (Valley Forge, PA: Judson Press, 1993); and on his church, Jeremiah A. Wright, Jr., *The Sankofa Moment: The History of Trinity United Church of Christ* (Dallas: St. Paul Press, 2010). On the increasing diversity of contemporary American religious practices and the consequences of that diversity for political engagement, see Robert D. Putnam and David E. Campbell, *American Grace: How Religion Is Reshaping Our Civic and Political Lives* (New York: Simon and Schuster, 2010).

On the shift in American politics from the New Deal to the Reagan revolution, see *The Rise and Fall of the New Deal Order*, ed. Steve Fraser and Gery Gerstle (Princeton: Princeton University Press, 1989); and an influential collection of essays interrogating the shift from egalitarian to individualist assumptions, *Beyond Self-Interest*, ed. Jane Mansbridge (Chicago: University of Chicago Press, 1990). Tracing the tradition of cooperation between radicals and moderate liberals that has only recently—and, for the

Left, disastrously—been severed is Doug Rossinow, *Visions of Progress: The Left-Liberal Tradition in America* (Philadelphia: University of Pennsylvania Press, 2008).

The seminal assessment of the evidence of increasing economic inequality in the United States since the 1970s is Thomas Piketty and Emmanuel Saez, "Income Inequality in the United States," *Quarterly Journal of Economics* 118, 1 (2003): 1–39. Updated versions of their data, the most recent of which run through 2007, are available at their website at the University of California, Berkeley: http://elsa.berkeley.edu/~saez/. See also the essays in *Inequality and American Democracy: What We Know and What We Need to Know*, ed. Lawrence R. Jacobs and Theda Skocpol (New York: Russell Sage, 2005); and Benjamin I. Page and Lawrence R. Jacobs, *Class War? What Americans Really Think about Economic Inequality* (Chicago: University of Chicago Press, 2009).

On the civil rights movement and its consequences, see Jacquelyn Dowd Hall, "The Long Civil Rights Movement and the Political Uses of the Past," *Journal of American History* 91, 4 (2005): 1233–63, which provides an excellent guide to the scholarly literature; James R. Ralph, Jr., *Northern Protest: Martin Luther King, Jr., Chicago, and the Civil Rights Movement* (Cambridge: Harvard University Press, 1993); Thomas Sugrue, *Sweet Land of Liberty: The Forgotten Struggle for Civil Rights in the North* (New York: Random House, 2008); and Taylor Branch, *America in the King Years*, 3 vols. (New York: Simon and Schuster, 1999–2006), a popular account that Obama told a friend he recognized as his own story. On the transnational dimensions of the civil rights movement, see Carol Anderson, *Eyes Off the Prize: The United Nations and the African-American Struggle for Human Rights, 1944–1955* (Cambridge: Cambridge University Press, 2003); and Nico Slate, *Reflections of Freedom: Race, Caste, and the Long Struggle for Democracy in the United States and India* (Cambridge: Harvard University Press, forthcoming).

On the agreements masked by the idea of a "culture war," see E. J. Dionne, *Why Americans Hate Politics* (New York: Simon and Schuster, 1991); Alan Wolfe, *One Nation, After All* (New York: Viking, 1998); Morris P. Fiorina, Samuel J. Abrams, and Jeremy C. Pope, *Culture War? The Myth of a Polarized America*, 3rd ed. (Boston: Longman, 2010); and the related issues addressed in Page and Jacobs, *Class War?*

On pragmatism and feminism, see Joan C. Williams, *Unbending Gender: Why Family and Work Conflict and What to Do about It* (New York: Oxford University Press, 2000); Joan C. Williams, *Reshaping the Work–Family Debate: Why Men and Class Matter* (Cambridge: Harvard University Press, 2010); Nancy Fraser, *Unruly Practices: Power, Discourse, and Gender in Contemporary Social Theory*, 2nd ed. (Minneapolis: University of Minnesota Press, 2008); Elizabeth Warren and Amelia Warren Tyagi, *The Two-Income Trap: Why Middle-Class Parents Are Going Broke* (New York: Basic Books, 2003); and *Feminism and Political Theory*, ed. Cass Sunstein (Chicago: University of Chicago Press, 1992).

Many recent works probe the changing contours of race and ethnicity in America. See in particular David A. Hollinger, *Postethnic America*, 2nd ed. (New York: Basic Books, 2006); Danielle S. Allen, *Talking to Strangers: Anxieties of Citizenship since* Brown v. Board of Education (Chicago: University of Chicago Press, 2006); Tommie Shelby, *We Who Are Dark: The Philosophical Foundations of Black Solidarity* (Cambridge: Harvard University Press, 2005); Eddie S. Glaude Jr., *In a Shade of Blue: Pragmatism and the Politics of Black America* (Chicago: University of Chicago Press, 2007); *Pragmatism and the Problem of Race*, ed. Bill E. Lawson and Donald F. Koch (Bloomington: Indiana University Press, 2004); and José Medina, "James on Truth and Solidarity: The Epistemology of Diversity and the Politics of Specificity," in *100 Years of Pragmatism*, pp. 124–43.

Of the countless books on Lincoln and slavery, see Richard J. Carwadine, *Lincoln* (London: Pearson, 2003); John Stauffer, *Giants: The Parallel Lives of Frederick Douglass and Abraham Lincoln* (New York: Twelve, 2008); and Eric Foner, *The Fiery Trial: Abraham Lincoln and American Slavery* (New York: Norton, 2010). On the tragic aftermath of the Civil War and the abandonment of newly freed African Americans, see David W. Blight, *Race and Reunion: The Civil War in American Memory* (Cambridge: Belknap Press of Harvard University Press, 2001).

For thoughtful reflections on the first year of Obama's presidency, see the essays by Danielle Allen, William

Galston, Martha Nussbaum, Katha Pollitt, Robert Reich, Michael Sandel, and Michael Walzer in *Democracy: A Journal of Ideas* (Spring 2010). For assessments of the causes of the nation's economic collapse prior to the presidential election of 2008 and the dangers to democracy in continuing down the path taken by the Obama administration in its early stages, see Joseph E. Stiglitz, *Freefall: America, Free Markets, and the Sinking of the World Economy* (New York: Norton, 2010); and Robert Kuttner, *A Presidency in Peril: The Inside Story of Obama's Promise, Wall Street's Power, and the Struggle to Control Our Economic Future* (White River Junction, VT: Chelsea Green, 2010).

Acknowledgments

I HAVE PILED UP A LOT OF DEBTS while writing this little book. I am grateful to Tony Badger, Duncan Bell, Duncan Kelly, Dan Matlin, Michael O'Brien, Andrew Preston, and John A. Thompson, who welcomed me as Pitt Professor into the community of American historians at the University of Cambridge and arranged for me to deliver the lectures on American political thought that prompted me to think about locating Barack Obama in American intellectual history. While I was in Cambridge, Quentin Skinner and Susan James generously allowed me to live in their home, a kindness that cannot be repaid. In other ways the fellows and students of Jesus College likewise made me feel very much at home. I am grateful for their hospitality to the Master of Jesus, Robert Mair; President James Clackson; Veronique Mottier, who arranged for me to discuss Obama with students at Jesus; Rosalind Crone and Rebecca Flemming, with whom I had many delightful conversations; John B. Thompson, who first suggested that I transform my paper on Obama into a book; and especially Michael O'Brien and Duncan Kelly, generous hosts, guides, and interlocutors. To members of the extraordinary Cambridge faculties of Social and Political Studies, English, and History, particularly Stefan Collini, John Dunn, Geoffrey Hawthorne, Raymond Geuss, Istvan Hont, Charles Jones, Gareth Stedman Jones, Melissa Lane, Peter Mandler, Ruth Scurr, Michael Sonenscher, and Adam Tooze, I am grateful for having had the chance to eat, drink, and talk about ideas. I owe special debts to Anouch Bourmayan, Sophie King, Joy Labern, Sarah Mortimer, Sophus Reinert, and Francesca Viano for kindnesses large and small during my year in Cambridge.

Not only did President James Wright of Dartmouth College invite me to discuss Obama at a symposium in the fall of 2008, he gave me my first chance, as a Dartmouth undergraduate forty years ago, to do independent research, and he waited patiently for the result while I spent months in Washington, D.C., fruitlessly organizing against the Vietnam War. I am glad to be able to thank him for both opportunities. I learned from all my fellow discussants at Dartmouth, including Leah Daughtry, Annette Gordon-Reed, Rob Portman, David Shribman, and Jacques Steinberg. Many other people generously invited me to discuss Obama in the past two years. I journeyed twice to Oxford, once at the invitation of Marc Stears and once at the invitation of Richard Carwadine. Although Jim Livesey and Knud Haakonsen at Sussex asked me to address their faculty on the subject of Jean-Jacques Rousseau, James Madison, and James Wilson instead of Obama, my informal conversations about American politics in Sussex were very illuminating. Dan Scroop and Mike Braddick at Sheffield rounded up a large and engaging crowd full of questions about Obama, as did Richard Crockatt and Nick Selby at East Anglia, Richard King and Robin Vendome at Nottingham, and Joel Isaac at the London Institute for Historical Research. Maurizio Vaudagna arranged two memorable gatherings of students and citizens in Torino, Italy. Hans Joas and Emanuel Richter allowed me to present my argument on Obama at a conference of distinguished Dewey scholars, including Robert B. Westbrook and Richard J. Bernstein, at the Zentrum für interdisziphäre Forschung in Bielefeld, Germany. David Hollinger, Annette Gordon-Reed, and David Garrow provided insightful commentary at the annual meeting of the American Historical Association in San Diego. Peter Buttigieg, Sabeel Rahman, Ganesh Sitaraman, Previn Warren, and Tom Wolfe invited me to discuss Obama at a meeting of the Democratic Renaissance Project, a lively group of politically active young men and women that has restored my hope for the future of American democracy. Finally, the students who attended my lectures in Cambridge and the students enrolled in my undergraduate and graduate courses at Harvard in 2009–2010 have pushed me hard, again and again, to clarify my arguments about Obama and American democracy. To all these colleagues and students I am grateful.

Friends and former teachers of Barack Obama have been unfailingly helpful. Among the many people who agreed to speak with me, I am particularly indebted to Michael Baron, Roger Boesche, Michael Dorf, Bob Gannett, Mike Kruglick, Ken Mack, Martha Minow, Michael Sandel, Laurence Tribe, and Roberto Unger for insights that would have been unavailable otherwise. Other friends have helped me clarify my ideas through conversation, answering questions, or making helpful—and sometimes sharply critical—suggestions, including David Armitage, Thomas Bender, Vincent Brown, Angus Burgin, Charles Capper, Lizabeth Cohen, Kareem Crayton, Carl Degler, Carrie Elkins, Henry Louis Gates, Jr., Katharine Gerbner, Pierre Gervais, Glenda Goodman, Jonathan Hansen, Joan Hollinger, Morton Horwitz, Meg Jacobs, Walter Johnson, Jane Kamensky, Michael Kazin, David M. Kennedy, Andrew Kinney, Amy Kittelstrom, Kathleen McGovern, Elizabeth More, Darra Mulderry, Alice O'Connor, Jennifer Ratner-Rosenhagen, Sam Rosenfeld, Emma Rothschild, Manisha Sinha, Rachel St. John, Thomas Sugrue, François Weil, Cornel West, Robert Westbrook, Daniel Wewers, Ann Wilson, and Julian Zelizer.

A number of people read early versions of the book manuscript and gave me the benefit of their responses, including Sandy Baum, Richard J. Bernstein, Richard Fox, Peter Gordon, Annette Gordon-Reed, Bryan Hehir, Mike Kruglik, Zach Liscow, Michael McPherson, Martha Minow, Timothy Peltason, Robert Putnam, Michael Sandel, Nico Slate, Trygve Throntveit, and Laurence

Tribe. Although David Garrow is working on his own biography of Obama, and although he does not share my interest in the importance of ideas in Obama's life, he generously shared with me his research, his contacts, and his judgment. Daniel T. Rodgers, who had just finished writing his superb book *Age of Fracture*, which examines in detail many of the issues addressed in my book, generously read the manuscript for Princeton University Press; his judgment and his expertise greatly improved the book. David A. Hollinger, who had already talked through my arguments with me in England and worked through two earlier drafts, making valuable suggestions each time, nevertheless read the final draft with his characteristic thoroughness and acuity, thereby earning a triple dose of gratitude.

Scholars at different stages of their careers helped with the final stages of preparing the manuscript for publication. At a crucial moment, my friend Darra Mulderry offered her characteristically acute historian's insight, and Arjun Ramamurti's attention to detail saved me from a number of errors. Noah Rosenblum not only prepared the index with intelligence and care, his probing queries about passages in the text helped me clarify important arguments.

Working with Princeton University Press has been smooth and satisfying. From the start Brigitta van Rheinberg and Peter Dougherty shared my hopes for the book, and Brigitta's enthusiasm has grown along with the manuscript. Everyone involved in the design, editing, and production of the book, particularly Ellen Foos, Anita O'Brien, and Sarah Wolf, has shown the consideration and professionalism that all authors prize.

Finally, as always, my deepest debts are to my family. My wife Mary Cairns Kloppenberg, no matter how over-burdened with her own work, is the only person I can trust to read a first draft and a final draft. From start to finish, her insistence on clarity and her kindness never waver. Our children Annie Kloppenberg and Jay Kloppenberg also read drafts; they offered not only encouragement but among the most detailed and discerning, and the most blunt, critiques I received. After licking my wounds only briefly, I realized their ideas improved the book, and I realized how happy I am that they have grown into adults with sharp critical judgment and equally strong convictions.

Index